CRUEL COMPASSION

BOOKS BY THOMAS SZASZ

CRUEL COMPASSION

PSYCHIATRIC CONTROL OF SOCIETY'S UNWANTED

THOMAS SZASZ

JOHN WILEY & SONS, INC.

New York ▪ Chichester ▪ Brisbane ▪ Toronto ▪ Singapore

Library of Congress Cataloging in Publication Data:

Szasz, Thomas, 1920–
    Cruel compassion : psychiatric control of society's unwanted /
Thomas Szasz.
        p.   cm.
    Includes bibliographical references and indexes.
    ISBN 0-471-01012-X (alk. paper)
    1. Involuntary treatment—moral and ethical aspects.   2. Socially
handicapped—Mental health services.   3. Psychiatric ethics.
4. Paternalism—Moral and ethical aspects.   5. Social control.
6. Antipsychiatry.   I. Title.
    [DNLM: 1. Mental Disorders.   2. Social Control, Formal.   WM 100
S996c   1994]
RC451.4.S62S93   1994
362.2—dc20
DNLM/DLC
for Library of Congress   93-31600

Printed in the United States of America

10 9 8 7 6 5 4 3 2 1

For Isobel

I must be cruel only to be kind.
Thus bad begins, and worse remains behind.
—*William Shakespeare*[1]

PREFACE

A further objection to force is that you impair the object by your very endeavours to preserve it. The thing you fought for is not the thing which you recover; but depreciated, sunk, wasted, and consumed in the contest.

—Edmund Burke[1]

We can influence others in two radically different ways—with the sword or the pen, the stick or the carrot. Coercion is the threat or use of force to compel the other's submission. If it is legally authorized, we call it "law enforcement"; if it is not, we call it "crime." Shunning coercion, we can employ verbal, sexual, financial, and other enticements to secure the other's cooperation. We call these modes of influence by a variety of names, such as advertising, persuasion, psychotherapy, treatment, brainwashing, seduction, payment for services, and so forth.

We assume that people influence others to improve their own lives. The self-interest of the person who coerces is manifest: He compels the other to do his bidding. The self-interest of the person who eschews coercion is more subtle: Albeit the merchant's business is to satisfy his customers' needs, his basic motivation, as Adam Smith acknowledged, is still self-interest.

Nevertheless, people often claim that they are coercing the other to satisfy *his* needs. Parents, priests, politicians, and psychiatrists typically assume this paternalistic posture vis-à-vis their beneficiaries.* As the term implies, the prototype of avowedly altruistic domination-coercion is the relationship between parent and young child. Acknowledging that parents must sometimes use force to control and protect their children, and that the use of such force is therefore morally justified, does not compel us to believe that parents act this way solely in the best interest of their children. In the first place, they might be satisfying their own needs (as well). Or the interests of parent and child may be so intertwined that the distinction is irrelevant. Indeed, ideally the child's dependence on his parents, and the parents' attachment to him, mesh so well that their interests largely coincide. If the child suffers, the parents suffer by proxy. However, if the child misbehaves, he may enjoy his rebellion, whereas the parents are likely to be angered and embarrassed by it. Thus, what appears to be the parents' altruistic behavior must, in part, be based on self-interest.[2]

How do people justify the coercive-paternalistic domination of one adult by another? Typically, by appealing to the moral-religious maxim that we are our brothers' keepers. It is a treacherous and unsatisfactory metaphor. Interpreted literally, the maxim justifies only meddling, not coercing. Moreover, in the family, only an older and stronger brother has the option of coercing his younger and weaker sibling. The weaker brother must make do with verbal (noncoercive) helping-meddling.

The dilemma that members of the helping professions find particularly disturbing is this: If they coerce their clients, they cannot really help them; to help their clients noncoercively, the helpers must enlist the clients' cooperation; and they cannot enlist the clients' cooperation without respecting, and appealing to, their clients' self-interest, as the clients define it. If the helper refuses to respect the client's view of his world, or if the client rejects cooperating with the helper, the two are at an impasse that can be resolved in one of two ways. Either the helper must leave the client alone; or the state must grant the helper the power, and indeed impose on him the duty, to coerce the client to accept help, as the state defines help. Today, leaving a person authoritatively designated as "in need of professional help" (albeit legally competent) to his own devices is considered to be unfeeling, inhumane, perhaps even a neglect of professional duties. In ancient Greece, coercing him would have been considered undignified meddling, inappropriate for relations among free adults. We revere Socrates as a powerful persuader, not as a compassionate coercer.

---

* A paternalistic relationship—one person treating another as a child—may or may not entail the use of force.

Ours is a Christian world, and to Christianity we owe the moral foundations of some of our most important institutions. But there is a dark underside to Christian—as well as Jewish and Islamic—-monotheism. If there is only one God, and if He is a perfect and perfectly Benevolent Being, then individuals who reject His Will are rightly coerced, in their own best interest. In a theocracy, there is no need for political checks and balances; indeed, such counterweights are synonymous with heresy. Similarly, in a therapeutic autocracy, there is no need for safeguards against the guardians; in the psychiatric hospital, the desire for checks and balances against absolute power is synonymous with madness.

Saint Augustine (354–430), bishop of Hippo in Roman Africa, is usually credited with being among the first to articulate the Christian duty to persecute heretics, in their own best interest. The clarity of his argument for clerical coercion and its striking similarities to the modern psychiatric argument for clinical coercion merit quoting his relevant views in full. In a letter addressed "To Vincentius, My Brother Dearly Beloved," Augustine writes: "You are of the opinion that . . . no coercion is to be used with any man in order to [hasten] his deliverance from the fatal consequences of error; and yet you see that, in examples which cannot be disputed, this is done by God, who loves us with more real regard for our profit than any other can."[3] God, the coercer, is a loving parent. Man, the coerced, is a wayward child. Grant divine authority to God's deputy, and his right to righteously persecute such errants is unchallengeable. Augustine continues:

> You now see therefore, I suppose, that the thing to be considered when any one is coerced, is not the mere fact of the coercion, but the nature of that to which he is coerced, whether it be good or bad. . . . I have therefore yielded to the evidence afforded by these instances which my colleagues have laid before me. For originally my opinion was, that no one should be coerced into the unity of Christ, that we must act only by words, fight only by arguments, and prevail by force of reason . . . . But this opinion of mine was overcome . . . by the conclusive instances to which they could point.[4]

In pre-Christian antiquity, coercing the person who offended against the City of Man was considered to be justified by his offense. He was punished not to improve him, but to improve society. In the Christian world, coercing the person who offended against the City of God was considered to be justified by concern for his soul. He was coerced in order to perfect him, not merely to protect society. Thus originated the authorization for the "therapeutic" use of force.

Some time between the Reformation and the French Revolution, this meliorist rationalization became secularized. Error ceased to be deviation from religion (iconoclasm, heresy) and became deviation from reason (irrationality, insanity); doctors of divinity diagnosing error were replaced by doctors of medicine diagnosing madness; forcible religious conversion was transformed into involuntary psychiatric treatment; the Theological State was replaced by the Therapeutic State.

In this book, I examine the growing practice of coercing individuals, especially adults economically dependent on others, allegedly in their own best interest. Adult dependency, as we now know it, is a relatively recent social phenomenon. In the remote past, dependents were supported in extended families or perished. In the more recent past, adult dependents were called beggars, drifters, panhandlers, tramps, vagrants, hoboes, and so forth. Today, we call them homeless and mentally ill.

From the sixteenth to the nineteenth century, adult dependents were coerced primarily on economic grounds, because they were a financial burden on the productive members of society. Since then, they have increasingly been coerced on therapeutic grounds, because they are mentally ill and hence are a danger to themselves and others. Both remedies aggravate the problem. Even charity devoid of coercion demeans and antagonizes its recipient and pits him against his patron. Combine charity with coercion, and the result is a recipe for feeding the beneficiary's resentment of his benefactor, guaranteeing the perpetuation of adult dependency and counterproductive efforts to combat it.[5]

In war, those who wield force can achieve great things, because war *is* the use of force. That is what makes the war metaphor—as in the War on Poverty, the War on Drugs, or the War on Mental Illness—both effective and repellent. In peace, however, only those who eschew force can do great things, because peace *is* security from violence. By separating church and state, the Founding Fathers uncoupled coercion from the cure of souls and laid the foundations for the greatest political success story in history. Unfortunately, the power the Founders took away from the clerics, their twentieth-century followers handed back to the clerks, the bureaucrats of the Welfare State and of the Therapeutic State. As a result, many of the liberties secured in 1787 are now but a dim memory. Either we must revive the Founders' Great Experiment in liberty by separating coercion from the cure of bodies and minds, or we shall have to relinquish our much-vaunted claim to being a free people.

Regardless of the names or diagnoses attached to adult dependents, most post-Enlightenment efforts to remedy their condition have rested on the benefactor's self-interest disguised as philanthropy. More than a century ago, James Fitzjames Stephen, the great Victorian jurist, warned against this pious self-deception:

Philanthropic pursuits have many indisputable advantages, but it is doubtful whether they can be truly said to humanize or soften the minds of those who are most addicted to them. . . . The grand objection to them all is that people create them for themselves. . . . Benevolence is constantly cultivated by philanthropists at the expense of modesty, truthfulness, and consideration for the rights and feelings of others; for by the very fact that a man devotes himself to conscious efforts to make other people happier and better than they are, he asserts that he knows better than they what are the necessary constituent elements of happiness and goodness. In other words, he sets himself up as their guide and superior.[6]

No one, myself included, has a solution for the problem of adult dependency. However, I am persuaded that coercing competent adults solely because of their dependency or dangerousness to themselves—in an effort to make them more virtuous, industrious, or healthy—injures their dignity and liberty, is counterproductive, and is morally wrong.* Only in this century, and only begrudgingly, did we stop treating blacks and women as quasi children. Perhaps in the next century, we will extend fully human stature to the so-called mentally ill as well. If so, we must begin to give serious consideration to the moral and political justifications of psychiatric coercions and excuses. I have long maintained that we should reject infantilizing mental patients and the coercive psychiatric paternalism that goes with it, and accord the same rights to, and impose the same responsibilities on, these patients as we accord to and impose on patients with bodily illness or with no illness.

I believe we should condone coercive paternalism as morally legitimate only in the case of (young) children and persons legally declared to be incompetent.† For the care and control of incompetent adults, the principle of *parens patriae*, as applied to the comatose patient, suffices, and is the sole appropriate mechanism. The ostensibly altruistic coercion of a protesting, legally competent adult should always arouse our suspicion. We must never forget that adults—even immature, irrational, or insane adults—are not children.[7]

Finally, two brief caveats. In this book, I use many terms and phrases—such as mental illness, mental patient, mental hospital, schizophrenia, psychiatric treatment, and others—whose customary implications and

---

* I believe our economic magnanimity toward able-bodied dependents, especially those labeled mentally ill, is also counterproductive. But that is another story.

† By incompetent, I refer to adults who are severely mentally retarded or who have been rendered temporarily or permanently unconscious, delirious, or demented by injury or illness. Insanity and incompetence are separate and discrete legal categories. A committed mental patient is not legally incompetent, unless—like a nonmental patient—he is declared incompetent by a court.

conventional meanings I reject. To avoid defacing the text, I have refrained from placing such prejudging expressions between quotation marks each time théy appear. Also, I use the masculine pronoun to refer to both men and women, and the terms *psychiatrist* and *mental patient* to refer to all mental health professionals and their clients.

THOMAS SZASZ

Syracuse, New York
November 1993

ACKNOWLEDGMENTS

I owe special thanks to my daughter, Suzy, and brother, George, who, as usual, gave generously of their time and talents. I am also indebted to Jeffrey Friedman, Charles S. Howard, Dan Klein, and Peter Swales, for reading all or parts of the manuscript and suggesting important additions or corrections; to Sanford Kline, Ralph Raico, and Roger Yanow for their useful criticisms; to David Herman, for sending me clippings and other useful source materials; and to Peter Uva, librarian at the SUNY Health Science Center at Syracuse, for his inexhaustible patience in securing many of the bibliographical sources used in this study. Finally, I thank the van Ameringen Foundation for its support of my effort to present a systematic critique of the principles and practices of contemporary psychiatry. The first part of my critique, titled *Insanity: The Idea and Its Consequences*, was published in 1987. The present volume completes the project.

T.S.

CONTENTS

INTRODUCTION

A man receiving charity practically always hates his benefactor—it is a fixed characteristic of human nature.
                                                    —George Orwell[1]

Most people today believe that certain persons ought to be deprived of liberty, in their own best interest. Psychiatrists implement this belief by incarcerating such individuals in mental hospitals, and for doing so society authenticates them as scientifically enlightened physicians and compassionate healers. Suppose, however, that psychiatrists deprived certain persons of life or property, in their own best interest. Would society applaud them for those interventions as well? The analogy is not absurd, or even far-fetched. The right to life, the right to liberty, and the right to property are the sacred values of the Western liberal tradition, the American political system, and Anglo-American law. Their importance is reflected in the three types of criminal sanctions—deprivation of life, deprivation of liberty, and deprivation of property. The person who is executed, imprisoned, or fined experiences what is done to him—regardless of how the doers define it—as a punishment.

THE HAZARDS OF HELPING AND BEING HELPED

It is axiomatic that we ought to help persons who need help, such as children, elderly persons, the poor, and the sick. Some persons we call "mentally ill" belong on this list because they are or are perceived to be like helpless children, needy indigents, or suffering patients. Note, however, that these diverse individuals share only one basic feature, namely, dependency.

We fear being dependent on others because we rightly associate dependency with loss of control and hence the risk of having to submit to a treatment—in the widest sense of the term—whose consequences might be inimical to our best interests, as we see them. This apprehension accounts for the fact that the persons most dependent on others for help are often the ones who most fiercely resist being helped.

All the same, when faced with a suffering human being, most of us are moved to help him. Out of this noble impulse arises a treacherous personal temptation and a vexing political problem. How can we be sure that a benefactor is a genuine supporter who respects his beneficiary, and not an existential exploiter who imparts meaning to his life by demeaning his ward? How can the beneficiary be protected from the benefactor's coercion, ostensibly in the recipient's own best interest? Who shall guard the guardians? Thousands of years of human history have given us a resounding answer to this last question: No one.

The root of this perennial dilemma lies in our prolonged childhood, when care and coercion are inevitably intertwined. As a result, when our health or well-being is jeopardized, we re-experience an intense need for protectors and become vulnerable to our dependence on them. The maxim that there are no atheists in the foxholes illustrates this phenomenon. Moreover, it is probably also our prolonged childhood dependence that makes young adults so prone to coerce and demean others, as the brutal history of youthful revolutionaries bent on improving mankind illustrates.

The Ambiguity of Aid

How do we help a starving person? Confucius taught that we can give him a fish or teach him to fish. If we feed him, we are likely to make him dependent on us. If we refuse to feed him, he may die. We cannot hedge and say it all depends on circumstances, on the victim's ability or inability to help himself. It is precisely his ability or inability to help himself that we typically cannot assess in advance. Moreover, since everyone is responsive to the way he is treated, the hypothetical starving person's behavior will be influenced by the way we respond to him.

Similar dilemmas abound. A person is troubled, agitated, feels guilty, cannot sleep, suspects others of evil deeds. How do we help Othello, consumed with jealousy? Hamlet, tortured by the suspicion that his mother and uncle have murdered his father? Lady Macbeth, maddened by the memory of her murderous deeds? We may pretend that these are scientific questions about diagnosing and treating illness, but they are not. They are quandaries intrinsic to living, with which people have struggled since antiquity. The medical profession's classic prescription for coping with such predicaments, *Primum non nocere* (First, do no harm), sounds better than it is. In fact, it fails to tell us precisely what we need to know: What is harm and what is help?

However, two things about the challenge of helping the helpless are clear. One is that, like beauty and ugliness, help and harm often lie in the eyes of the beholder—in our case, in the often divergently directed eyes of the benefactor and his beneficiary. The other is that harming people in the name of helping them is one of mankind's favorite pastimes.[2]

A DISPASSIONATE LOOK AT COMPASSION

In our fervor to medicalize morals, we have transformed every sin but one into sickness. Anger, gluttony, lust, pride, sloth are all the symptoms of mental diseases. Only lacking compassion is still a sin. Guided by the light of the fake virtue of compassion, we have subverted the classical liberal conception of man as moral agent, endowed with free will and responsible for his actions, and replaced it with the conception of man as patient, the victim of mental illness.

However, compassion is a dangerous ally. Sir Matthew Hale (1609–1676), Lord Chief Justice of England, counseled: "Be not be biassed with compassion to the poor, or favour to the rich, in point of justice."[3] Nothing could be more politically incorrect today. Instead of expecting criminal courts to dispense justice tempered by mercy, we expect them to sentence defendants accused of crimes to treatment for their "abusive behavior." Instead of expecting civil courts to adjudicate the reciprocal rights and duties of the litigants, we expect them to dispense "social justice," redistributing money from deep to shallow pockets. In short, being compassionate is now synonymous with being virtuous.

Is Compassion (Necessarily) a Virtue?

A little self-scrutiny would quickly show us that compassion is not always or necessarily a virtue. Among my earliest and most vivid memories is the sight of amputees, blind men, and other cripples on the streets of Budapest, holding out their hands in a gesture of begging, and my feeling overcome with a sense of compassion for their misery. The intensity of this feeling gradually diminished, but neither the memory nor the feeling has disappeared.

Receiving a small allowance from my father, supplemented by additional sums for good grades, I fell into the habit at an early age of placing some coins, or even bills, into the outstretched hands of these *misérables*. I realized all along that my generosity was not wholly altruistic, that I was motivated by a vague sense of dread that a similar fate might befall me, together with a superstitious hope that my offering might propitiate a deity with mysterious powers over such matters, a being in whose existence I could not bring myself to believe, yet was still too insecure to disbelieve. I doubt that my childhood experiences were unusual. If not, they suggest that feeling compassion, like feeling fear or guilt, does not require much talent or sophistication.

Indeed, Greek and Roman philosophers distrusted compassion. In their view, reason alone was the proper guide to conduct. They regarded compassion as an affect, neither admirable nor contemptible. Aristotle put it this way:

> Now neither the virtues nor the vices are *passions,* because we are not called good or bad on the ground of our passions. . . . For he who lives as passion directs will not hear argument that dissuades him, nor understand it if he does. . . . Passion seems to yield not to argument but to force.[4]

Because compassion is a type of passion, we ought to view it, as Hannah Arendt cautioned, with the same suspicion with which the Greeks viewed it, rather than with the veneration Rousseau popularized. She wrote:

> [The philosophers of antiquity] took a position wholly at odds with the great esteem for compassion of modern times . . . the ancients regarded the most compassionate person as no more entitled to be called the best than the most fearful. The Stoics saw compassion and envy in the same terms: "For the man who is pained by another's misfortune is also pained by another's prosperity."[5]

The Roman goddess of justice is a blindfolded woman: Her virtue is dispassion, not compassion.

Justifying Coercion by Compassion

The coercive altruist who justifies his behavior by compassion must convince himself that he is acting for the benefit of the Other. How can he be sure of that? Since he cannot, he must be able to turn a blind eye to the suffering he causes. The best way to do this is to stop respecting the targeted beneficiary as a person and instead treat him as the member of a particular group. He then ceases to be a moral agent and becomes the object of our benevolence. Classifying a person as a mental patient is an especially treacherous enterprise, encouraging abstract compassion toward him as a patient, and concrete indifference toward him as a person. Hannah Arendt's remarks about the Grand Inquisitor are especially apposite. She wrote: "[The Grand Inquisitor] was attracted toward *les hommes faibles* . . . because he had depersonalized the sufferers, lumped them together into an aggregate—the people *toujours malheureux*, the suffering masses, et cetera."[6]

No contemporary professional helper has more compassion for people as patients, and less for them as individuals, than the psychiatrist. He pledges to help millions suffering from mental illness, and harms the self-defined interest of virtually everyone whose life he touches as a professional. Arendt's remark about the political revolutionary fits the psychiatric reformer: "Since the days of the French Revolution, it has been the boundlessness of their sentiments that made revolutionaries so curiously insensitive to reality in general and to the reality of persons in particular."[7]

The revolutionist-reformist posture romanticized by Rousseau and realized by Robespierre faithfully expresses the guiding principle of collectivist benevolence toward mankind en masse, and hostility toward the individual as moral agent. "The common enemy," declared Rousseau, "is the particular interest of the particular will of each man."[8] It is no coincidence that modern psychiatry traces its birth to the mythologized "liberation" of the mental patient by Philippe Pinel during the French Revolution.

A RETURN TO DISPASSION

Observation, reason, and science are useful only for clarifying relations among particular valued ends and identifying the most effective means for attaining them. They are powerless to resolve conflicts among competing ends or values. For example, the person who claims he is Jesus Christ is not, ipso facto, irrational. He may simply be trying to enhance his self-esteem or gain admission to a mental hospital.

The Case against Compassion

The ethics of psychiatric therapy is the very negation of the ethics of political liberty. The former embraces absolute power, provided it is used to protect and promote the patient's mental health. The latter rejects absolute power, regardless of its aim or use. By definition, the powers of constitutional government are limited. Hence, there is no room, in such a political framework, for psychiatric power over mental patients that, by definition, is unlimited. A person not declared incompetent by a court of law has the right to be left unmolested by psychiatrists. Whereas a person declared incompetent—for example, a comatose patient—need not be diagnosed as mentally ill to justify his physician's treatment of him without his consent.[9] The whole history of psychiatry then, may be said to come down to the history of the repudiation of limited therapeutic powers. Ever since Pinel's successful recasting of psychiatric imprisonment as liberation, every so-called psychiatric advance has consisted of a shameless celebration of the psychiatrist's unlimited power over his patient. Awarding a Nobel Prize in medicine to the inventor of lobotomy is an example. In 1945, Portuguese neurosurgeon Egas Moniz (1874–1955) received this honor "for his discovery of the therapeutic value of leucotomy in certain psychoses." At the Nobel Award ceremonies, famed Swedish neurosurgeon Herbert Olivecrona hailed Moniz's work with these words: "Prefrontal leucotomy . . . must be considered one of the most important discoveries ever made in psychiatric therapy, because through its use a great number of suffering people and total invalids have recovered and have been socially rehabilitated."[10]

The promise of curing sick people against their will—especially people whose illnesses we do not understand or who may, in fact, not even be ill—is fraught with perils we seem determined to deny. Despite the ghastly mayhem wrought by psychiatrists in Nazi Germany and the Soviet Union, we continue to venerate the coercive-compassionate psychiatrist. Indeed, there is no popular interest in, or professional support for, a psychiatry stripped of political power. On the contrary, improving the Other by coercion in the name of mental health has become a characteristic feature of our age.[11]

Valuing and Disvaluing Persons

How do we know what a person values? One answer lies in the classic rule that people value what they pay for, and pay for what they value. The trouble with this formula is summed up by Oscar Wilde's maxim: "Cynics know the price of everything and the value of nothing." Indeed, the value of some of the most important things in life cannot be measured by the yardstick of payment. In the end, we infer a person's values from the way he lives. A man cares for and respects his parents, spouse, and children, and we conclude that he values his family. Another cares for and collects works of art, and we conclude that he values art.

The worth we attach to a person, activity, or object may be positive or negative, a value or a disvalue. We value the individuals and institutions we cherish (our children or church), and disvalue the persons and happenings we demonize and fear (drug pushers and disabling diseases). When we value others, our response to them does not generate a social problem. It is only when we disvalue them—when we deem their behavior to be dangerous or deranged and view them as unwanted—that the result is a social problem. I want to add here that the distinction between a person and his behavior is contrived. Only angels are capable of the existential gymnastics of hating the sin but loving the sinner. Ordinary mortals are more likely to practice the sin in private and hate the sinner in public. Although separating sin from the sinner is beyond human capacity, separating virtue from the virtuous is not. The politics of envy so popular today is, in effect, loving virtue and hating the virtuous.

Since I am concerned here with mental illness as a social problem—not as a private experience of anguish or life problem—my focus is on the mental patient as an unwanted Other. The question we must never lose sight of is: Who is unwanted by whom and why? Actually, most people are wanted by some, are unwanted by others, and are of utter indifference to the vast majority of mankind. The terms *wanted* and *unwanted* refer to a person's relationship to others. Many ugly and untalented individuals are wanted, and many beautiful and talented persons are unwanted. I regret saying such trivialities and do so only to emphasize that before we can effectively help an unwanted person, we must first ask, Why is this person unwanted? Why do I want to help him? What do I want to help him be or do?

In every society, certain persons are unwanted. Their identity varies from time to time, and place to place. In some, the unwanted are female babies; in others, old persons unable to care for themselves. In the United States today, the most unwanted are drug abusers, chronic mental patients, and the homeless.[12] Every politician and psychiatrist now proclaims his determination to help these persons, by enlisting the coercive apparatus of the state in a therapeutic crusade against the sickness that supposedly causes their being unwanted. What the politicians and psychiatrists actually mean is that it is their duty to lead, and the taxpayers' to fund, prohibitively expensive campaigns to save the victims, viewed as defective objects, devoid of both rights and responsibilities.

I do not doubt that the desire to help is often genuine. The issue is not the benefactor's motive but his method, and the misfit between the treatment and the disease it is supposed to cure. We can help victims of famines or floods *impersonally,* by shipping them food or medicines. But we cannot help people impersonally who are the victims of their own religious beliefs, lifestyles, or intentional misconduct. Although the misfortunes of such persons may also manifest themselves in material deprivations and personal suffering, the cause and character of their problem is spiritual. Hence, we can help such "victims" only *personally,* by establishing and maintaining a bond of intimacy with them. Obviously, this is impossible if the moral values of the benefactor and his beneficiary oppose one another. Thus, although we can institutionalize helping the victims of natural disasters, we cannot institutionalize helping the "victims" of personal disasters.*

How, then, do we help chronic mental patients? For the reasons I set forth, this question cannot be answered in the abstract. It is possible to suggest, however, how to avoid harming them. C. S. Lewis put it this way:

> Of all the tyrannies a tyranny sincerely exercised for the good of its victims may be the most oppressive. . . . To be "cured" against one's will and cured of states which we may not regard as disease is to be put on a level with those who have not yet reached the age of reason or those who never will; to be classed with infants, imbeciles, and domestic animals. . . . For if crime and disease are to be regarded as the same thing, it follows that any state of mind which our masters choose to call "disease" can be treated as a crime; and compulsorily cured. . . . Even if the treatment is painful, even if it is life-long, even if it is fatal, that will be only a regrettable accident; the intention was purely therapeutic.[13]

To help the unwanted Other, we must therefore first relinquish the quest to classify, cure, and control him. Having done so, we can try to help him the same way we would try to help any person we respect—asking what he wants and, if his request is acceptable, helping him attain his goal or accept some compromise. Would that help him or be good for him? Who is to say? Moreover, in our secular world, where is the individual or institution ready to meet Shakespeare's requirement: "'Tis is not enough to help the feeble up,/ But to support him after"?[14] And how are we to respond to the person who is not feeble but only pretends to be, to secure our support?

---

* This generalization requires a slight qualification. Alcoholics Anonymous and some other self-help groups illustrate the possibility of organizing some types of personal help. However, such groups are in perpetual danger of losing their integrity by yielding to the temptation of accepting court-referred "clients" and government funds, a fate that has already befallen AA.

THE HUMAN CONDITION AND THE PROBLEM OF DEPENDENCY

Although we are animals, we are radically different from other creatures we call by that name. As children, we are extraordinarily dependent, for an extraordinarily long period, on our parents or parent surrogates. As adults, most of us possess an awesome capacity for symbolic experience and expression. As a result, many of us do not simply reproduce. Instead, we desire and dread having children and go to great lengths to implement our desires. If we are unable to procreate, we try desperately to undo the handicap. If we are able to reproduce and have children, we often neglect them, give them away, even kill them.[15] Although it seems self-contradictory, the generalization that children are both the most wanted and most unwanted human beings is, I think, profoundly true.

In this book, I shall view the history of civilization as, inter alia, a catalog of the various methods man has developed to dispose of unwanted persons and the pretexts with which he has justified doing so. Infanticide, abandonment, oblation, consignment to the foundling home, adoption, education, and mental hospitalization are some of the methods and pretexts that have been used, or are used, to dispose of unwanted children. The methods and pretexts used to dispose of unwanted adults are even more familiar—the poorhouse, the school, the concentration camp, the mental hospital, the nursing home. In short, I shall present the familiar subject of mental hospitalization from this somewhat unfamiliar perspective. Ordinarily, this subject is addressed as a medical problem, that is, as a problem of illness, treatment, and mental health policy. I shall address it as a problem of adult dependency and unwantedness, that is, as a problem of the political-economic and power relations between producers and nonproducers, stigmatizers and stigmatized, intrinsic to modern society.

The nature (or existence) of mental diseases presents an impasse that, for the moment, we ought to finesse. Although the question of the biological basis of mental illness, if any, is important, we need not resolve it to pursue our inquiry. That is, we need not decide whether mental patients suffer from brain diseases; or if they do, whether such diseases account for their unproductiveness and lawlessness. It is enough to acknowledge that a clear recognition of both *our* conception of the mental patient and *his* conception of himself are crucial for such an undertaking. Changes in psychiatric and social perspectives on the masturbator and the homosexual as mental patients illustrate the validity of this assertion.[16]

Do we regard the mental patient as a moral agent or not? Does he treat himself as a person responsible for supporting himself, or as a victim entitled to the support of others? Do we regard him, and does he regard himself, as sick and hence responsible for seeking medical care and cooperating with physicians? Or do we regard him, and does he regard himself, as not sick, the victim of an intrusive-coercive medical-legal system? Should we treat him, and does he want to be treated, as a responsible adult, or as an irresponsible child? Actually, such conceptions and presumptions, rather than any medical findings, determine our psychiatric policies.

Few of us are free of disease. However, suffering the slings and arrows of outrageous diseases—such as diabetes, epilepsy, or heart disease—does not diminish our rights as citizens or our responsibilities as persons. Perhaps the time will come when we shall base our psychiatric policies on such a "medical model"; that is, when instead of mouthing the cliché that mental illness is like any other illness, our mental health policies will rest on the principle that adults have rights and responsibilities that are unaffected, much less annulled, by psychiatric diagnoses. In practice, that would mean treating the psychiatrically diagnosed person as a moral agent who is expected to cope with his problems and obey the law. If he asks for help, we offer to help him on terms agreeable to both him and us. If he does not, we leave him alone. And if he breaks the law, we treat him as we would want to be treated by a policeman who stopped us for a traffic violation.

Psychiatry: Solution for the Problem of Adult Dependency

Although producers are ambivalent toward the nonproducers they must support, the dependency of young children, aged persons, and those temporarily disabled by genuine diseases is universally recognized as legitimate. These dependencies are tolerable because they are temporary. Children become adults. Old people die. The sick (usually) recover enough to cease being dependents or die. Last but not least, we tolerate the dependency of our kin better than that of the stranger. We do not regard our own children as parasites, but that is exactly how we tend to regard the able-bodied stranger who lives off the welfare or psychiatric system.

Although most mental patients appear to be able-bodied adults, we pretend that they suffer from genuine diseases that are genuinely disabling, and pledge ourselves to treat them as genuine dependents. It is important to understand how this view and policy arose.* Modernity is the mother of twins. One twin is science, technology, and limited government. The other is the able-bodied but unproductive adult and the efforts of producers to control and support him. Initially, the members of this new dependent class were categorized as indigents and dealt with by means of poor laws and workhouses. Gradually, the effort to cope with the problem of adult dependency merged with the new pseudoscience of psychiatry and led to storing adult dependents in mental hospitals. In short, I view our statist-institutional psychiatric practices not as specialized medical technics for treating mental diseases, but as socially approved procedures for disposing of unwanted persons, similar to such past social practices as segregating paupers in workhouses, incarcerating defaulting debtors in prisons, and exiling epileptics to colonies.

---

* I develop this story more fully throughout this book.

PART ONE

STORING THE UNWANTED

1

THE INDIGENT

To remove a man who has committed no misdemeanour, from a parish where he chooses to reside, is an evident violation of natural liberty and justice.

—Adam Smith[1]

Poverty is a fact of life. "You always have the poor with you," the Bible assures us.[2] However, society's criteria of poverty and its responses to it change from time to time and place to place.

Throughout most of history, indigence was the near-normal condition of the majority of mankind. However, in subsistence economies and feudal societies, with people bound to the soil and the clan, there were no individuals in our present sense of that word. The homeostasis of premodern communities thus precluded the possibility of poor persons, as indigent *individuals*, becoming social problems.

A BRIEF HISTORY OF POOR RELIEF

In Jewish and Christian communities, helping the poor was a familial and religious duty. The medieval establishments that provided for the poor, called "hospitals" in England and *Maisons Dieu* (God's houses) in France, were attached to monasteries, were supported by public donations, and functioned as guesthouses for "free to all . . . poor travellers as well as the sick, infirm, and aged."[3] The root meaning of the word *hospital* is to give shelter to a guest or traveler. In sixteenth-century England, there were some 800 such "hospitals."[4]

Until modern times, the population in virtually all societies consisted of masses of indigents, a few rich families, and one opulent "house," that of a pharaoh, emperor, or king. The material advancement of large numbers of ordinary people and the development of a so-called middle class are recent historical phenomena, originating in England, Scotland, and the Low Countries with the Reformation, the industrial revolution, and the free market. Widespread material advancement generated a heightened awareness of poverty, the appearance on the social scene of large numbers indigents, and an exploding vocabulary for naming them. In a study of Elizabethan "low life," Gamini Salgado describes "a vast army of wandering parasites . . . a ragged and motley band whose names in their own private tongue are as variously fascinating as their tricks and trades—patriarchos, palliards and priggers of prancers, autem-morts and walking-morts, fraters, Abraham men and rufflers . . . the list is all but endless."[5]

The Invention and Interpretation of Indigence

Although state and church are still not formally divorced in England, the two have long lived apart, their separation reflected, among other things, by the transformation of poor relief from a religious to a secular enterprise. In the sixteenth century, as the English people set out on the road to modernity, working became a virtue and idleness a sin, indeed a crime. Parliament undertook to define and curb vagrancy. The Act of 1531 defined a vagrant as "any man or woman being whole and mighty in body and able to labour, having no land, master, nor using any lawful merchandise, craft, or mystery whereby he might get his living."[6] David Little emphasizes that during the reign of Elizabeth there was a "widespread aversion . . . to 'that loathsome monster Idelness (the mother and breeder of Vacabounds) . . . that pestilent Canker . . . which is the root of all mischief.'"[7] The great English jurist, Sir Edward Coke (1562–1634) demanded the suppression of "that root evil, from whence all mischiefs proceed, and that is idleness."[8] In public, paupers were at all times required to wear the letter *P* on their clothes.

Consistent with this outlook, the Elizabethans regarded the idleness of an able-bodied person as a commission rather than omission and were prepared to punish it with the utmost severity. The Act of

1572 prescribed: "He [the sturdy beggar] was to be whipped and bored through the gristle of the right ear, and if he continued his roguery he was to suffer, in the last resort, death for felony."[9] We have inverted this outlook. According to the politically correct view, the idleness of an able-bodied person is an omission rather than a commission, indigence is a no-fault status of victimage, and the pauper is endowed with a constitutional right not only to the franchise but to welfare benefits and health care as well.

In 1597 and 1601, Parliament enacted the first English Poor Laws, mandating each parish to maintain its indigents and initiating the use of tax revenues to support them. From the start, the cost was considerable. In the seventeenth century, approximately 600,000 "cottagers and paupers"—more than 10 percent of the population of England and Wales—were dependent on the parish.[10] Thenceforth, the history of poor laws, like the history of mental health laws, is a tale of successive reforms, each seeking to correct the abuses of former practices, each in turn generating fresh abuses. "It is a singular curse in the records of our race," remarked Edward Bulwer-Lytton, British novelist and Member of Parliament, "that the destruction of one evil is often the generation of a thousand others. The Poor-laws were intended to prevent mendicancy; they have made mendicancy a legal profession."[11]

The drafters of the early poor laws were deeply conscious of both the economic and moral significance of work. Their aim was to rehabilitate the pauper by setting him to work. To this end, parishes began to erect Bridewells, named after the London penitentiary near St. Bride's Well, to "receive[d] vagrants and beggars who could not be convicted of any crime save that of wandering abroad and refusing to work."[12] In 1714, an Act authorized the "detention, restraint, and maintenance" of lunatics in Bridewells as well.[13] Gradually, Bridewells "degenerated into mixed receptacles of misery where every class of pauper, vicious or unfortunate, young or old, sick, well, or lunatic, was dumped."[14]

Contemporary observers quickly realized that the social processes that liberated the person, transforming him from clan member into individual, were also responsible for defining him, if he was poor, as indigent. Gertrude Himmelfarb described this metamorphosis thus:

> Before the introduction of manufacturing . . . there had been no "poor." It was manufacturing that liberated an entire class of people from bondage to the soil, and liberated them at the same time from territorial lords who had assumed responsibility for them in times of drought or war. In that earlier condition of servitude there had been no "poor," only "slaves." The poor were thus a "new class," a product of emancipation.[15]

The insane were also a new class, a product of replacing a theological with a medical perspective on dissent and deviance. Both indigence and insanity are thus the products of modernity, specifically, of individualism and of the new political relationship between the individual and the state. "It is a great law of social development," Arnold Toynbee observed a century ago, "that the movement from slavery to freedom is also a movement from security to insecurity of maintenance. There is a close connection between the growth of freedom and the growth of pauperism; it is scarcely too much to say that the latter is the price we pay for the former."[16] There is a similarly close connection between the growth of freedom-as-reason and the growth of insanity-as-unreason.[17] The factors responsible for the individualization of poverty as a *personal trait* were thus also responsible for its initial identification as a *political problem,* and its present perception as a *medical illness.*

Poor Relief and the Perception of Poverty

When poor relief was a religious affair, producers supported nonproducers out of their sense of duty to God, rather than out of a sense of duty to the poor themselves. So long as that was the case, the engine of poor relief was driven more by the donors' rectitude than by the recipients' need; and the donors, feeling ennobled by their charitableness, were relatively unconcerned about the corrupting effect of the dole on the paupers' character.

As the focus of poor relief shifted from pleasing God to reclaiming the pauper, from voluntary donation to compulsory taxation, peoples' perspective on helping the indigent underwent a radical change. Helping the poor by giving to charity salves a person's conscience. Being taxed so the state can support parasites vexes a person's soul. This is the reason secular programs of poor relief immediately excited the fear that maintaining able-bodied poor persons on the dole would seduce them into lives of parasitism. "You [the English] offered a premium for the encouragement of idleness," observed Benjamin Franklin in 1766, "and you should not now wonder that it has had its effect in the increase in poverty."[18]

Albeit Franklin's remark had merit, as we now know only too well, it was too simplistic, failing to distinguish between "real" and "perceived" poverty. England was then the most rapidly developing and most powerful country in the world. Some observers were awestruck by the magnificent tusks of this mammoth, seeing England as a land of incredible prosperity. Others were appalled by the beast's ugly rear end, seeing

England as a country full of destitute people.[19] The two images fed off one another. From the market point of view, "Pauperism is the product of freedom."[20] From the Marxist point of view, it is a product of oppression.[21] The point is that the market is responsible not for poverty per se, but for poverty publicly identified and politically ratified. No student of history or economics doubts that there was far more privation in old, feudal societies than there is in modern, industrialized nations. However, unlike the perceived and acknowledged poverty of capitalism, feudal poverty was unperceived and unacknowledged.* With the advance of the free market, prosperity diffused over ever wider portions of the population, and the collective poverty of the peasant on the land was transformed into the individualized poverty of the urban laborer. The impoverishment of the former was veiled, whereas that of the latter was glaring. The conspicuous cost of maintaining the poor lifted his visibility to a new plane. Once poor relief became a politically centralized enterprise funded by the government, its cost began to explode, from less than 2 million pounds in 1785, to more than 4 million in 1805, and to 8 million by 1817.[22] The rest is history.

STORING THE UNPRODUCTIVE

After millennia of unrelieved scarcity and slavery, the dream of prosperity and liberty for many members of society first appears on the stage of history as a grand Scottish-English-Protestant vision. It is a vision that places exceptionally high value on effort and productivity, by persons as well as property, exalting hard work and savings as the engines of prosperity, and debasing idleness and indigence as impediments to it. Thus, the owners of land, factory, and machinery, in cooperation with the workers whose labor turns raw materials into consumer goods, are perceived as virtuous providers; whereas idle paupers, lacking both employment and property, are perceived as warped parasites.

The Market Economy and Its Outcasts

The existence in society of a large class of adult dependents, requiring government-mandated relief, presents a irksome problem for society. If

---

* Poverty in the Soviet Union was similarly unacknowledged within the system, and often unperceived outside it. Even today, after the collapse of the Soviet empire, left-liberal ideologues in academia systematically mask poverty in Marxist countries, and dramatize it in capitalist countries.

the model citizen of a free-market society is a producer, the able-bodied adult nonproducer is bound to be disdained as a deviant. Not surprisingly, an obsession with work, both as economic necessity and emblem of virtue, dominated debates on poor relief right through to the end of the nineteenth century. Society's economically motivated inclination to exclude the idle pauper from the ranks of normal adults (citizens) was reinforced by the traditional exception of "infants, idiots, and the insane" from the body politic. Since infants, idiots, and the insane could neither support themselves nor enter into binding contracts, they were required to be under the tutelage of competent adults. It was tempting to assimilate the idle pauper to this group. Himmelfarb writes:

> In that contractual world [of the free market] the pauper had no part. . . . Since the framework defined the boundaries of society, the pauper was, by definition so to speak, an outcast—an outcast not so much by virtue of his character, actions, or misfortunes, but by the mere fact of his dependency, his reliance on relief rather than his own labor for his subsistence. From being an outcast it was only a short step to being regarded a criminal. Hence the workhouse, the visible confirmation of his status as an outcast was also, in popular parlance, a prison, a "Bastille."[23]

In a market economy, logic dictates juxtaposing industriousness with idleness, the productive with the unproductive adult. In a therapeutic society, logic dictates juxtaposing mental health with mental illness, the self-caring with the self-neglecting person. Casting out the unproductive (parasitic) person was thus intrinsic to eighteenth- and nineteenth-century English society, just as casting out the unreasonable (psychotic) person is intrinsic to contemporary society. The workhouse, Himmelfarb cogently observes, "was meant to be cruel—not in terms of food or physical conditions, or arduous labor, but conceptually."[24] For the same reason, cruelty is intrinsic to the mental hospital and accounts for the futility of mental health reforms.[25]

The Criminalization and Decriminalization of Poverty

English and Scottish scholars were the first and foremost supporters both of the free market and political liberty, epitomized by Adam Smith (1723–1790), and of the principles and practices of storing unwanted persons, epitomized by Jeremy Bentham (1748–1832). When Bentham entered on the stage of social reform, secular poor relief was an integral part of the British social fabric. Bentham's main contribution to the subject lay in his efforts to abolish outdoor relief, on the ground that it

allowed able-bodied individuals to shirk their duty to support themselves. His motto was: "No relief but upon the terms of coming into the
house."[26] In 1834, when outdoor relief to the able-bodied poor was abolished, the Poor Law Commissioners vindicated this measure as follows:

> In no part of Europe except England has it been thought fit that the provision
> of relief . . . should be applied to more than the relief of *indigence,* the state of
> a person unable to labour, or unable to obtain, in return for his labour, the
> means of subsistence. It has never been deemed expedient that the provision
> should extend to the relief of *poverty;* that is, the state of one who, in order to
> obtain mere subsistence, is forced to have recourse to labour.[27]

Yet, after drawing a distinction between the poor (who did not merit
relief) and the indigent (who did), the Commissioners complained about
"the mischievous ambiguity of the word *poor.*"[28] History does repeat itself. Today, psychiatrists draw a distinction between nondangerous
mental illness (that is not a ground for commitment) and dangerous
mental illness (that is), and complain about the ambiguity of the
term *mental illness.*

Denying liberty to recipients of poor relief was consistent with Bentham's view that they were unruly children who needed to be controlled
by a paternalistic state. "The persons in question," he wrote, "are a sort
of forward children—a set of persons not altogether sound in mind, not
altogether possessed of that moral sanity without which a man cannot in
justice to himself any more than to the community be intrusted with the
uncontrolled management of his own conduct and affairs."[29] Note the
merging of the images of infancy, indigence, and insanity, yielding a construct closely resembling our image of the homeless mental patient.
Seemingly unaware of Bentham and the history of controlling the poor,
psychiatrists now advance arguments very similar to Bentham's in their
effort to defend restricting the liberty of the mental patient.

Producers are rarely happy about supporting dependents, even when
they are their own children or aged parents. When the dependents are
strangers, the producers' resentment of them cannot be denied and must
be dealt with. That is why, formerly, people tried to distinguish between
the able-bodied and the disabled pauper, and now try to distinguish between mentally healthy homeless persons (able to work) and mentally ill
homeless persons (unable to work). The impulse for wanting to make the
distinction is understandable. However, unless we are willing to resort
to unacceptably brutal measures to compel nonproducers to work, it is
impossible to distinguish between persons who cannot and those who
do not want to work. "Nothing," warned Tocqueville, "is so difficult to

distinguish as the nuances which separate unmerited misfortune from adversity produced by vice."[30]

The Workhouse: The Emblem of Secular Poor Relief

Administering institutionalized poor relief required criteria for identifying the persons who qualified for it. Initially, the list included only orphans, women without husbands or kinfolk, the "decrepit aged" lacking family support, and the sick. Although the dependency of these persons was economically troubling, it was morally unproblematic. The dependency of the able-bodied adult male was a very different matter. The community's moral expectation of him was that if he did not work, he did not deserve to eat, and if he was supported by charity, he did not deserve the blessings of liberty.*

While the text of the history of poor relief is assisting the indigent, its subtext is the providers' consuming concern that poor people might yield to the temptation to take advantage of society's largesse. Assistance was thus deliberately organized to be disagreeable and demeaning. The workhouse, declared George Crabbe in a poem famous in its day (1783), "is a prison with a milder name/ Which few inhabit without dread or shame."[31] In a similar vein, George Nicholls wrote: "Let the poor see and feel, that their parish, although it will not allow them to perish through absolute want, is yet the hardest taskmaster, the closest paymaster, and the most harsh and unkind friend they can apply to."[32] The cruelty intrinsic to the workhouse system was excused by the need to discourage idleness, much as the malice intrinsic to the mental hospital system has been excused by the need to provide treatment.

Despite all efforts to reduce indigence, it grew, illustrating the bitter truth of the maxim that what the government pays for, it gets more of. Poor relief encouraged the relativization of poverty, defining it "as a function of 'felt wants' rather than of basic needs."[33] "The accommodation of an European prince," wrote Adam Smith, "does not always so much exceed that of an industrious and frugal peasant, as the accommodation of the latter exceeds that of many an African king, the absolute master of the lives and liberties of ten thousand naked savages."[34] In 1833, Alexis de Tocqueville visited England and arrived at the same conclusion as Smith: "The countries appearing to be the most impoverished, are those which in reality account for the fewest indigents. In

---

* In those days, Englishmen would have considered the idea of giving the franchise to nonproducers as absurd as we would consider the idea of giving the franchise to noncitizens.

Portugal, there are hardly any paupers, [whereas in England] one-sixth of the inhabitants . . . live at the expense of public charity."[35]

The upward relativization of poverty has advanced rapidly since then. Today in the United States, the Census Bureau identifies more than 30 million Americans as "poor," and 1 in 10 qualifies to receive food stamps.[36] By the standards of our own recent past, not to mention those of less developed countries, most of the poor people in the United States are well off. According to a report in *The Wall Street Journal*, 40 percent of officially poor householders own their own homes:

> The average home owned by a "poor" person is a three-bedroom house with a garage and a porch or patio. . . . One million "poor" people own homes valued at more than $80,000. . . . The average American poor person has twice as much living space as the average Japanese citizen and four times as much as the average Russian. . . . Most "poor" Americans today are better housed, better fed, and own more personal property than average Americans throughout most of the 20th century.[37]

These statistics cannot be attributed to the *Journal's* conservative leanings. In an essay on American affluence in *Parade Magazine*, financial writer Andrew Tobias writes: "Not every American has these things [faxes, etc.], but even among our poor, 60 percent own automobiles. Compare that with Somalia or Russia or China or India or Africa or Mexico. Or even Japan."[38] We have redefined the meaning of the word *poor*. It no longer means destitute, in the sense in which Orwell might have used this term a mere half century ago.[39] Instead, it denotes anyone in the bottom 10 or 20 percent of the income scale. This relativization of poverty, as I noted earlier, explains why the richest countries have the greatest number of persons officially classified as poor, that is, qualified to receive public assistance. The analogous relativization of insanity explains why the technologically most advanced countries have the greatest number of persons officially classified as mentally ill, that is, qualified to receive services from the psychiatric and Social Security systems.

Although contemporary observers were quick to note that the poor laws were "pauperizing the poor," once the state assumed the role of dolemaster—and stripped the churches of access to the taxpayers' money—the foundation for the welfare state was firmly set. By the nineteenth century, reformers stopped trying to abolish the poor laws and concentrated instead on developing methods to distinguish among various types of impoverished persons, hoping to rationalize bestowing benefits by matching them against need and merit. The result was that they had almost as many diagnostic categories for poverty as we have for mental illness. Not so long ago, people thought they could distinguish between the "beggar," the "sturdy beggar," the "industrious poor," the "laboring poor," the "pauper," the "indigent," and the "impotent." Their strategic fictions, whose aim was to regulate poor relief, were no more or less ridiculous than are our strategic fictions for regulating psychiatric relief, which include categories such as "pathological gambling," "pyromania," "factitious disorder," and "insomnia."[40]

In a society as deeply committed to the protection of individual liberty as Victorian England, the incarceration of the poor as quasi criminals could not go unchallenged forever. For people who love liberty, nothing can change the fact that a person detained against his will is a prisoner, regardless of how his guards define his status or describe his place of detention. A person may be deprived of liberty for good or bad reasons, but deprived of liberty he is. This fact set the stage for the demise of the workhouse.

The opening salvo in the battle to abolish imprisonment for indigence was fired by Benjamin Disraeli in 1837, when he declared: "In England, poverty is a crime."[41] That rebuke challenged the principle behind the penalizing of poverty. Henceforth, the struggle on behalf of the poor was fought not for more *material relief*, but for more *political power*; it was exemplified by the Chartist movement, whose goal was universal male suffrage. That effort failed. In the nineteenth century, popular opinion was not yet ready to embrace the view that the dependent poor, who do not contribute to the maintenance of society, should be given the franchise. Englishmen on relief did not receive the vote until 1918, when women were enfranchised as well.*

In retrospect, the poor laws clearly rested on an unresolved conflict between personal freedom and freedom of property.† The person incarcerated in the workhouse had a right to the freedom of his person, and the person whose taxes supported him had a right to his property.[42] The identical conflict reappears in our mental health policies. The person incarcerated in the mental hospital has a right to freedom, and the person whose taxes support him has a right to property.

After the workhouse was unmasked as a de facto prison, it gradually fell into disrepute. However, it disappeared only in our century,

---

* I am narrating these events without wishing to imply that I believe giving the franchise to persons with no material stake in their society is a good thing.
† Another manifestation of this conflict was the debtor's prison, discussed in Chapter 2.

replaced in part by the state hospital, and in part by the social programs of the welfare state.

The Merging of Indigence and Insanity

In the eighteenth century, social practices aimed at controlling the indigent and the insane developed in tandem, and both became intertwined with policies aimed at controlling criminals. During the nineteenth century in the United States, agencies providing relief for the poor, insane asylums for the mentally ill, and prisons for the criminal converged into a single, bureaucratic system, called Boards of Charity and Corrections, whose main responsibility was "the direct administration of prisons, reformatories, mental hospitals, and other welfare institutions."[43]

The similarities between the nineteenth-century workhouse and the modern mental hospital extend far beyond both being incarnations of total institutions.[44] Faced with contradictions between each institution's avowedly benevolent aims and manifestly social-control functions, reformers tried to placate the public and their own consciences by performing semantic surgery on the institutions' names. In 1904, the Poor Law Commissioners declared that "the name 'workhouse' should be done away with and the term 'state home' or 'state infirmary' substituted."[45] Insane asylums have similarly been renamed state hospitals, psychopathic hospitals, psychiatric hospitals, psychiatric centers, community mental health centers, and John Doe Centers (the name often commemorating some former madhouse superintendent).

The arguments advanced for and against the workhouse and the madhouse also resemble one another. Critics of the workhouse asked: Is poverty a crime? Isn't the workhouse "a prison with a milder name"?[46] Its defenders replied: No, poverty is not a crime; it is a misfortune. Incarceration in the workhouse is not imprisonment; it is a means of maintaining those unable to care for themselves and helping them become productive citizens. Today, critics of commitment ask: Is mental illness a crime? Isn't psychiatric incarceration simply a form of imprisonment? Apologists for psychiatric power answer: No, mental illness is not a crime; it is a disease. Incarceration in the mental hospital is not loss of liberty; it is a means of restoring the patient to liberty, lost as a result of insanity.[47]

There is, however, a dramatic difference between the workhouse and the mental hospital, namely, the posture of the press toward each. In 1834, the London *Times* bluntly declared that the workhouse was a prison: "Such a system amounts to a declaration that every pauper is a criminal, and that, under the name of workhouses, prisons shall be erected throughout the land for their safe custody and punishment."[48] Today, the American press enthusiastically embraces the canard that involuntary mental hospitalization is bona fide medical treatment and a blessing for the "patient."

The Pauper: Criminal, Client, Patient

It was one thing for the disenfranchised pauper to acquire political rights, formerly belonging only to members of the propertied classes; acquiring their habits of industry, self-discipline, and delayed gratification was quite another matter. Despite valiant efforts by the Victorians to solve the problem of poverty, their remedies seemed only to increase the number of poor persons and the "problem of poverty." At the dawn of the twentieth century, Charles Booth (1840–1916), a wealthy businessman and prominent antipoverty warrior, claimed that one-third of the people in London were "poor" and were his, and society's, "clients."[49] The welfare state, based on the principle of providing state support not only for the poor but for all "needy" persons, had arrived. Soon, its mandate was extended to supplying a variety of social services, initially only to those who could not purchase such services on the open market, and subsequently to virtually the entire population.

An inevitable consequence of the principle of welfarism was that access to a so-called basic level of decent subsistence, which could only escalate with the passage of time, became perceived as a political right or entitlement. The "last" of the Scriptures did not become the "first," but they did become "special." In feudal times, the aristocracy, by virtue of birth, was entitled to the services of the laboring poor. Today, the roles are almost reversed: The indigent and the insane, by virtue of material and mental insufficiencies, are entitled to a proportion of the producers' earnings.

In tandem with the metamorphosis of the pauper from disgraceful quasi criminal into no-fault client possessing entitlements, a new bureaucratic-professional class came into being, charged with the task of mediating between providers and parasites. Called "social welfare workers" or simply "social workers," their ostensible mandate was to help the poor obtain food and shelter and prepare them to enter the job market. In reality, they became functionaries of the policymakers, stigmatizing and controlling their clients while ceaselessly expanding their client base. Society's responses to poverty, unemployment, lawlessness, and craziness have thus merged in a vast quasi-therapeutic bureaucracy whose basic mandate is storing the unwanted.

2

THE DEBTOR

Belief in the obligatory force of contracts and respect for the given word are going, if not in some spots actually gone, in the law of today.
—*Roscoe Pound*[1]

If insanity is due to brain disease, it is partly a medical matter. Although insolvency might also be partly the result of disease, it is not considered to be a medical matter. The history of the practice of imprisonment for failing to respect financial obligation (debt) thus forms a particularly instructive background against which to view our present practice of imprisonment for failing to respect personal and social obligation (mental illness).

Although lending, borrowing, and defaulting are universal phenomena, imprisoning the defaulting debtor is a singular social response to nonpayment of debt. The belief that the only proper response to a particular social problem is the policy prevailing in a person's own society is a mark of parochialism or stupidity. Although it is understandable why people hold such ethnocentric views, there is nothing admirable about doing so. Admittedly, social policies rest on, and reflect, the values of the community. Hence, so long as people are satisfied with their customary moral priorities, they refuse to entertain other, possibly more "rational," policies as valid alternatives.

CONTRACT: THE PILLAR OF ORDERED SOCIETY

The Framers of the Constitution never doubted that among the principles on which the United States was founded the sanctity of private property and the inviolability of contracts ranked very high. Property was the foundation for liberty, contract the bulwark against force and fraud. It is "a source of especially keen distress to students of political theory," writes Clinton Rossiter in his Introduction to *The Federalist Papers,* "that they [the Framers] apparently found it unnecessary to make more than a handful of explicit observations on private property as a right of man . . ."[2] Alexander Hamilton did warn against the danger of individual States showing favoritism to their citizens by enacting "Laws in violation of private contracts . . ."[3] James Madison insisted that ". . . laws impairing the obligation of contracts are contrary to the first principles of the social compact and to every principle of sound legislation . . . [and] are prohibited by the spirit and scope of these fundamental charters."[4] Finally, Article I, Section 10, of the Constitution states: "No State shall . . . pass any . . . Law Impairing the Obligation of Contracts." That this principle is now observed more in the breach than in the observance is widely recognized. Roscoe Pound attributed the phenomenon, I think rightly, to

> "contractual dirigism" . . . and the humanitarian idea of rendering a service to debtors or promisors by the state lifting or shifting burdens or losses, and hence the burden of promises, so as to put them upon those better able to bear them. The two are closely related. When contracts are made for the people by the service state, they do not feel any strong moral duty to perform them. If the state makes the contract, let the state perform it or compensate the disappointed promisee.[5]

The Creditor: Benefactor or Malefactor?

The practice of lending and borrowing—persons, animals, objects, money—must be as old as civilization itself. Owning what another lacks and covets, and hence what he has an incentive to borrow or steal, provokes sentiments in both lender and borrower whose roots extend into the deepest recesses of our nature. Jeremy Bentham astutely located the source of the debtor's resentment against his creditor in the child's intemperance and incompetence. In his classic, *Defense of Usury,* he wrote:

> The business of a money-lender . . . has no where nor at any time been a popular one. Those who have the resolution to sacrifice the present to the

future, are natural objects of envy to those who have sacrificed the future to the present. The children who have eat their cake are the natural enemies of the children who have theirs. While the money is hoped for, and for a short time after it has been received, he who lends it is a friend and bene-factor: by the time the money is spent, and the evil hour of reckoning is come, the benefactor is found to have changed his nature, and to have put on the tyrant and the oppressor. It is oppression for a man to reclaim his own money; it is none to keep it from him.[6]

When two persons exchange goods or services, the transaction is rarely simultaneous. Usually, one party delivers his part of the bargain first, and the other reciprocates after a certain delay, which may run from a few seconds to many years. The potentiality for nonreciprocity is inherent in this lapse of time. In addition, the relationship between creditor and debtor is often informal and the borrower may not be re-quired to repay his debt in time, or in full, or perhaps at all. For exam-ple, a man may give his friend food, clothing, or money, and expect to be repaid only if and when the borrower is able to do so. This sort of arrangement tends to be based on bonds of mutual affection and obli-gation between the parties, such as prevail in families and among friends, and typically remains a private affair.

Outside the family, lending and borrowing tends to be more formal, based on a legally binding contract. Still, patterns of lending, borrowing, repaying, and penalizing the defaulting debtor are very diverse, each cul-ture representing its values through this mechanism. In ancient Rome, for example, imprisoning a criminal was not a recognized legal sanction, but enslaving him was. The delinquent debtor, called *addictus*,* was sen-tenced to be his creditor's slave.[7]

THE BIBLE, THE CLAN, AND THE CRIME OF USURY

In Exodus, God prohibits the Israelites from charging interest to their coreligionists.[8] In Leviticus, the injunction is repeated: "And if your brother becomes poor . . . you shall maintain him. . . . Take no in-terest from him, but fear your God."[9] Finally, there is the momentous Deuteronomic directive from God to his Chosen People:

---

* The prefix *ad* means "in the direction of"; and *dictus* means to speak solemnly, as does a judge when he pronounces a sentence. The etymological root of our present concept of addiction, as when we speak of a person being addicted (enslaved) to a drug or to gam-bling, lies in that ancient practice.

At the end of every seven years . . . every creditor shall release what he has lent to his neighbor; . . . Of a foreigner you may exact it; but whatever of yours is with your brother your hand shall release. . . . You shall not lend upon interest to your brother. . . . To a foreigner you may lend upon interest.[10]

The rationale of these rules—to strengthen the bonds of solidarity among members of the clan and weaken them with outsiders—was appropriate for regulating relations among people living in a tribal, agricultural society. By the same token, such rules are unsuitable for regulating relations among strangers engaged in trade. People unrelated by bonds of kinship do not treat each other as brothers.*

The transition from Judaism to Christianity marks a major advance in social consciousness, from tribal exclusivism to universal brotherhood (at least in principle). The New Testament rules transform lending into giving, credit into charity: "It is well with the man who deals generously and lends. . . . He who is kind to the Lord lends to the poor, and he will repay him for his deed."[11] In an often-quoted passage, Jesus exhorts his disciples to follow what might be called the fundamental rule of antibanking: "But love your enemies, and do good, and lend hoping for nothing in return; and your reward will be great, and you will be sons of the Most High."[12] Here, the destitute displace the Jews as God's favorite children, and almsgiving is raised to the level of religious worship. The goodness of God, not the borrower's exertion, repays the lender. The contrast between the Old and New Testament precepts concerning credit are the sources of the two stereotypical images of the creditor—the Jew, as greedy exploiter of the helpless pauper, and the Christian, as God-fearing benefactor selflessly aiding the needy.[13] The Jewish, Deuteronomic standard became a source of anti-Semitism, and the Christian, antibanking standard, a source of hypocrisy.†

Neither the Jewish rule, imposing different obligations on creditors and debtors depending on whether they are or are not members of the Tribe, nor the Christian rule, requiring lenders to be self-sacrificing altruists, meets the requirements of trade between strangers. The growth of commerce during the Middle Ages led to the abandonment of both sets of Biblical rules and gave birth to modern banking. Contrary to common belief, moneylending was never primarily a Jewish occupation. Christian bankers in Italy and the Low Countries—especially in

---

* I disregard here the unbrotherly relations between Cain and Abel.
† All three major Western religions lay down strict rules about lending and borrowing, regulating or prohibiting charging interest ("usury").

Siena, Florence, Venice, and Amsterdam—laid the foundations for mer-cantilism and capitalism.

After the Reformation, the influence of the Deuteronomic law on Western morals disappeared altogether. This happened not because the great Reformers were devout free-marketeers, but because, turning the tables on the Church, they attacked the papacy as a usurious ex-ploiter of the poor. "Luther stands forth," wrote Benjamin Nelson, "as the spokesman of the German nation against the 'usurious' extortions of the Roman Church and ecclesiastical foundations. All Germany, he charges, is being exhausted by usury."[14] Luther's anticapitalist agita-tion was simultaneously an attack on the Church's secular power and a summons to reembrace a primitive proto-Christianity, leading some Lutherans "to declare not only interest taking, but even private prop-erty, to be incompatible with brotherly love."[15] As a result, Luther's greatest influence was not on economics, but on politics. In economic affairs, Calvin proved to be the prophet.

Calvin, Capitalism, and Contract

Like every person engaged in the business of molding public opinion, John Calvin was a rhetorician. And as he was a priest, he claimed that the will of God ratified his pronouncements. His unique talent lay in endow-ing with religious legitimacy hard work and frugality that generated prosperity and wealth.

The Church held that poverty is blessed. Calvin declared that pros-perity is even more blessed: "Riches in themselves and by their na-ture are not at all to be condemned; and it is even a great blasphemy against God to disapprove of riches, implying that a man who pos-sesses them is thereby wholly corrupted. For where do riches come from, if not from God?"[16]

The Church insisted that lending money at interest is a sin. Calvin rejected this proposition and deployed a tactic that makes him appear very modern. He proposed banishing the word *usury:* "Only those exac-tions are condemned as unjust in which the creditor, losing sight of equity, burdens and oppresses his debtor. . . . I wish the name [usury] itself were banished from the world."[17]

Calvin's attack on the traditional interpretation of the Deuteronomic passage marks a turning point in the history of Western thought. Since Calvin was not about to spurn the Old Testament, he offered an inspired reinterpretation of the Jewish rule on usury, arguing that lending money at interest could not be an unqualified evil because God permits no evil, and He permitted Jews to engage in this practice when dealing with

Gentiles. Furthermore, the Deuteronomic commandment applied to Jews only, and was not binding on Christians: "God had laid the Jews alone and not foreign nations under the obligation of the law against usury."[18]* This ingenious tactic enabled Calvin to sanction business and trade as positively godly vocations: "For the life of the godly is aptly compared to business, since they ought to deal with one another in order to maintain their fellowship."[19] Veritably, Calvin is the patron saint of contract, commerce, and capitalism. "Adversity," he declared, "is a sign of God's absence, prosperity of his presence."[20]

In two grand leaps, (Protestant) Christianity transcended the Jewish tribal ethic and established interpersonal reciprocity as a moral ideal, respect for private property as an economic ideal, and the faithful execution of contracts as a legal ideal. The first leap, executed by Jesus and his disciples, consisted of proclaiming the *brotherhood of all men (persons) in God.* The second, executed by Calvin and his disciples, consisted of exalting *reciprocity in human relations, especially economic relations.* Calvin astutely reinterpreted charging and paying interest as two sides of the same coin, "since otherwise a just reciprocity would not have been preserved, without which one party must needs be injured."[21]

The immense success of Calvin's teachings about usury is reflected by the fact that "Calvinist pastors were under pressure to toe this line. In 1564–65, Bartholomew Gernhard of St. Andrews, Rudolstadt, was forced out of office for refusing communion to men who had loaned money at interest; and in 1587 at Ratisbon five preachers were expelled for insisting on preaching against usury."[22]

Probably because even before the Reformation, the English and the Scots were successful seafaring and trading people who had embraced the values of private property and individual liberty, Calvinism proved to be especially influential in Britain. In 1545, the English parliament formally approved lending at interest.[23] "Englishmen's fundamental rights," declared William Penn (1621–1670), "included right and title to your own lives, liberties, and estates: in this every man is a sort of little Sovereign to himself."[24] Note that Penn characterized the rights to life, liberty, and property as the rights not of mankind in the abstract, but as those of Englishmen.

These remarks linking Calvin to contract must not be interpreted as implying that he supported a right to self-ownership. As a devout Christian, Calvin believed that God owns man and viewed market relations

---

* Calvin might have noted that the divine commandment requiring male circumcision also applied only to Jews.

simply as His design of the proper social order.[25] Nor was Calvin a supporter of the open society. Just the contrary. My remarks are intended only to emphasize that modern capitalism required respect for property; respect for property begot respect for persons as proprietors; and respect for proprietors generated respect for the satisfaction of contract, a story to which I now turn.[26]

THE DEBTOR'S PRISON AND THE SANCTITY OF CONTRACT

Imprisoning the defaulting debtor, first mentioned in English Common Law in 1285, became a frequent practice in the sixteenth century, when the English people began their rapid ascent up the ladder of economic and political development. Soon, the debtor's prison appeared to be an indispensable social institution, and remained so until the second half of the nineteenth century. Calvin's profound influence on English thought regarding credit and the obligations of the debtor is dramatically illustrated by Jeremy Bentham's classic, *Defense of Usury*. In that work, he declared:

> Among the various species or modifications of liberty, of which on different occasions we have heard so much in England, I do not recollect ever seeing any thing yet offered in behalf of the *liberty of making one's own terms* in money-bargains . . . this meek and unassuming species of liberty has been suffering much injustice. In a word, the proposition I have been accustomed to lay down to myself on this subject is the following one, viz. that no man of ripe years and of sound mind, acting freely, and with his eyes open, ought to be hindered, with a view to his advantage, from making such bargain, in the way of obtaining money, as he thinks fit: nor, (what is a necessary consequence) any body hindered from supplying him, upon any terms he thinks proper to accede to.[27]

In 1787, when Bentham offered this argument, England was already the world's leading industrial and commercial power, and the system of debtor's prisons was an indispensable feature of the English social landscape.

Imprisonment for Debt

Imprisonment for debt has a long and colorful history, richly documented in *belles lettres* as well as in legal literature. Sir William

Holdsworth summarized the basic premise underlying the practice as follows:

> If it is advantageous to commerce that the standard of commercial morality should be high, and that credit should be given, it is necessary to bring home to such persons, in the only way in which they will feel it, the consequences of their conduct. It is true that the imprisonment of a debtor, who is unable or unwilling to pay his debt, will not necessarily give the creditor his money; but it will tend to stop such abuses of confidence.[28]

The promise to discharge commercial obligations was taken so seriously that the principle could also be enforced against a "delinquent" worker, that is, one who did not show up for work as pledged: "In the middle of eighteenth century, Statutes were passed giving justices power to jail workmen who absented themselves from work in breach of contract 'to the great disappointment and loss of the persons with whom they so contract.'"[29]

It did not matter why the debtor was insolvent. Failure to repay debt as due made the delinquent borrower appear to be like a thief or able-bodied beggar, a predator or parasite living off the labor of others. So secure was the place of debtor's prisons in eighteenth-century English society that no Englishman could imagine life without them, just as no American today can imagine life without mental hospitals. The "abuses" of debtor's prisons, like those of mental hospitals, came with the territory.

Everyone realized that once an impecunious debtor was imprisoned, he could no longer earn any money and he and his family sank ever deeper into destitution. However, imprisoning the delinquent debtor was not merely a utilitarian act, it was also a ceremonial and symbolic performance. The sanction combined the contract-violator's punishment for his wrongdoing and society's ritual observance of the sanctity of contracts. Involuntarily hospitalizing the mental patient serves the same dual purpose. Nearly everyone realizes that psychiatric coercion does not cure the mental patient and aggravates his conflicts with his relatives, but it punishes the patient (by means of so-called treatments) and discourages people from taking advantage of the largesse of the state (free room and board in return for being "psychotic").

Certain peculiarities of English customs and laws gave the practice of imprisoning debtors a unique piquancy. English legal tradition placed a mythic importance on landed property. Only a debtor's liquid assets could be confiscated; freehold land and certain other nonmonetary assets were protected from the creditor's reach. This practice was a relic of feudalism, in which the integrity of family estates was protected from the profligacy of their owners, who were regarded as temporary occupants of a privileged position rather than as individual proprietors. Prior to 1830, the delinquent debtor was sometimes richer than his creditor. The creditor had the power to deprive him of liberty, but not of land. When people valued the sanctity of contract more highly than individual liberty, they viewed such an arrangement as rational and desirable.

Criticisms of the "Abuse" of Debtor's Prisons

The seemingly antiquated criticisms of debtor's prisons and the modern criticisms of mental hospitals are amazingly similar. In each case, the critics supported the institution in principle, and objected only to certain practices they considered to be "abuses."

Reformers of debtor's prisons believed that the delinquent debtor is justly deprived of liberty. They deplored only the suffering of the impoverished inmates and the frequency of imprisonment for debt. A typical eighteenth-century critic referred respectfully to "that necessary part of the Law, call'd *Imprisonment for Debt*, [which ought to] be executed with *Humanity* and with *Equity*," and protested only against the "*Cruelty* and Inhumanity of *Jaylors* and Prison-keepers."[30] Another critic acknowledged:

> Therefore if we will support *Trade*, we must encourage *Petty Credit*; and if you will support *Petty Credit*, you must not take away the *Security* to the *Creditor*; the Security of the Tradesman's trusting his Neighbour is the Power he has by Law to *enforce* his Payment, and of arresting and imprisoning the Debtor if he fails or refuses. . . . If you take away this *Right*, you take away the *Credit*; for no Man will sell his Goods upon a *Faith* which the Debtor is not obligated to *keep*.[31]

As late as the nineteenth century, a reformer pleaded that "the benevolent principles of genuine Christianity . . . [must inspire people] to persevere in relieving those Debtors, who may be found worthy, distressed, and friendless."[32]

Although it is unlikely that such lamentations helped the victims, they no doubt made the reformers feel much better. Moreover, imprisonment for debt had become so common that the very number of detained debtors offered reformers a limitless opportunity to ventilate their sympathies on behalf of these victims.

As one might expect, the system of imprisoning debtors worked differently for the poor and the rich. The propertyless delinquent was dispatched to a dungeon where he languished in misery and often soon perished. Samuel Johnson estimated that each year a quarter of all imprisoned debtors died, "overborne with sorrow, consumed by famine, or putrefied by filth."[33] In contrast, the propertied delinquent could "voluntarily" enter a posh private residence, called "sponging house,"* and live comfortably under a kind of house arrest while negotiating for a settlement with his creditor. Indeed, he could make use of an even more shameful legal fiction: He could reside, unguarded and unsupervised, in a house or apartment located within certain areas— for example, in the Southwark district of London—and be "legally considered [to be] in prison."[34] This injustice moved the anonymous critic cited earlier to propose that rich and poor debtors be regarded as two distinct classes: "When I argue against the Knavery of the Debtor, in making himself a *voluntary* Prisoner, on purpose to defraud and delude his *Creditors*, it naturally follows that the prisons should be purged from all such voluntary, fraudulent People."[35]

The fact that some persons were confined in debtor's prisons "voluntarily" may surprise people.† However, the debtor who made such a decision was neither mad nor masochistic. He simply chose what he regarded as the least of three evils. Paying for his keep in a sponging house and thus pressuring his creditor to settle was preferable to paying him in full or going to a common debtor's prison.

The Demise of Debtor's Prisons

In 1758, Samuel Johnson—who had himself been imprisoned for debt— wrote:

> The end of all civil regulations is to secure private happiness from private malignity; to keep individuals from the power of one another; but this end is apparently neglected, when a man, irritated with loss, is allowed to be the judge of his own cause, and to assign the punishment of his own pain; when

---

* According to the Oxford English Dictionary (OED), the term *sponging house* was first used in 1700. A debtor entered a sponging house nominally voluntarily, but actually under duress by creditors, just as most patients enter a mental hospital ostensibly voluntarily, but actually under duress from relatives, employers, or judicial authorities.

† Many people who read Ken Kesey's novel, *One Flew over the Cuckoo's Nest,* or saw the film, were similarly surprised that the mental hospital in which the protagonist was confined against his will also housed patients who chose to be there voluntarily. The reason for this is that, in each case, the actor's motives disturb his audience. In the eighteenth century, some people preferred to lose their liberty rather than their property; today, some people prefer to lose their liberty rather than their pretensions.

the distinction between guilt and unhappiness, between casualty and design, is intrusted to eyes blind with interest, to understanding depraved by
resentment. . . . It is vain to continue an institution, which experience
shows to be ineffectual.[36]

The only justification for depriving a debtor of liberty, Johnson
maintained, was to discover his hidden assets and compel him to dis-
gorge them: "If such property can be discovered, let it be given to the
creditor; if the charge is not offered, or cannot be proved, let the prisoner be dismissed."[37]

Almost a century had to elapse for these views to become acceptable.
In 1832, echoing Johnson, the Commissioners of the British Common
Law Procedure declared that "the system [of imprisoning debtors] was
too harsh towards the person and too relaxed towards the property of
the debtor."[38] In the same year, the creditor was granted the right to attach the debtor's banknotes, stocks, bonds, and other negotiable instru-
ments. In 1854, he was granted the right to garnish his wages as well.[39]
Gradually, the aim of the laws regulating lending ceased to be the ceremonial chastisement of the delinquent debtor, and instead became the
satisfaction of the creditor's just demands balanced by the protection of
the debtor's right to liberty. The eighth edition (1859) of the *Encyclopaedia
Britannica* gave the following account of this transformation:

> A revolution has been almost noiselessly made in this department by the re-
> adjustment of the laws of debtor and creditor. Formerly the creditor was de-
> nied access by form of law to the debtor's estate, and he took vengeance on his
> person; hence the industrious man might be kept idle, separate from the
> means of supporting his family, or even paying his creditor; and on the other
> hand the man of fortune might live in jail, spending his money, and defying
> his creditors to touch his estate. The procedure for realizing and appropriat-
> ing the property of the debtor has now, however, been rendered more com-
> plete and effective. At the same time, the honest and fair debtor can obtain a
> speedy discharge under one of the bankruptcy or insolvency statutes. It hence
> arises that those who are now long detained in prison for debt are in some
> measure criminals as well as debtors, having been guilty of fraud or culpable
> recklessness.[40]

After the 1850s, laws authorizing the imprisonment of debtors gradually atrophied and were replaced by procedures for bankruptcy.*

---

* The OED states that in 1700 the term *bankruptcy* was synonymous with "willful fraud";
and that, in 1776, Adam Smith observed that "bankruptcies are most frequent in the
most hazardous trades."

The Debtor's Prison in America

The American experience with the practice of imprisoning debtors differed considerably from that of the English. The two principal reasons for the difference were that many Americans had come to the New World to escape imprisonment for debt and that Colonial America was an agricultural rather than a commercial society. There were debtor's prisons in the Colonies, however, and some famous Americans had been imprisoned in them. Robert Morris, who helped to finance the Revolution and signed the Declaration of Independence, spent three years in a Philadelphia jail for "incurring debts of about $12 million." James Wilson, an early justice of the Supreme Court, fled from Pennsylvania to North Carolina to avoid imprisonment for debt.[41]

In the United States, opposition to debtor's prisons rested from the start on the principled rejection of the right of a private person to deprive another of liberty.* In 1823, Thomas Hertell challenged the legitimacy of the practice with the following incisive statement: "I will not deny the right of government to punish, by imprisonment or other reasonable means, a *fraudulent* debtor, because he is a criminal, and ought to be punished; but it is the *fraud* and not the *debt,* which constitutes his crime."[42] The policy Hertell proposed was similar to the policy I have advocated for managing mental patients.† He wrote: "I would have fraudulent debtors punished; but it should, as in other criminal cases, be done agreeably to the constitutional law of the state . . . for the law of imprisonment for debt, levelling all the boundary marks of innocence and guilt, involves the fraudulent and the honest debtor in one common fate."[43]

Much of what Hertell said about debtor's prisons applies to mental hospitals: "The law authorizing imprisonment for debt was passed; it became an engine of oppression, to prevent which, another law became necessary; this produced fraud and perjury, which other laws were enacted to punish, but did not prevent those crimes."[44] Similarly, once commitment laws are enacted, they become an engine of oppression; other laws are then enacted to prevent this from happening, such as laws guaranteeing the patient's right to treatment, to refuse treatment, to a lawyer, to a hearing, and so on; and the more laws, the less protection for the patient, and the more power for his oppressors.

---

* This principled rejection of depriving insolvent debtors of liberty was, of course, inconsistent with the principled acceptance of Negro slavery, a contradiction that was overcome by viewing black slaves as nonpersons.

† Such persons should be restrained/punished only if they are guilty of a criminal offense, in which case they should be punished for their crimes, by the criminal law.

ECONOMICS VERSUS IDEOLOGY: BANKRUPTCY AS COMPROMISE

In a society committed to the protection of private property and the sanctity of contracts, the defaulting debtor could not be allowed to escape his obligation. If a borrower failed to repay his debt, he was mercilessly punished. Contrariwise, in a Communist society, committed to viewing the production of goods as a means of strengthening the state, no (industrial or commercial) debtor could be found in default. If he failed to repay his loan, it would mean he needed another. Because creditor and debtor alike were agents of the state, admission of imprudence, impropriety, or incompetence by either party would have reflected negatively on the state and was thus ruled out of court.

Eventually, both systems had to compromise. Capitalism accepted and accommodated to the reality of the hopelessly, sometimes innocently, insolvent debtor. Communism accepted and accommodated to the reality of the irresponsible, economically unmotivated, bureaucrat as both lender and borrower. The charade of Communist commerce, accurately diagnosed at the very moment of its birth by Mises, was finally unmasked after the disintegration of the Soviet empire. In 1989, the Polish government proposed an economic package that was labeled "revolutionary"— because it decreed that companies "must be allowed to go bankrupt."[45]

The Abuse of Bankruptcy: Caveat Creditor

In capitalist and socialist countries alike, economic necessity and political ideology continue to influence the regulations governing the relations between unsatisfied creditors and insolvent debtors. For example, in the 1980s, the French government revised the bankruptcy laws "to enable the authorities to seize an insolvent company in the name of preserving jobs."[46]

In the United States, Florida law allows "debtors [to] shield from creditors up to 160 acres of land in rural areas and half an acre inside city limits—no matter how much it's worth . . . and keep all wages, annuities, partnership profits, pension plans, and property jointly owned with a spouse."[47] Bankruptcy is now an American growth industry, students in business school and law school flocking to specialize in the subject.[48]

During the past decades, the American people, aided and abetted by courts and the press, have steadily retreated from contract, caveat emptor, and personal responsibility, and advanced toward blaming all manner of personal failures and suffering on agents with deep pockets, regardless of the latter's responsibility for the accuser's grievance.

Transferring responsibility for business failure from the user of credit to the provider of it is merely one facet of this pervasive trend.[49] Inverting the principle that justified imprisoning the delinquent debtor, courts now recognize the concept of "lender liability," that is, the creditor's duty to extend loans to clients with failing businesses to enable them to keep their enterprise afloat. Lawyers representing debtors attribute the phenomenon to the "recession in the energy, farming, and real-estate industries," and claim that "lenders moved too aggressively to call in loans from those troubled companies."[50] Bankers contend that "hapless borrowers are looking to pin the blame for their failure on institutions with deep pockets." During the decade of the 1980s, borrowers have won at least $1 billion in so-called lender-liability suits.[51] *Caveat creditor.*

IMPRISONMENT FOR DEBT AND MENTAL ILLNESS

The practices of imprisoning delinquent debtors and involuntarily hospitalizing dangerous mental patients resemble one another in two important ways: Each practice affected/affects virtually every aspect of daily life;[52] and the victim of each was/is deprived of liberty by means of a *civil* procedure.

The Civil Law as Quasi-Criminal Sanction

Unlike Roman and Continental laws, English and American laws are exceedingly protective of individual liberty. In our system, only a successful *criminal* action—that is, an action brought against an individual by the state—carries with it the penalty of loss of liberty. The normal penalty for a successful *civil action*—that is, an action brought against a person by a private plaintiff—is a fine.

How could a civil law procedure be used to imprison debtors? How can such a procedure now be used to incarcerate mental patients? The answer in each case is, by legal legerdemain, supported by professional and popular opinion. The confinement of the debtor was rationalized on the ground that he was neither imprisoned nor punished; he held the keys to his cell door; to regain his liberty, all he had to do was repay his debt. Similarly, the confinement of the mental patient is rationalized on the ground that he is neither imprisoned nor punished; he is holding the ticket for his trip to both health and freedom; to regain his liberty, all he has to do is accept treatment and recover from his treatable illness. This legally sanitized despotism, which is coeval with psychiatry, has become immensely popular in the United States since World War II. Consider the striking parallels between the past use of the civil law against debtors and its present use against mental patients.

The debtor:

- Was accused by his creditor—a person with close and important economic ties to him—of defaulting on his financial obligation to him.
- Was brought into court by his creditor.
- Was imprisoned by his creditor—because that is what the creditor demanded (he had the option to extend the loan or forgive it).
- Was freed only when he satisfied his creditor.
- Ergo, the debtor forfeited his liberty to his creditor.

The mental patient:

- Is (typically) accused by a parent or spouse—a person with close and important emotional and economic ties to him—of defaulting on his personal obligation to him (being mentally ill).
- Is brought to the mental hospital (or some intermediate place of detention) by his relative (or an agent of the state he has summoned).
- Is involuntarily hospitalized—because that is what his relative wants (the concerned kin has the option of taking the patient into his home or leaving him to his own devices).
- Ergo, the mental patient forfeits his liberty to his kin (or to a psychiatrist who is his kin's agent).*

The parallels between imprisonment for debt and mental hospitalization extend to the conceptual and legal controversies about the legal status of debtor's prisons and mental hospitals. In the eighteenth century, jurists pondered whether a debtor in a sponging house was imprisoned, and decided that he was not. Today, jurists ponder whether a voluntary patient in a mental hospital is imprisoned, and decide that he is not. Jurists thus supported, and continue to support, the legal fiction that the subject—albeit he acts under duress of potential "literal"

---

* The parallel now ends here. Historically, the mental patient was usually confined indefinitely, unless a relative requested his release and took him back into his home.

imprisonment—is nevertheless a free agent.* The wisdom of our language tells a different story. The OED offers "Locked up in a sponging house" as a typical example of the use of this term in 1838. The term "locked up" also fits the situation of the voluntary patient in a mental hospital.

It remains for me to mention an important difference between imprisonment for debt and mental hospitalization, namely, the role of the state in the proceeding. With respect to the debtor, the role of the state was limited to enforcing the laws. Prosecutors did not petition to have debtors imprisoned. With respect to the mental patient, the role of the state goes far beyond enforcing laws. Prosecutors and judges regularly instigate and initiate commitment proceedings, especially if the patient is indigent and deemed to be dangerous to himself or others. At the same time, the state plays, or pretends to play, the role of umpire as well, courts being entrusted with the duty of protecting the citizen from abuses of the mental health laws. This dual role of the state makes the practice of civil commitment especially corrupt, farcical, and tragic.†

---

* The legal fiction of the freedom of the voluntarily hospitalized mental patient stands in ironic contrast to the legal fiction of the unfreedom—attributed to his irresistible impulse (i.e., insanity)—of the perpetrator of a premeditated crime to which he wants to plead guilty (e.g., John W. Hinckley, Jr.).
† I continue and conclude my analysis of the parallels between imprisoning debtors and committing mental patients in the Epilogue.

3

THE EPILEPTIC

The criminal classes contain a considerable portion of epileptics and other persons of instable, emotional temperament, subject to nervous explosions that burst out at intervals and relieve the system . . . in all cases it [epilepsy] is a frightful and hereditary *disfigurement of humanity.*

—Sir Francis Galton[1]

In 1938, when I came to the United States, there were 13 epileptic colonies in the country, housing tens of thousands of inmates. Yet, neither the 15th edition (1987) of the *Encyclopaedia Britannica* nor current textbooks of medicine, neurology, or psychiatry even mention epileptic colonies.[2] Save for some historians of medicine, hardly anyone today has heard of an epileptic colony. And who remembers that, as recently as the 1950s, the U.S. Immigration and Nationality Act stipulated that "Aliens afflicted with . . . epilepsy . . . shall be excludable from admission into the United States"?[3]

A BRIEF HISTORY OF EPILEPSY

Because of its dramatic symptoms—loss of consciousness, convulsions, tongue-biting, and other accidental injuries—epilepsy is one of the oldest recognized diseases. It is a relatively common ailment, affecting 1 to 2 percent of the population.

Like many diseases, epilepsy may be mild, requiring no treatment or easily controlled with medication, severe and difficult to control, or even fatal. Although Hippocrates attributed the disease to natural causes, that view proved to be premature. For millennia, people preferred to believe that seizures were caused by deities or demons and regarded the disease as either sacred or accursed.

From Possession by Demons to Possession by Madness

The demonic origin of epilepsy, accepted by the Gospel writers, meant that its cause was possession, and hence its proper treatment was exorcism by holy men skilled in the practice of casting out devils. Jesus regularly engaged in this practice:

> And when they came to the crowd, a man came up to him and kneeling before him said, "Lord, have mercy on my son, for he is an epileptic and he suffers terribly; for often he falls into the fire, and often into the water. And I brought him to your disciples, and they could not heal him." And Jesus answered, "O faithless and perverse generation. . . . Bring him here to me." And Jesus rebuked him, and the demons came out of him, and the boy was cured instantly.[4]

When the religious explanation of epilepsy was replaced by the medical explanation of it, the belief that the disease is due to possession was replaced by the belief that it is due to madness. But madness was not so easily cast out. Indeed, the first tangible result of the medicalization of epilepsy was that suffering from the disease became a major social handicap. Only after World War II did physicians change their attitude toward the epileptic, from demeaning him as a defective dependent, to respecting him as an individual with the same rights and responsibilities as anyone else. To be sure, not all experts on epilepsy agree with this thumbnail sketch. For example, William G. Lennox, a professor of neurology at Harvard and a world-renowned authority on epilepsy, declared: "The emancipation of the epileptic by physicians began some three hundred years ago and has proceeded with increasing success."[5]

The Physician and Epilepsy

Modern medicine begins in the nineteenth century, with the study of the structure and function of the human body, in health and disease. In practice, this meant the study of normal and pathological anatomy and physiology, the clinical examination of sick patients, and the post-mortem study of cadavers. Examination of the brains of persons dying from nervous diseases, carried out mainly by British and French pathologists, demonstrated certain connections between abnormal brain structures and functions (brain diseases) and abnormal behaviors (some of which were considered "diseases of the nervous systems," others, "nervous diseases"). Convulsions or so-called grand mal seizures were among the earliest maladies identified as the manifestations of neurological malfunction.

The first physicians to observe patients suffering from epilepsy were general practitioners who knew their subjects as persons, not as specimens. They concluded that, in the main, epileptics were not seriously disabled. Sir John Russell Reynolds, the most prominent nineteenth-century English physician writing on epilepsy, stated: "Epilepsy does not necessarily involve any mental change . . . considerable intellectual impairment exists in some cases; but that is the exception, not the rule . . . ulterior mental changes are rare."[6] When the psychiatrist looked at the epileptic, he saw a very different phenomenon.

The medical stigmatization and persecution of the epileptic may be dated from 1873, when Sir Henry Maudsley, the acknowledged founder of British psychiatry, renamed epilepsy "epileptic neurosis" and cast the epileptic in the role of a Frankensteinian monster. He wrote:

> [E]pileptic neurosis may exist for a considerable period in an undeveloped or masked form, showing itself not by convulsions, but by periodic attacks of mania, or by manifestations of extreme moral perversion. . . . The epileptic neurosis is certainly most closely allied to the insane neurosis. . . . A character which the insane neurosis has in common with the epileptic neurosis is that it is apt to burst out into a convulsive explosion of violence.[7]

Maudsley maintained that insane persons are biologically disposed to engage in destructive behavior, for which they are not morally or legally responsible; and that they must, therefore, be permanently incarcerated under the watchful eye of the psychiatrist.[8] His approach to epilepsy, based on commingling it with insanity, reflected this bias: "The two diseases most closely related in this way [that is, being hereditary], are insanity and epilepsy; the descendant of an epileptic parent being almost if not quite as likely to become insane as to become epileptic, and one or other of the descendants of an insane parent not infrequently suffering from epilepsy."[9]

Maudsley had not a shred of evidence to support the claim that epilepsy and insanity are closely related diseases. But he had the power of his authority—unmatched and uncontested at that time, not only in the English-speaking world but in all advanced countries—and he used it to incriminate the epileptic, along with the insane, as a crazed killer:

> I shall now, then, proceed to point out what I conceive to be the most impor-
> tant conditions which are precedent of an outbreak of insane homicidal im-
> pulse. These are the *insane neurosis* and the *epileptic neurosis* in both of which
> the tendency is to convulsive action. . . . It is a remarkable and instructive
> fact that the convulsive energy of the homicidal impulse is sometimes pre-
> ceded by a strange morbid sensation, beginning in some part of the body
> and mounting to the brain, very like that which, when preceding an attack
> of epilepsy, is known in medicine as the *aura epileptica.*[10]

This melange of metaphors is typical of Maudsley's rhetoric in the service of maligning the madman as a menace. Note the treacherous use of the oxymoron, "convulsive action." Properly speaking, we call the involuntary movement of a *muscle* a reflex, convulsion, or seizure. Whereas action is the name we attach to the deliberate, voluntary movement of a *person.* This is why we do not hold people morally or le-gally accountable for reflex movements, but do hold them accountable for actions. I shall not belabor the obvious, namely, that the evidence for Maudsley's assertions is purely analogical or rhetorical. In fact, Maud-sley's epileptic killer was a creature who, by definition, could not com-mit a murder. He was merely an innocent bystander who happened to inhabit a body filled with "the convulsive energy of the homicidal im-pulse." In the scriptural view, the epileptic is possessed by demons. In Maudsley's view, he is possessed by "homicidal impulses." This was not medical progress, replacing superstition with science. It was medi-cal propaganda, replacing clerical with clinical superstition.*

By the end of the nineteenth century, the view that epileptics are potential criminals—specifically, that they are afflicted with an ir-resistible urge to commit violent acts—became psychiatric dogma. Hungry for the spooky and the sensational, journalists and the public eagerly embraced this view, which still lingers in the back of the popular mind. The Italian psychiatrist, Cesare Lombroso (1836–1909) became world famous largely on the grounds of popularizing this nonsense.[11]

The Treatment of Epilepsy

At the end of the nineteenth century, physicians did not yet understand that the proximate cause of an epileptic seizure was an abnormally

---

* From the patient's point of view, Maudsley's treatment of epilepsy by lifelong imprisonment rather than exorcism was hardly an improvement.

heightened excitability of the cerebral cortex. However, they knew from experience that sedatives, such as opium, were useful for controlling convulsions. In 1835, potassium bromide was discovered and was soon employed in the treatment of insomnia. About 20 years later, Sir Charles Locock learned of a person who, after medicating himself with bromides, complained that the drug virtually eliminated his sexual desire. Like every knowledgeable person at that time, Locock believed that masturbation caused epilepsy and reasoned that potassium bromide was an "anaphrodisiac" that might be an effective treatment for the disease. He tried it on 14 patients and had good results in 13.[12] The drug treatment of epilepsy had arrived.

For the next half-century, bromide was the standard treatment for epilepsy. Its use, however, left much to be desired, as adequate suppression of seizures often required doses large enough to cause sedation, interfering with normal existence. The next advance in the treatment of epilepsy occurred in 1903, with the discovery of barbiturates. The long-acting barbiturate, phenobarbital, proved to be especially helpful, enabling many epileptics to take enough of the drug to reduce the frequency of seizures without making them too sleepy in the bargain. Phenobarbital remained the drug of choice for treating seizure disorders until 1938, when it was displaced by Dilantin, the first in a class of drugs with specifically anticonvulsant properties. Today, several anticonvulsant drugs are available for treating seizure disorders.

COLONIZING THE EPILEPTIC

In 1872, an new type of institution was established at Bielefeld, in Germany. Resembling the large public mental institutions popular at the time, the Bielefeld facility was devoted to housing and caring for epileptics. It soon attracted the attention of American psychiatrists, who began to agitate for the construction of similar institutions in the United States. Their efforts were successful. In the 1890s, legislatures in the more populous states appropriated funds for the construction of so-called epileptic colonies.

A Brief History of American Epileptic Colonies

Prior to the end of the nineteenth century, most epileptics lived like other people, with their families and relatives. Insane epileptics were confined in madhouses, like other insane persons. By the time the century ended, epileptics were slaves, and psychiatrists masters, in state facilities popularly known as "epileptic colonies." The institutions were so called because they were run largely by the inmates themselves, who received little or no pay. In those bygone days, such an arrangement was considered to be generous. Most of the inmates were poor, unemployed, or unemployable. They received room and board and medical care, gratis. Like grateful children, the least they could do was help their "parents."

The first American institution for epileptics, initially called the "Asylum for Epileptics and Epileptic Insane," was established at Gallipolis, Ohio, in 1891. Before the first inmate was admitted in 1893, the institution's name was changed to the "Ohio Hospital for Epileptics."[13] Thus began the American experience with storing epileptics, allegedly because they had epilepsy, ostensibly in order to treat them.

I want to remark here briefly on the history of a famous epileptic colony in upstate New York. Established at Sonyea, in Livingston County, this institution's name was also changed before it opened its doors in 1894, from Sonyea Colony to Craig Colony, in honor of Oscar Craig of Rochester, then the president of the State Board of Charities.[14] Two years later, the facility was renamed the Craig Colony for Epileptics. After 1920, renamed once more the Craig Colony, it became one of the largest and best known epileptic colonies in the United States, housing about 1,600 inmates in 1928. In 1951, the facility became the Craig Colony and Hospital; in 1966, the Craig Colony School and Hospital; in 1968, the Craig State School; and in 1969, the Craig Developmental Center. This series of euphemisms reflect society's changing fashions for concealing the stigmatization and storage of epileptics, mental patients, and retarded persons.

Packaged as "therapeutic communities," the advocates of epileptic colonies directed their sales pitch to the families of epileptics, offering them a legitimate, indeed laudable, means of getting rid of their unwanted relatives. The doctors promised that the inmates would receive better treatment in the institutions than they could receive at home. Since the colonies were state facilities, the inmates were housed and fed at taxpayers' expense. Institutionalizing the epileptic thus relieved nonepileptics not only of their obligation to care for their afflicted dependents, but also of their feelings of guilt for rejecting them.

Of course, the colonists were conscious of their self-interests. They knew that with every increase in the number of persons housed in their institutions, their power and profit would increase as well. Even before the first epileptic colony in the United States opened its doors, the New York State Lunacy Commissioners declared: "There can be no question as to the desirability of the State making special provisions for epileptics of the *dependent and semidependent class, apart from the insane.*"[15] A century earlier, physicians had gained control over lunatics. It was time to go after the nonlunatics. Epileptics were the perfect targets. "The entire question [of how best to care for epileptics] can be solved," declared the clinicians bent on colonial conquest, "by the creation of colonies, the admission to which is *not to be regulated by the mental condition of the patient.*"[16] If the mental condition of the patient was irrelevant to the business at hand, why was their care delegated to specialists in mental diseases? No respectable physician or jurist asked that question, then or later.

During the 1940s, partly as a result of the development of Dilantin, the policy of segregating epileptics began to lose its appeal. By 1950, only one epileptic colony remained, the Indiana Village for Epileptics. In 1955, it became the New Castle State Hospital.[17] Most of the buildings formerly used to store epileptics were renamed and used for storing retarded persons.

The Medico-Legal Rationalization for Epileptic Colonies

In the 1890s, epilepsy was considered to be a type of insanity. Nevertheless, epileptic colonies were not intended to be special types of insane asylums. The main reason for this was that the colonizers were eager to expand their clientele to include sane epileptics.

William Pryor Letchworth, a celebrated colonist, explained the legal procedure for storing sane epileptics as follows: "*Sane* epileptics are committed [in Ohio] by the probate judge . . . upon the application of parents, guardians, or friends."[18] Because the persons committed were considered to be sane, physicians were not associated with these commitment proceedings. Nevertheless, the committed subject was placed under the custodial care of medical professionals. Because mental patients are now incarcerated for many of the same reasons formerly used to incarcerate epileptics, Letchworth's justifications for his policies are timely and worth pondering: "Special institutions or colonies, besides benefiting the unfortunate sufferers, may be made to serve the economy of the State. . . . In colonizing epileptics, society is relieved in some measure of a dangerous element and the public safety promoted."[19]

Professional articles published during the early decades of this century reveal that the incarceration of epileptics had, in fact, nothing to do with their illness. Diagnosis and treatment were mere pretexts. Epileptics were institutionalized because they were poor, unwanted, or both. The colonizers guaranteed the success of their enterprise with the surefire formula of heads-I-win, tails-you-lose. *Insane epileptics* needed to be confined in colonies because epilepsy was best treated there. *Sane epileptics* needed to be so confined because epilepsy was untreatable and hence the patients' best interests required their lifelong protection from the demands of normal society. "A cure of epilepsy," remarked a Scottish physician in 1906, "is not to be expected in more than about 10 per cent of those affected with this disease." This did not prevent him from proffering this remarkable reasoning for storing sane epileptics in colonies: "The purpose of the present contribution is to expose the unfortunate position of the sane epileptic, to advocate the advantages of the colony system in dealing with individuals of this class, and to indicate the need for further extension of this system."[20] Some colonizers candidly acknowledged that their goal was to remove unwanted persons from the community:

> The National government has provided for the Mute, the Negro, and the Indian—then, why not for this branch of population [epileptics], increasing as rapidly as they, and becoming yearly more inimical to national prosperity? A reservation set apart, affording facilities for agricultural pursuits as well as all the varied industries of a town, would provide an outlet for the surplus population.[21]

Despite the experts' self-contradictory rationalizations, members of the legal profession and the public eagerly embraced their claims as valid therapeutic prescriptions. At the 1903 annual meeting of the National Conference of Charities and Correction, William E. Sprattling, M.D., medical superintendent of the Craig Colony for Epileptics at Sonyea, declared:

> Epileptics cannot be cared for successfully, or even with partial success, in any other way than under the colony plan. . . . [The colonies] provide home life . . . , vocations ranging from . . . weeding the cabbage patch to the making of brick, . . . amusements and recreation . . . the highest treatment for the disease, . . . [and] segregating epileptics in colonies has a too often forgotten value in that it keeps them from reproducing.[22]

Alexander Johnson, the chairman of the Conference's official Committee, went further, pleading for the medical segregation of all "the degenerates who either physically, or morally, are so far below the normal that their presence in society is hurtful to the fellow citizens, or that their unhindered natural increase is a menace to the well being of the State."[23] Here is a partial list of the persons Johnson classified as "degenerates," fit for permanent involuntary storage:

> The chronic insane, the epileptic, the paralytic, the imbecile and idiotic of various grades, the moral imbecile, the sexual pervert, the kleptomaniac;

many, if not most, of the chronic inebriates; many of the prostitutes, tramps, and minor criminals; many habitual paupers, especially the ignorant and irresponsible mothers of illegitimate children . . . many of the shiftless poor ever on the verge of pauperism; some of the blind, some deaf-mutes, some consumptives.[24]

EPILEPSY AND EUGENICS

By the end of the nineteenth century, the practice of medicine was solidly based on the principles of pathological anatomy and pathophysiology. Many serious illnesses—tuberculosis, syphilis, and the contagious diseases of childhood—were understood as being caused by infections with microbial agents. Others, such as feeblemindedness and dementia praecox (later renamed schizophrenia), were believed to be due to heredity. The nature and causes of many other diseases, including epilepsy, remained shrouded in mystery. Meanwhile, the condition was closely linked to idiocy (feeblemindedness) and insanity, all three of which were attributed to heredity.

Eugenics: Theory, Ideology, Politics

Sir Francis Galton (1822–1911), the father of the eugenics movement, was confident that he knew what caused epilepsy. In 1883, he wrote:

> The criminal classes contain a considerable portion of epileptics and other persons of instable, emotional temperament, subject to nervous explosions that burst out at intervals and relieve the system . . . . The highest form of emotional instability is often associated with epilepsy; in all cases it is a frightful and *hereditary* disfigurement of humanity.[25]

Though not trained as a physician, Galton was a highly educated person. He must have known that epilepsy is often the result of head injury and, in those cases at least, it is not hereditary. However, Galton was more interested in controlling epileptics, especially preventing them from reproducing, than in understanding epilepsy. His snobbish lucubrations about "race improvement" supported the movement to forcibly sterilize persons categorized as epileptic or feebleminded. He declared:

> I do not see why any insolence of caste should prevent the gifted class, when they had the power, from treating their compatriots with all kindness, so long as they maintained celibacy. But if these continued to procreate children, inferior in moral, intellectual and physical qualities, it is easy to believe the time

may come when such persons would be considered as enemies to the State, and to have forfeited all claims to kindness.[26*]

Here Galton, who was Charles Darwin's cousin, departed from the evolutionist belief that the individuals and groups that most successfully procreate are biologically the most fit. To check the reproductive superiority of the "unfit," Galton proposed replacing "Natural Selection by other processes that are more merciful and not less effective. This is precisely the aim of Eugenics. Its first object is to check the birth-rate of the Unfit."[27] Galton was not alone. Long before the National Socialists in Germany adopted his Weltanschauung, prominent English and American scientists embraced it as their version of psychiatric humanism. Declared Elmer E. Southard (1876–1920), director of the Boston Psychopathic Hospital, professor at the Harvard Medical School, and the most revered psychiatrist of his time:

> [Psychiatry] has neglected feeble-mindedness . . . . The interest of us all must primarily be a humanitarian interest . . . it becomes a question with us, what to do with these waste materials . . . I am told that we make car wheels from the refuse of cheese factories and that all the great firms are putting research men to work on the disposal of their by-products. Let us, then, look upon the feeble-minded as in some sense by-products of society.[28]

Sterilizing the (Female) Epileptic

The title of an early twentieth-century medical journal, *The Journal of Psycho-Asthenics: Devoted to the Care, Training and Treatment of the Feeble-Minded and the Epileptic,* illustrates the doctors' dogmatic bracketing of seizure disorders with severe mental retardation. A typical article—devoted to "Surgical Sterilization as a Eugenic Measure," by Bleecker van Wagenen, Chairman of the Eugenics Section of the American Breeders' Association—advocated the sterilization of "the Feeble-minded . . . the Pauper class . . . the Criminaloids . . . Epileptics . . . [and] the Insane."[29] The author described one of his "cases" as that of "a high grade, feeble-minded, epileptic girl, twenty-three years of age. The operation (salpingectomy) was performed . . . to overcome if possible excessive masturbation, to which they [her parents] attributed the epileptic

---

* I should note that, once again, the issue is not science but politics. My remarks here are intended to be a critique of state-sponsored coercions legitimized by eugenic claims and should not be construed as a criticism of eugenics as scientific inquiry or as a voluntary practice by private persons. Individuals who know they suffer from a genetically transmitted disease often abstain from procreating. That is eugenics uncontaminated by politics.

seizures which began when she was seven . . . So far as can be ascertained, the bad habit is no longer practiced."[30]

It would be a mistake to dismiss this report as a quaint relic of a bygone era. The modern reader knows, because the new science of sexology tells him, that masturbation is not a bad habit but a good method of sex therapy.[31] But the story of the sterilization of epileptics did not end there. In 1938, as the greatest experiment in eugenic sterilization in human history was gathering steam in Germany, G. B. Arnold, a physician at the State Colony in Virginia, delivered an address at the annual meeting of the American Association on Mental Deficiency, in which he enthusiastically endorsed the involuntary sterilization of epileptics. "The Virginia sterilization law," he explained, "well protects the patient's interests . . . provid[ing] that no person legally participating in the execution of the provisions of the law shall be liable therefore either civilly or criminally."[32] Twenty-two percent of Arnold's patients were diagnosed as epileptics, the rest as feebleminded. But the diagnoses were mere pretexts. The patients' most important common characteristic was poverty: "The majority of our patients . . . came from families of the definitely low class—and by 'low class' we mean families whose heads are barely eking out an existence."[33] In addition to being poor, most of the female patients displayed what Arnold calls "sex delinquencies . . . . Of these women, 404 [out of a total of 607] had been guilty of sexual immorality prior to admission."[34] Feminist historians have yet to discover epilepsy, eugenics, and female sterilization as chapters in the persecution of "immoral" women by "moral" male physicians.*

EPILEPSY, SCHIZOPHRENIA, AND SHOCK TREATMENT

As we saw, no sooner did psychiatrists begin to take an interest in epilepsy than they detected remarkable connections between having convulsions and being crazy. Although these alleged connections bore no relation to reality, that fact did not diminish the psychiatrists' influence on legislators, as the history of epileptic colonies and the sterilization of epileptics illustrates. It was enough that the psychiatrists were useful. It was not necessary that they also be right. In psychiatry (as in religion), the maxim "Seeing is believing" works better when it is inverted. When you are very powerful or very powerless, believing is seeing.

---

* During the early decades of this century, unmarried women engaging in sexual activity, including masturbation, were defined as being guilty of "sexual immorality"; whereas male physicians performing surgical operations on women—without the patients' consent and aimed at unsexing them—were defined as paragons of ethical professionalism.

In the 1930s, the psychiatrists' perception of the relationship between convulsions and craziness reversed course. Instead of seeing epilepsy and insanity as fraternal twins, psychiatrists suddenly saw the two conditions as mutually antagonistic. The person who fabricated this falsehood, and devised the prototype of the diabolical "shock treatment" based on it, was the Hungarian psychiatrist Ladislaus von Meduna. Despite all the evidence to the contrary, most historians of psychiatry accept Meduna's rationalizations and repeat the mendacious legend of his "discovery" as if it were legitimate scientific history. For example, in their best-selling *History of Psychiatry*, Franz Alexander and Sheldon Selesnick write:

> In the late 1920's Ladislaus Joseph von Meduna (1896–1964) . . . observed that the glial tissue [in the brain] had thickened in epileptic patients. When he compared their brains with those of deceased schizophrenic patients he noted that the latter showed a deficiency of glial structure. On the basis of these findings . . . Meduna became convinced that schizophrenia and epilepsy were incompatible diseases and that a convulsive agent administered to schizophrenics would therefore cure them.[35]

Actually, Meduna *invented* the inverse relationship between the incidence of epilepsy and the incidence of schizophrenia to justify his use of metrazol. Moreover, like Meduna, Alexander and Selesnick are also guilty of conscious misrepresentation: They fail to mention that in his classic text on schizophrenia, Bleuler still claimed that there is a direct, rather than an inverse, relationship between schizophrenia and epilepsy. He wrote: "Many of our patients were first sent to us with the diagnosis of epilepsy, and were so labeled in the clinics."[36] Neither Meduna nor Alexander could possibly have been unfamiliar with Bleuler's classic text, the veritable bible on schizophrenia.

Iatrogenic Epilepsy as Psychiatric Treatment

The American Psychiatric Association's centennial celebratory volume, *One Hundred Years of Psychiatry* (1944), summarizes the official psychiatric version of the story of the origin of shock treatment as follows: "Somewhat as the treatment of general paralysis with tryparsamide paralleled malaria therapy . . . so was the treatment of schizophrenia by means of insulin shock paralleled by the use for the same purpose of pentamethylenetetrazol (metrazol), as a convulsive agent."[37]

The comparison is absurd. When the malaria treatment of paresis was introduced, neurosyphilis, unlike schizophrenia, was a clearly defined disease, known to be due to infection with the trepona pallidum. As I see this period in psychiatric history, what happened was that, after the 1920s, schizophrenia gradually displaced paresis as the core "clinical entity" of psychiatry. There was a treatment for paresis, but not for schizophrenia. Naturally, psychiatrists wanted to be able to treat "it." But they had not the foggiest notion what this alleged disease was, much less what to do about it. At this point, coincidental advances in medicine once again determined the course of psychiatric quack-therapeutics.

In 1922, insulin was discovered and diabetes became a treatable disease. The early preparations of insulin were crude and made it especially difficult to regulate the diabetic's blood sugar level. Patients often received too little or too much insulin. The consequence of receiving too little insulin is hyperglycemia (too much glucose in the blood); if severe and protracted, this condition leads to diabetic coma and death. The consequence of receiving too much insulin is hypoglycemia (too little glucose in the blood). If mild, hypoglycemia causes light-headedness; if moderately severe, loss of consciousness and involuntary, epilepticlike movements, a condition called "insulin shock"; and if severe and protracted, brain damage and death.

Diabetes is a common disease. Many patients in mental hospitals had diabetes. Treated with insulin, some developed episodes of hypoglycemia, after which they appeared to be "better." Presto, a cure for schizophrenia. The psychiatrist who claimed to have made this discovery was Manfred Sakel, the place was Vienna, the year was 1933, and the name of the cure was "insulin shock treatment." The era of "modern somatic treatment in psychiatry" had arrived.

The trouble was that psychiatrists had no objective criteria or tests for diagnosing schizophrenia. One could never really be sure that a particular patient had the (alleged) disease or whether a particular treatment for it was effective. (This is still the case.) But now at least doctors knew how to give people artificial epilepsy. Before psychiatrists could subject nondiabetic persons to the risks of an insulin overdose, they had to find a reason and a justification for doing so. It was this need to rationalize inducing artificial convulsions in mental patients that generated the theory of epilepsy and schizophrenia as antagonistic conditions and justified giving schizophrenics seizures.

Insulin shock was an instant success. Insulin wards, with hundreds of people subjected to hypoglycemia, became a standard fixture of progressive mental hospitals. However, the procedure had two major drawbacks. It was dangerous for the patient, and time-consuming and troublesome for the staff. The search was on for a simpler and safer method of inducing convulsions that did not require a laborious intervention to bring the patient out of the coma.* In 1935, Meduna, as I mentioned, observed that an overdose of metrazol by injection causes convulsions. Three years later, in Rome, Ugo Cerletti and Luigi Bini observed the slaughtering of pigs tranquilized by electric current passed through their brains. Thus were metrazol shock and electroconvulsive therapy (ECT) "discovered."[38]

Today, seizure disorders are no longer considered to be mental diseases. The term *epilepsy* is absent from the *Diagnostic and Statistical Manual of the American Psychiatric Association (DSM-III)*.[39†] Yet, as if in an unconscious embrace of the old, Maudsleyan bracketing of epilepsy and madness, and despite the *Physicians' Desk Reference's* firm assertion that there are no psychiatric indications for the use of the antiseizure drug, Tegretol (carbamazepine),[40] psychiatrists claim that it is "effective in certain patients with behavioral dyscontrol, alcohol and sedative-hypnotic withdrawal, eating disorders, anxiety disorders, and post-traumatic stress disorder."[41] In short, psychiatrists now treat some mental patients with convulsions, others with anticonvulsant drugs, maintain that both are cures for mental diseases—and most people believe them.

THE EPILEPTIC COLONY IN HINDSIGHT

Galton, Maudsley, Lombroso, and their followers assembled the rhetorical building blocks necessary for scapegoating epileptics. The epileptic ceased to be a person and became instead the feared and persecuted carrier of an "epileptic neurosis," a term that conjured up images of unpredictable violence. "The consequence of this approach," observed Sir Dennis Hill, Emeritus Professor of Psychiatry at the University of London, "was the enormous stigma attached to the epileptic. . . . By destiny he was seen as mad and bad, liable to explosive and unpredictable attacks of violence and insanity, perhaps murder or at least moral depravity."[42] Hill failed to mention that this image of the epileptic justified depriving him of the rights, and excusing him from the responsibilities, of the citizen. Moreover, although Hill's account is correct, his attribution is not. It was not abstract destiny that made the epileptic

---

* Comatose patients had to be given glucose, by nasal tube, to bring them out of hypoglycemic shock.

† Evidently, psychiatrists now consider epilepsy a neurological disease, meriting no more special attention than, say, multiple sclerosis. Nevertheless, they continue to use the diagnosis of epilepsy to support a defendant's insanity plea.

appear as mad-and-bad; instead, it was psychiatrists who had cast him in that role (to which they now assign the "dangerous" mental patient).

The Myth of the Dangerous Epileptic

The antiepilepsy agitators, posturing as the compassionate protectors of the patient as well as the public, identified three distinct clinical states or phases that supposedly made the epileptic dangerous. The first phase, called the "aura," occurred just before the seizure and was characterized by visual, auditory, or olfactory sensations. The second, manifested by automatic behavior, occurred when the convulsive process did not progress to a grand mal seizure. And the third, called the "fugue," occurred following a grand mal seizure and was characterized by confusion and perhaps headache. During each phase, especially the last, the epileptic was believed to be liable to automatic, spontaneous violence. He was also thought to be dangerous because of his "epileptic personality," manifested by moral degeneration and a general lessening of the ability to exercise self-control.[43]

During the first half of this century, experts on epilepsy ceaselessly trumpeted the message that epileptics were dangerous unless confined in colonies. The medical directors of the Ohio Hospital for Epileptics and of the Craig Colony in New York both stoutly maintained "that epileptics were liable to attack others, frequently with deadly violence."[44] No contemporary medical or legal authority challenged that claim. The belief that any epileptic is susceptible to sudden, unpredictable, random violence, even homicide, thus became a scientific "fact." Ironically, the very existence of epileptic colonies, housing large numbers of epileptics in close quarters, demonstrated that this belief was a libelous falsehood. The inmates of epileptic colonies, as Janet Colaizzi states,

> . . . were neither sedated, restrained, nor closely supervised . . . . [They] lived in cottages housing twenty-five to a hundred residents . . . . The concentration of large numbers of epileptics did not precipitate the anticipated violence . . . . Despite this evidence to the contrary, medical superintendent William H. Pritchard of the Ohio Hospital . . . asserted [in his annual report for 1909], that the epileptic was "dangerous to others. During the mental disturbance which precedes, replaces, or follows an attack he frequently commits acts of violence or may be guilty of homicide or other revolting crimes for which he is not really responsible." William D. Sprattling, the first medical superintendent of the Craig Colony for Epileptics, also believed that the affliction was characterized by the "meanest violence." Yet the Craig Colony was as free from injuries as the Ohio Hospital.[45]

Few people then cared about the truth concerning epileptic *persons,* and perhaps even fewer now care about the truth concerning schizo- phrenic *persons.* The myth of the dangerous epileptic justified a popular social policy, and that was all that mattered.

Eventually, thanks to the efforts of conscientious neurologists, the epileptic was freed from psychiatric slavery. Sadly, the psychiatrist's disastrous encounter with the epileptic has not impaired his authority vis-à-vis the mental patient.

Contemporary Reassessments

The practice of confining epileptics in colonies lasted about half a cen- tury. While it was in vogue, people believed that epileptic colonies were progressive, therapeutic institutions, and that incarcerating epileptics in them was the best treatment for the patients. As late as 1949, Albert Deutsch, the widely admired journalist-historian of psychiatry, wrote:

> Among the major advantages of separate care for the epileptics in colonies are the following: The model colony provides the patient with an environ- ment from which many of the dangers he faces in normal community life, as well as stresses injurious to his *mental health,* are eliminated . . . . It re- lieves society in some measure of a source of potential danger to public safety, since certain types of epileptic seizures are often accompanied by *homicidal impulses.* [46]

Similar falsehoods appeared in medical textbooks as well. The 1942 edition of *Cecil's Textbook of Medicine* (the standard text when I was a med- ical student) explained:

> Between attacks, the frank epileptic is usually a constitutional psychopath of the most disagreeable sort. . . . [Epileptics] are self-centered, unable to grasp the viewpoint of others, and childishly uncomprehending when forced to accept the opposite view. . . . Like manic-depressives and other psychotics, they are apt to adjust their depressions through this means [alcoholism], and are likewise easy victims of delirium tremens . . . . Insti- tutional treatment properly directed along strictly modern lines affords the best possible means of handling [epileptics]. . . . In properly conducted in- stitutions the epileptic . . . [is] taught to view his malady in its proper light, and learn to enjoy the inestimable advantages of outdoor life. [47]

Thirty years later, when one of my daughters was a medical student, gone were the "constitutional psychopathy" of the epileptic and the ad- vantages of "institutional treatment." Passing over the long history of the medical persecution of epileptics in discreet silence, physicians were now (1974) advised: "It is important to emphasize that the patient should be allowed to live as normal a life as possible . . . . Every effort should be made to keep children in school, and adults should be encouraged to work."[48] Since then, neurologists have gone even further, enjoining the physician to treat the person afflicted with epilepsy as an autonomous moral agent. A current textbook of neurology counsels: "It is important to remember that the goal of treatment is to assist patients in their efforts to overcome or at least adapt to the consequences of epilepsy. This means that treatment consists of things done in collaboration with patients rather than to or for them."[49]*

The differences between the neurological and psychiatric attitudes toward patients could hardly be more dramatic. The neurologist eschews dominating, much less coercing, patients suffering from *demonstrable* brain diseases. The psychiatrist, protesting more stridently than ever that mental patients suffer from brain diseases, clings to his power to impose unwanted interventions on nonconsenting nonpatients.

The modern medical history of epilepsy is full of ironies. Until relatively recently, when epilepsy "belonged" to psychiatry, psychiatrists emphasized the similarities between epilepsy and insanity. Today, when epilepsy no longer "belongs" to psychiatry, neurologists emphasize the differences between it and mental illness. The Epilepsy Foundation of America states: "Not many years ago, people with epilepsy . . . were sometimes treated as if they were insane. . . . No state allows commitment based solely on a person's epilepsy. . . . The EFA does not believe that epilepsy is a reason to take an individual's freedom away."[50] Will there ever come a day when the American Psychiatric Association makes the same statement about mental illness?

Believing is indeed seeing. The disease we call epilepsy is the same today as it was in 1893. But the beliefs of physicians about epilepsy and our social policies toward epileptics are very different indeed. Michael Trimble, an English authority on the relationship between epilepsy and psychiatry, comments: "By the 1950s, the view was that patients with epilepsy were exactly like anybody else and did not have any special susceptibility to psychopathology."[51] Unfortunately, not every expert on epilepsy was willing to relinquish his power. As late as 1960,

---

* If we were to replace "epilepsy" with "schizophrenia," the statement would read: "It is important to remember that the goal of treatment is to assist patients in their efforts to overcome or at least adapt to the consequences of schizophrenia. This means that treatment consists of things done in collaboration with patients rather than to or for them." Were a psychiatrist to write a textbook containing this paragraph, he would not a find a publisher for it.

William G. Lennox, the great Harvard authority on epilepsy, advocated killing certain epileptic children. He wrote:

> Epilepsy belongs to the specialty of neurology, but the need for custodial care of public patients has caused epilepsy to be bracketed with the psychoses in state departments of mental disease and in the American Psychiatric Association . . . "Thou shalt not kill" and "Be ye merciful." Can the two commands be combined in mercy killing? . . . Society systematically and cruelly kills its best members by the means called "war," and unmercifully prolongs the lives of its hopeless liabilities [idiotic epileptic children].[52]

While Lennox's brand of humanism no longer dominates medical-legal opinion concerning epilepsy, it remains firmly in control of such opinion concerning mental illness. When the doctor cannot cure the patient, he can still kill him and thus demonstrate his usefulness to the society he cravenly seeks to serve.*

A recent historical-political event merits notice here. In 1964, in the aftermath of the assassination of President Kennedy, there was a momentary revival of the psychiatric myth that epilepsy causes murder. Soon after Lee Harvey Oswald, Kennedy's alleged assassin, was taken into custody, he was assassinated by Jack Ruby. Celebrity lawyer Melvin Belli came to Ruby's defense, claiming that his client was not guilty because he suffered from an epileptic fugue when he shot Oswald. The defense failed, not because it was ridiculous—it was no more ridiculous than other insanity defenses that have succeeded—but largely because the American neurological profession united in refuting the claim. Belli was unable to find a single neurologist willing to testify for the defense. In an editorial in the *Journal of the American Medical Association,* Samuel Livingston, a prominent neurologist, warned:

> The "average reader" who has recently been exposed to the many newspaper articles relative to the Jack Ruby murder trial can understandably get the impression that epilepsy, murder, and crimes of passion are related. . . . I find no evidence of a higher rate of criminal activity among epileptics than among nonepileptics. . . . I certainly would not question the fact that an epileptic might kill, not because he has epilepsy, but because he is a human being.[53]

Similarly, a psychotic might kill, not because he is psychotic, but because he is human. A recent work on epilepsy aimed at the public re-emphasizes precisely this point: "There is no scientific or medical

---

* Unlike Nazi psychiatrists, democratic psychiatrists do not literally kill their patients. They kill them metaphorically, by incarcerating, shocking, and drugging them.

evidence that epilepsy causes violent behavior. . . . Of course, people with epilepsy sometimes become violent, just as people without epilepsy sometimes do."[54]

The Unlearned Lesson of Epilepsy

A hundred years ago, people found it intolerable to witness a person having a seizure, falling down, perhaps injuring himself. The public wanted to be spared this spectacle. To accommodate this desire, psychiatrists declared that epileptics needed to be confined in institutions. Today, people find it intolerable to witness a person talking to himself, depressed, contemplating suicide. The public wants to be spared this spectacle. To accommodate this desire, psychiatrists declare that (seriously ill) mental patients need to be confined in institutions.

That is not the official version of the story. It is considered unprofessional to acknowledge that doctors dispose of unwanted persons at the behest of society. The professionally correct perspective on the incarceration of epileptics and mental patients is that such policies serve the purpose of caring for sick and dependent person. As recently as 1944, Samuel W. Hamilton, psychiatric advisor to the Mental Hygiene Division of the United States Public Health Service, stated:

> Still another group that *needs* special institutional accommodation is the convulsive disorders. Some of these are found in mental hospitals. . . . Many more are cared for along with mental defectives. . . . The idea of the separation of buildings into many different groups was thoroughly carried out at the Craig Colony in western New York, to create for *appreciative* patients homes where they could be comfortable and have suitable occupation for life.[55]

The rhetoric of the therapeutic segregationist creating ghettos for "appreciative patients" sounds eerily similar to that of the racial segregationist creating ghettos for "appreciative Negroes." Hamilton was not satisfied with institutionalizing only epileptics and mental defectives (and, of course, the mentally ill). He added: "Since many alcoholic persons are unable to control themselves, the necessity of institutional control is obvious."[56]* The hypocrisy intrinsic to this rhetoric makes the predicament of the person caught in the web of

---

* In the United States, this tactic has been used to justify the segregation and coercive treatment of "sex offenders" (a category that used to include homosexuals) and "drug abusers" (including alcoholics).

therapeutic segregation even worse than that of the person caught in the web of punitive segregation. When we imprison a murderer, we do not say he *needs* to be deprived of liberty; we say he *deserves* to be punished. But when we imprison the epileptic or the mentally ill, we say he *needs* to be treated; we do not say that we don't like his behavior and want him to change it.

Finally, there is an important medical-political lesson in the history of epileptic colonies that we are eager to ignore. When the treatment of epilepsy was nonexistent or rudimentary, psychiatrists used the epileptic's alleged need for treatment as a pretext for confining him. Subsequently, as the physician's *pharmacological* power to treat epilepsy increased, his *political* power to deprive him of liberty, in the name of therapy, diminished and quickly disappeared. Let us apply this formula to psychiatry. If the psychiatrist has no effective remedies for mental illness, then he cannot appeal to treatment as a justification for depriving the patient of liberty. And if the psychiatrist does possess effective treatments for mental illness, then, as the lesson of epilepsy has shown, the patient's alleged need for treatment ceases to be a legitimate reason for depriving him of liberty.

4

THE CHILD

Come away, O human child!
To the waters and the wild
With a faery, hand in hand,
For the world's more full of weeping
than you can understand.

—*William Butler Yeats*[1]

Adults are larger, stronger, and more experienced than children, and can survive without them. Children cannot survive without adults.* This basic inequality defines and shapes the child's relationship to the adult world.

Childhood is a sociolegal status that, in the modern West, lasts 18 to 21 years. In the past, childhood ended earlier with respect to some activities, such as entrance into the labor force and marriage, and ended later (or never) with respect to others, such as achieving personal independence.

---

* I use the words *child* and *childhood* in this chapter to identify a biological condition of immaturity, a chronological condition of minority, and a sociolegal status of dependence on adults.

CHILD ABUSE

Because parents have power over children, there have always been parents who abused their children. The truth is that childhood is a prison sentence that lasts until the young person is able and allowed to cast off the chains of his status as a minor. Saying this, I do not mean to imply that childhood is pure torment. I mean only that the kind of childhood a person has depends overwhelmingly on the wardens he happens to have. Many parents are good parents. Some are too indulgent, with the result that when the child reaches adolescence he refuses to relinquish the security of his sanctuary and remains a ward for the rest of his life. Others are too indifferent, with the result that the child becomes permanently disabled from independent existence and is doomed to spend the rest of his life in one institution or another.

History teaches us not only that parents have always abused their children but also that every socially sanctioned abusive practice was, by definition, so well integrated into the culture it served that, to a properly acculturated person, it did not appear to be an abuse at all.[2] For some reason, Americans have long regarded their culture as especially sensitive to the needs of children, a collective self-delusion that may in part account for the popularity of psychoanalysis in the United States. The falsehood that childhood is a state of blissful dependency, to which adults perpetually long to return or "regress," is one of the doctrinal tenets of the Freudian cult. Although perhaps true for some people, such a longing is an exception, not a rule.

A Historical Glimpse at Child Abuse

In every culture, children have been subordinated to adults. Their inferior, captive status is illustrated by etymological evidence. In the antebellum South, the male slave was called "boy," and the female slave was called by her first name. "The terms for 'child,' 'boy,' and 'girl,'" John Boswell explains, "are regularly employed to mean 'slave' or 'servant' in Greek, Latin, Arabic, Syriac, and many medieval languages."[3] The status of inferiority is intrinsic to the idea of childhood, much as the notion of irrationality is intrinsic to the idea of insanity.[4]

The oldest method of (what we would now call) child abuse appears to be child sacrifice. The practice must have been prevalent among the ancient Hebrews, as Moses tried to prohibit it: "The Lord said to Moses, 'Say to the people of Israel . . . who gives any of his people to Moloch, shall be put to death.'"[5] Still, Abraham was ready to sacrifice Isaac, not to Moloch, but to Jehovah.

The Oedipus legend is the classic Western case of an unsuccessful infanticide. The failure of Freud's moral vision is starkly revealed by his neglect of Laius's initial murderous act and his reframing of Oedipus's self-defense into a symbol of mankind's primal sexual sin and enduring infantilism.[6]

Pre-Christian cultures provided many legally sanctioned forms of relief for parents who wanted to dispose of their unwanted children. In Egypt, a woman could abandon her child. In Rome, a father could kill his child, even after he had reached (biological) adulthood. Almost everywhere, parents could sell their children into slavery. Boswell lists other examples of child-disposal, both real and legendary: Kronos devoured his children; Jupiter was abandoned; Zeus, Poseidon, Aesculapius, Attis, and Cybele were exposed.[7] Today, we call "child abuse" a symptom of mental illness, obscuring personal agency and responsibility for acts motivated by some of the oldest and most enduring human passions.

Oblation: Committing the Child to the Church

In the Middle Ages, a parent could donate his unwanted child to the church, a practice called "oblation." Boswell's account of this custom suggests certain parallels with our practice of "psychiatric oblation." He writes: "There is no reason why oblation could not have been a religious act on the part of the parents and still have functioned socially as a means of divesting the family of children."[8] Mutatis mutandis, there is no reason why the practice of committing children to mental hospitals may not be a nominally medical act and still function socially as a means of divesting the family of children. "Far from constituting antisocial behavior," Boswell adds, "it [oblation] ostensibly involved altruism, sacrifice, and devotion to the major benevolent institution of the day."[9] Continuing the parallel, the staff of the monastery functioned as a substitute family for the oblate, just as the staff of the children's madhouse functions as a substitute family for the child mental patient. The hierarchy of the religious institution replicated that of the family: The word *abbot* is Aramaic for "father"; a monk was called "brother," and a nun, "sister." Similarly, the children's mental hospital is furnished and decorated to resemble a home, and other trappings of family life are contrived to make it resemble a residence rather than a hospital. The oblate was, in effect, a slave on a clerical plantation; the child mental patient is a slave on a clinical plantation. Boswell writes: "It was the child, obviously, who bore the costs of these benefits to family and community. . . . His diet, drink, education, labor, and occupation were determined by his superiors in the community."[10]

When Boswell turns to the abuses of oblation, his remarks read almost as if he were writing about child psychiatry. An eleventh-century cleric's apology is telling: "Anything born of honest and pious motivation can, indeed, be turned to bad use, and this holy institution [oblation] has been corrupted by the greed of parents, who, for the benefit of the family, commit to monasteries any hump-backed, deformed, dull, or unpromising children they have."[11] It is easier to state than to resolve the dilemma: Either we consider oblation and child psychiatry morally impermissible, in which case we must abolish such practices. Or we consider them morally permissible, in which case we have no meaningful way to distinguish between the uses and abuses of the practices.[12]

Child Abandonment: The Church as Depository

The most common medieval method of disposing of unwanted children was abandonment. Typically, a parent or servant would leave the unwanted child in or near a church, many of which provided special receptacles, built into their walls, where infants could be deposited unobserved.* In the eighteenth century, about 14,000 foundlings a year were officially registered in the city of Lyons alone.[13] In fact, it was the ubiquity of child abandonment that gave rise to the foundling home, the first social welfare institution ostensibly devoted to child care, but actually serving the interests of the rejecting parents. The mortality rate in foundling homes was staggering, most children dying within a few weeks or months of admission. That did not matter. Boswell's remarks highlight the similarities between the foundling home and the children's mental hospital:

> A major benefit of the foundling-home system was that the problem of unwanted children was removed from the streets and the view of ordinary citizens. The children disappeared behind institutional walls, where specialists were paid to deal with them, so that parents, relatives, neighbors, and society could forget. How would a parent know that the vast majority of such children died?[14]

---

* The practice must have made many people feel guilty and was probably partly responsible for the popular belief that Jews habitually stole and murdered Christian children, to use their blood for baking matzo. Hospital emergency rooms now offer a similar opportunity for children to deposit their unwanted, elderly parents, a practice called "granny dumping."

Probably this is the sort of thing the parent who has deposited his child in a mental hospital tells himself after he realizes what psychiatry has done to his "loved one."

I might add that child abandonment, functioning as a kind of postnatal birth control, has remained a common practice to this day. In the United States, unwanted children are often deposited in trash cans or left in bus stations, train stations, or hospitals. In China, at least 700,000 infant girls are abandoned annually.[15]

CHILD PSYCHIATRY*

The conventional definition of child psychiatry is that it is a medical specialty devoted to the diagnosis, treatment, and prevention of the mental diseases that afflict children. From a sociological viewpoint, child psychiatry is a secular institution for regulating domestic relations. From my point of view, it is a form of child abuse.

Because the mental diseases that supposedly afflict children are undeniably misbehaviors, and because the child mental patient is in an even more helpless position than the adult mental patient, child psychiatry is a doubly problematic enterprise. John S. Werry, professor of psychiatry emeritus at the University of Auckland, in New Zealand, comes close to admitting this, and more. He writes:

> . . . many children seen in clinics do not have true disorders but problems of living—developmental conflicts with parents, schools or peers. . . . Poverty, untreatability, chance and the desire to escape punishment, rather than need for medical attention are often the tickets of entry to child psychiatric services. Child psychiatry has persistently avoided debating this issue.[16]

Here is an example from the daily press. A five-year-old boy gets up early one morning, helps himself to the car keys, and takes off in the family's Honda Accord. He drives about a mile and a half without incident but then, according the news report, "got into trouble when he stopped at a gas station and struck a pickup truck."[17] No one is injured. The boy is placed in the psychiatric wing of a hospital and is held there against the wishes of his parents and their lawyer, "Thomas Stickle, [who] said a psychiatrist at the hospital told him that 'any little kid who gets up at 5:30 in the morning and drives the family car for 31 blocks is

---

* I use the term *child psychiatry* to refer to any intervention vis-à-vis children under mental health auspices. Although it is not an American invention, the promiscuous practice of child psychiatry is a characteristically American social phenomenon.

psychiatrically unbalanced.'" A hospital spokeswoman added: "We're still evaluating him. . . . We are in the proces of developing a good after-care program for him."[18]

By definition, children are under the age of consent. They are not free to choose when or what to eat, when to go to bed, what religion to profess. Obviously, they are not free to accept or reject medical or psychiatric examination and treatment. Hence, every mental patient who is a minor is, ipso facto, an involuntary patient. Because psychiatric relations are intrinsically intimate-invasive, in a way that resembles sexual relations, I oppose involuntary psychiatric relations, just as nearly everyone opposes involuntary sexual relations.* I have no intention of depriving parents of their rights and responsibilities as guardians of their children. On the contrary. I propose only that we prohibit them from violating the bodily and spiritual integrity of the child.†

In the West, a parent cannot consent to his minor child's having sexual relations with an adult ("in the best interest of the child"). Similarly, a parent should not be allowed to consent to his minor child's having psychiatric relations ("in the best interest of the child"). Sexual relations between adults and children are outlawed, as statutory rape; child psychiatry ought to be outlawed, as psychiatric rape. This recommendation is consistent with, and is merely an extension of, my view that all involuntary psychiatric interventions should be outlawed.‡

The Child as Mental Patient

The child mental patient is doubly disfranchised, as a minor and as mad. Every encounter between a child psychiatrist and his denominated patient entails this double handicap for the child.

Typically, the child is brought to the psychiatrist by one or both of his parents. Many of the child psychiatrist's patients are adolescents, that is, individuals who no longer feel like children but are not yet adults. What do parents expect of the psychiatrist? The same thing as Macbeth did:

---

* All intimate relations are invasive, literally or figuratively. Therein lies much of their beauty and value. In the case of females, the invasive nature of the sexual act is anatomically obvious. In the case of males, it is anatomically less obvious, but psychologically no less relevant. What makes a bodily or spiritually invasive relationship valuable is the person's desire for it; and what legitimizes it, morally and legally, is consent.
† This is the reason we do not let parents mutilate their children's bodies. What constitutes mutilation is, of course, also culturally defined. We consider female circumcision a mutilation, but not male circumcision.
‡ Voluntary psychiatric relations ("treatment") are a very different matter. Like voluntary religious relations ("worship"), they ought to be protected as a basic human right.

They want to believe that their child is sick and want the doctor to cure him. The "patient," however, is likely to experience the intervention as a tactic to thwart him from reaching the position of power and freedom represented by adulthood.

Unusual is the psychiatrist who, like James Simmons, the author of a textbook of child psychiatry, acknowledges: "The child psychiatric patient is similar to the committed adult patient in that usually he had no part in the decision to seek professional help and has been brought for examination against his will."[19] Most psychiatrists ignore the involuntary and stigmatizing character of child psychiatry and dismiss the child patient's realistic perceptions as cognitive errors due to his "primitive thinking." For example, child psychiatrist John Markowitz distorts the child's justified fear of psychiatry as a symptom of his "initial resistance to psychotherapy" and insists: "The child knows that the psychiatrist is only rarely enlisted 'against' children and then only when the child is especially 'bad' (uncontrollable, crazy, dangerous)."[20]

Aided and abetted by psychoanalysis, child psychiatrists have perfected a professional jargon well suited for concealing the simplest social realities behind a semantic facade of illness and treatment. The following sentence is typical: "The neurotic child coming for analysis has frequently lived in a home where he had not adequate opportunity to express himself or to feel."[21] A child does not *come* for analysis; he is *brought* to the doctor's office, clinic, or hospital. Lest it appear that I quote out of context, consider the next sentence: "The child who comes in for his first therapeutic session may not be consciously aware of his difficulties or of his need for help."[22] Again, the author writes that child *comes in*, when, in fact, he is *brought in*. Moreover, now the child is also said to be *unaware of his own needs*. The very language of child psychiatry perverts the truth, denying that the reason the child submits to psychotherapy is because adults force him to do so.

The Mentally Ill Child: The Metaphor of Development

Although child psychiatry's root metaphor is the same as that of its parent discipline, namely disease, their respective concepts of disease are informed by different models. The psychiatrist's model of disease is the abnormal brain, exemplified by neurosyphilis.[23] The child psychiatrist's model of disease is abnormal development, exemplified by undescended testicles in the male or delayed menarche in the female.

Like the word *disease*, the word *development* may be used literally or metaphorically. The growth of the child's body is an instance of literal development. The growth of the child's intellectual and interpersonal skills is an instance of metaphorical development. One happens to the organism. The other is something a person does or learns. Measles is a literal disease. Oppositional disorder is a metaphorical disease.

Unless a child has a proven brain disease, we have no more reason to believe that his misbehavior, called "mental illness," is due to organic causes than we have to believe that any other human behavior is so caused. Prima facie, a child's mental illness is simply behavior that upsets the adults who have legal authority and power to define and control him.

Actually, the developmental model of disease has scant bearing on the child psychiatrist's everyday practice. The patients brought to the pioneer child psychiatrists were referred to them by family court judges. The psychiatrists had no reason to suspect that such children suffered either from brain diseases or from somatic developmental arrests. The children were denominated as mentally ill because they were unruly, difficult to manage, or guilty of behavior deemed criminal in adults (theft, assault, or murder). The child psychiatrists' vested interest in psychopathologizing the misbehavior of children is illustrated by the sorts of phenomena they consider to be children's mental diseases. Herewith a few examples:

Oppositional Disorder, 313.81
The essential feature is a pattern of disobedient, negativistic, and provocative opposition to authority figures. . . . The oppositional attitude is toward family members, particularly the parents, and towards teachers . . . . Usually, the individual does not regard himself or herself "oppositional," but sees the problem as arising from other people.[24]

This is the description of a conflict between two persons of unequal power, the superior person defining the inferior person as mentally ill. The child's "oppositional behavior," just like a political protestor's "dissident behavior," is motivated action, not disease. However, if we accept the view that motivated action may be a form of mental illness, then we can interpret the deliberate infliction of injury on others as disease, as the following diagnosis illustrates:

Conduct Disorder, Socialized, Aggressive, 312.23
A repetitive and persistent pattern of aggressive conduct in which the basic rights of others are violated, as manifested by . . . physical violence against persons or property (not to defend someone else or oneself), e.g., vandalism, rape, breaking and entering, fire-setting, mugging, assault.[25]

Welcome to the "Bonfire of the Psychiatric Vanities."

Child Psychoanalysis

Freud defined the psychoanalytic relationship as a contract between two independent, legally competent adults,[26] a definition that renders the concept of child psychoanalysis a self-contradiction. Freud also warned against the therapist's "attempt to gain the confidence or support of parents or relatives,"[27] a rule obviously incompatible with the practice of child therapy. In short, child analysis is a contradiction in terms.[28]

Anna Freud, Freud's daughter and the exemplar of child analysis, acknowledged that the child "does not enter analysis of his own free will, and makes no contract with the analyst. . . ." However, she then added that "he [therefore] does not feel bound by any analytic rules."[29] But why should he? Although there is no contract between the child patient and the analyst, Anna Freud blamed the child for not being "bound by any analytic rules." In the same vein, she interpreted the child's rejection of her meddling as a symptom of his "resistances" to analysis: "Since habitually his ego sides with his resistances, every child wishes to abscond from analysis in times of heightened pressure from unconscious material or intense negative transference, and would do so if not held in treatment by the parents' support."[30] One more example of Anna Freud's pretentious gaffes should suffice:

> The most seriously disturbed children are completely oblivious of their illness. . . . Children suffer less than adults from their psychopathology. . . . Obviously, we have become accustomed to the paradoxical situation that the correspondence between pathology and suffering, normality and equanimity, as it exists in adults, is reversed in children.[31]

My critical estimate of child psychoanalysis and of Anna Freud's baneful influence on children is supported by the testimony of one of her former patients, Peter Heller. In a memoir written some 50 years after the event, Heller describes Anna Freud as having "spun, in all innocence, the spiderweb of the older generation in which later so many of us, beneficiaries and victims [i.e., her child patients], got caught"; chronicles her "fateful embrace stifling the unfolding lives of these children"; and concludes with this remonstrance: "My most bitter reproach to Anna Freud, Dorothy Burlingham, and the circle of orthodox, presumptuously authoritative psychoanalysts has always been that they had an infantilizing and often debilitating influence on their patients."[32]

History is replete with injustices for which there can never be reckoning. The injustice done to children by psychoanalysts, illustrated by the outcome of the first "child analysis," is an example. The first so-called child psychoanalyst, accredited as such in 1910 by Freud himself, was a

Viennese physician named Hermine Hug-Hellmuth. Her first patient was her nephew, Rolf. When Rolf was 18, he murdered and robbed his aunt. When he came to trial, he told the court that he killed her because she treated him as "her experimental guinea pig [*Versuchskaninchen*]."[33] Nevertheless, the authors of a recent biography of Hug-Hellmuth, laboring under the delusion that child psychoanalysis is a genuine treatment for real illnesses, try to whitewash this sordid affair by casting Hug-Hellmuth in the role of innocent victim and Rolf in the role of ungrateful "rotten kid."[34]

THE CHILDREN'S MENTAL HOSPITAL

The systematic confinement of children denominated as mentally ill, in psychiatric wards for children only, is a recent phenomenon. Before 1910, there was not a single such psychiatric facility in the United States. At this point, it would be logical to ask: If mental illnesses are real (bodily) diseases, why did they not affect children in the past? The answer to this question is instructive.

Children were always especially vulnerable to bodily diseases, often dying of intestinal or infectious illnesses during the first year of life. In the old days, a real disease was something that killed the patient. Thus, before the twentieth century, people did not "recognize" that children suffered from mental illnesses because they regarded the youngsters now so diagnosed as unruly or wicked.

The Orphanage and Other Precursors of the Children's Madhouse

In the nineteenth century, when child-care institutions came into being, dependency and delinquency were not clearly differentiated, both conditions being regarded as intrinsic to the problem of pauperism. Abandoned or orphaned children were then often housed in the same institutions as adult dependents, that is, in workhouses and insane asylums. At the end of the 1800s, there were more than 50,000 children under the age of 16 in English workhouses.[35] In the United States, orphanages were first established in the early 1800s. By midcentury, in New York State alone, there were 27 public and private child-care institutions, mainly reformatories.[36] Unwanted children were also confined in madhouses. In 1823, the Bellevue Asylum in New York City housed 553 children, and in 1848, over a thousand.

At the end of the nineteenth century, there were 140 facilities in New York State, housing more than 100,000 unwanted children or one child out of every 100. In New York City, one child in 35 was publicly housed. In the United States as a whole, hundreds of thousands of children were stored in nearly 800 public institutions.[37] The only requirement for admission to such children's prisons was the caretaker's desire to discard the child. Psychiatric historian David Rothman describes the admission criteria thus: "The reformatory, like the orphan asylum, maintained a flexible admission policy, prepared to accept the commitment decisions of a judicial body, the less formal recommendations of overseers of the poor, or the personal inclination of the head of the household."[38]

The Children's Madhouse

Until the middle of the twentieth century, children deemed mentally ill or retarded were usually incarcerated, along with adults, in public mental hospitals. The 1955 Mental Health Study Act stated that "there is reason to believe that many emotionally disturbed children are being placed in mental hospitals, which have no proper facilities to administer to their needs."[39]

The systematic confinement of children in psychiatric institutions devoted specifically to housing them began during the 1950s, and became a large-scale phenomenon only in the 1970s. Today, hundreds of thousands of children are imprisoned in psychiatric hospitals, most of them, even according to psychiatric authorities, unnecessarily.[40] A 1993 study by the New York State Commission on Quality Care for the Mentally Disabled found that more than half of all children in state-run children's psychiatric residences did not belong there, and that "three quarters of the children . . . had no psychotic symptoms but almost all were receiving psychotropic drugs."[41] Like fast-food chains, child psychiatric inpatient units and the wholesale psychiatric drugging of children, in and out of hospitals, are recent, typically American, and remarkably popular products and practices.

The cornerstone of the children's madhouse movement was laid in Chicago by William Healy, a general practitioner with an interest in "problem children." Healy's curiosity about such children was sparked by a woman friend engaged in trying to help delinquent children whose cases came before the Cook County (Illinois) court system. Feeling unqualified to assist her in her endeavor, Healy traveled to Europe, for special training in *neurology*. After returning to Chicago in 1909, with help from associates and philanthropists, he founded the Juvenile Psychopathic Institute (soon renamed the Institute for Juvenile Research), which was intended to act as "an administratively nonaffiliated adjunct of the court."[42]

Trained in law and feeling unqualified in matters of child care, family court judges were bewildered by the cases of unruly and unwanted children brought before them. Because there were no special institutions to house such children, the judges welcomed with open arms the doctors who offered to take their problems off their hands. Thus was child psychiatry, the last refuge of psychiatric scoundrels, born.

Healy's book, *The Individual Delinquent*, became the instant bible of the child psychiatry movement. Inadequate physicians, unable to make a go of their professional lives even as psychiatrists, became child psychiatrists, working as glorified governess-guards, while posing as medical specialists. Naturally, any suspicion that the child psychiatrist's job was to confine and control unwanted children had to be denied and disguised. That was accomplished by means of the legal-psychiatric code phrase, "in the best interest of the child"; the preposterous proposition that the child psychiatrist was the person best qualified to define and protect the child's best interest; and the fiction that this enterprise was therapeutic in character and required medical qualifications.

In 1917, Healy moved to Boston and established the Judge Baker Foundation. Soon renamed the Judge Baker Child Guidance Center, this facility became the mecca of the new profession of child psychiatry. In 1924, the American Orthopsychiatric Association was established and assumed formal control over the child mental health movement. The language in which the child psychiatrist's work was couched is, as usual, revealing. The Greek prefix *ortho* means straight or to straighten, as in orthopedics. The child psychiatrist's task was thus to straighten out the mentally crooked child.

Although psychiatrists define these events as milestones of medical progress, nothing could be further from the truth. In 1941, the year I entered medical school, Foster Kennedy, one of the leading psychiatrists in America, declared:

> I am in favor of euthanasia for those hopeless ones who should never have been born—nature's mistakes . . . . I believe it is a merciful and kindly thing to relieve that defective of the agony of living. . . . The social organism [will] grow up and [move] forward to the desire to relieve decently from living the utterly unfit, sterilize the less unfit, and educate the still less unfit . . . and thereafter civilization will pass on and on in beauty.[43]

After the end of World War II, American psychiatry, and child psychiatry along with it, entered a period of explosive growth. By 1945, there were enough child psychiatry clinics to organize a special society for their directors and staff, called the American Association of Psychiatric

Clinics for Children. Two years later, special training standards for child psychiatrists were created, which, in turn, led to the establishment of the Subspecialty Board of Accreditation in Child Psychiatry by the American Board of Psychiatry and Neurology.[44] In 1957, the Board recognized Child Psychiatry as a subspecialty of Psychiatry.

THE TRADE IN CHILD LUNACY

Like the trade in adult lunacy, the trade in child lunacy quickly became a two-class phenomenon: Children of poverty, diagnosed as delinquents, became psychiatric patients; children of privilege, diagnosed as neurotics, became psychoanalytic patients.

In the 1920s, Anna Freud founded a psychoanalytic "school" in Vienna. With the mixture of naiveté and arrogance characteristic of her work, she declared: "Psychoanalysis, whenever it has come into contact with pedagogy, has always expressed the wish to limit education. Psychoanalysis has brought before us the quite definite danger arising from education."[45] Nevertheless, we continue to delude ourselves that mental health professionals in schools help rather than hinder the development of children.

Ostensibly, the students in this Freudian parody of education had mental problems "treated" at the school; actually, they were the pampered rejects of rich parents. Typically, the children were denominated as sick because they were upset by the parents' extramarital affairs. For a fee, Anna Freud took the troubled and troubling children off their parents' hands. But she and her colleagues evidently convinced themselves that they were engaged in a more lofty enterprise, rationalizing the school's aims in terms that echo the rationalizations of the Jacobins and Bolsheviks—making a new and better human being. Victor Ross, an eyewitness—his mother, Eva Rosenfeld worked at the school and was a close of friend of Anna Freud—puts it thus: "The reform of life through psychoanalysis, traceable in the founding of the school . . . was *in truth* meant to be a reform of humanity. What was to be created was the new, the truly truthful and truly human being."[46] The school closed when the analysts had to flee the Nazis, who had their own ideas about the making of the New Man.

Along with psychoanalysis, child analysis was brought to the United States where, wed to child psychiatry and the family court system, it has flourished. During recent decades, the trade in child lunacy grew even faster than the trade in adult lunacy.[47] The lure of government and other third-party payments for mental health services for minors was more than parents or psychiatrists could resist. Child psychiatrists offered parents a medically legitimized program to dispose of their troublesome children. To discard his disobedient child, a parent had only to call him "mentally diseased," bring him to a mental health professional, denounce him to the doctor, and presto, the child was taken off the parent's hands. The supreme beauty of the arrangement was that the parent was praised for his concern for the child's mental health, disposing of the child cost him nothing, the children's madhouse was lauded as a marvel of modern medical science, and the child psychiatrist who oversaw the operation basked in his glory as guardian of the best interests of the mentally ill child.

Certain economic and social changes in post-World War II American life laid the ground for this new, psychiatrically-sanctioned, form of child abuse. The disintegration of the extended family made child rearing more demanding and more difficult than ever. Then, beginning in the 1950s, the nuclear family itself started to unravel. More children were being raised by single mothers; more married women, with young children at home, joined the labor force; and more unmarried women raised children relying on welfare. Millions of youngsters were left without adequate adult supervision. Demographer Peter Morrison wisely remarks: "What we are now doing is contracting out for family care. If you contract out everything, you have an enterprise, not a family."[48] Actually, television has become the American family's principal child-care robot/worker. Many parents' idea of minding their child is letting him sit in front of the boob tube, so long as he causes no trouble; as soon as he causes trouble, taking him to a child psychiatrist and putting him on Ritalin; and if that doesn't fix the sick kid, sending him to a children's madhouse for more intensive treatment.

The Boom in Madhousing Children

Once Medicare, Medicaid, and private health insurance programs began to pay for hospital care, the American public witnessed the realization of the adage, "He who pays the piper, calls the tune." Health care managers assumed control over who gets hospitalized and for how long. As a result, the use of hospital beds for nonpsychiatric patients *decreased* dramatically, while the use of hospital beds for psychiatric patients, especially in children's mental hospitals, *increased* even more dramatically.[49] The practice of madhousing children grew so spectacularly that it attracted widespread media attention. In 1987, *American Medical News*, the American Medical Association's official newspaper, reported:

Psychiatric admissions to private hospitals nearly tripled between 1980 and 1986 for those younger than 18. . . . Patients are hospitalized for periods consistent with their insurance coverage and discharged with diagnoses that question whether hospitalization is appropriate. . . . The cost of inpatient psychiatric care is estimated at about $1,000 a day per patient . . . The hospitalization rates have been particularly startling given that the population of 10- to 19-year-olds has declined 11 percent from 1980 to 1987.[50]

One psychiatrist opined that mental hospitals "have become the new jails for upper-and middle-class children." Another called the practice of madhousing children "a racket." A third explained: "Hospitalization often increases in June as parents begin to make plans for vacation . . . . The presence of full payment by medical insurance stimulates the use of maximum treatment measures, incorrect diagnoses, untrustworthy records, and full units."[51] The psychiatrically abused children were not fooled: "Many children refer to the mental hospital as a jail."[52]

Instead of examining the dubious premises on which child psychiatry rests, the media preferred to dramatize its "abuses." The following report from *The Wall Street Journal* is typical:

For-profit chains have concentrated on building psychiatric wards and on advertising services to parents frightened by teen-age suicide, sex, and drug use. . . . These new psychiatric hospitals aren't the stark wards of late-night slasher movies. . . . [One] looks like a condominium. . . . The hospital has a tennis court, two swimming pools, and a fully equipped gym.[53]

Horribile dictu, maybe this hospital is not a hospital at all. Maybe the patients are not really sick. The reporter does not consider these possibilities. Instead, once inside the madhouse, he encounters psychiatry's paradigmatic therapeutic procedure, coercion, and concludes that the dwelling is really a hospital: "In a windowless 'quiet room' . . . an 11-year-old boy is lying motionless, his wrists and ankles strapped to a bed." The restraints, the reporter assures us, are used only "as therapy . . . as a sort of metaphorical hug."[54] The hug is metaphorical, but the disease is real.

Between 1980 and 1987, the number of teenagers incarcerated in madhouses increased by nearly 50 percent. Children's madhouses became the private hospital industry's cash cows. *Newsweek* reported:

Difficult, disruptive, disobedient adolescents—kids who once might have been sent to military schools or even juvenile-detention centers—are now being locked up in mental hospitals. . . . The diagnoses . . . cover a wide variety of teenage behavior: running away, aggression, persistent opposition to parental values and rules, engaging in "excessive" sexual activity . . . or serious antisocial behavior. . . . [Teenagers] do not enter full-time hospitalization willingly. That's why hospitals sometimes even advise parents to trick their teenagers by saying that the visit is for a brief evaluation. . . . A California girl—whose mother said she had to stop off at the hospital on her way home from the beach to make an appointment for future counseling—was forcibly committed while still in her bathing suit . . . . Getting out of the hospital is a lot harder than getting in. . . . They are minors, their parents' decision to hospitalize them is binding, and the commitment is considered voluntary.[55]

None of this dampened Americans' enthusiasm for child psychiatry. The prestigious Institute of Medicine declared: "At least 7.5 million children, or 12 percent of the nation's population under 18, suffer from a mental disorder or emotional disturbance, [yet] few are getting treatment."[56] A report in the *New York Times*, fittingly placed in the business section, told of hospitals converting "large sections into locked units for kids, whom they admit on the signature of a parent and a physician."[57] A Prudential Securities investment letter colorfully informed its readers: "Insane Demand—Psychiatric Hospitals. It may strain investment credulity, but there seems to be no limit to the demand for, and the supply of, psychiatric hospital care."[58] At the Hartgrove Hospital in Chicago, psychiatrists created "one of the nation's first treatment programs to wean teenagers away from Satanism."[59] The hospital, with an expert on the "treatment of Ritualistic Deviance" on its staff, "plans to inaugurate a program in which teenagers will spend four to eight weeks as inpatients . . . to undermine Satanism's underlying belief system."[60] Never has the manufacture of madness been more popular, or the trade in lunacy more lucrative.

Does hospitalizing children for psychiatric treatment help them? Even child psychiatrists acknowledge that there is no evidence that it does. Martin Irwin, co-editor of a textbook on the psychiatric hospitalization of children, writes: "Despite there being many advocates for inpatient and residential treatment, the efficacy of the treatment is in doubt." He cites a recent study of children who received individual residential treatment "considered, at the time of discharge, to have benefited from treatment," and notes that even these supposedly successfully treated children "fared poorly at follow-up according to objective measures used to assess outcome."[61]

THE CHILD PSYCHIATRIST AND SUICIDE

Few things in today's world unsettle a normal American more than suicide, especially if the person who kills himself is neither very old nor very ill. The suicide of an adolescent, perceived as the death of a young person "with his whole life before him," is the most upsetting of all. One of the child psychiatrist's jobs is to explain away the lure of suicide for the young person facing the challenge of life. Since the American public thirsts for the authoritative attribution of suicide to mental illness, it is not a difficult task.[62]

Once a mental health professional attributes suicidality to a person, no one dares to oppose his recommendation for the subject's preventive psychiatric detention. Thus, when a child psychiatrist meets an ostensibly suicidal adolescent, the requirements of his professionally correct conduct negate the possibility of his being able to help the youngster. This antitherapeutic posture is intrinsic to the child psychiatrist's professional role.* As an agent of the parents, he is expected to prevent the child's suicide. Prevented from being the youngster's agent, the psychiatrist cannot support his uncertain self-esteem by siding with his strivings for autonomy, and hence cannot help him to clarify and master his confusions and conflicts. Instead, the psychiatrist must "discover" and diagnose the mental disease that causes the adolescent to want to kill himself. As a result, he is bound to impair the adolescent's ability to cope with his first truly serious fight-or-flight dilemma in life. The literature of child psychiatry supports this view.

John Donaldson and James Davis, the authors of a chapter titled "Evaluating the Suicidal Adolescent," present the case history of a "17-year-old adolescent male," whose problem they describe thus: "Current Complaints. Recent suicidal gestures."[63] This cannot be true: No one calls his own suicide attempts "gestures." The authors' final diagnoses of their patient are "Adjustment reaction with depressed mood. 2) Personality disorder . . . 3) Homosexuality."[64] The book I cite was copyrighted in 1980, seven years after the APA abolished the diagnosis of homosexuality. Nine years after the authors' treatment ended, the patient committed suicide. I am not faulting the authors for the suicide. I am faulting them for using this case as support for psychiatric coercion as a rational method of suicide prevention.

---

* The same antitherapeutic posture is intrinsic to the adult psychiatrist's professional role as well.

Anyone familiar with the mental health industry knows that suicide is now the single most effective tool for promoting, justifying, and selling psychiatry. The threat of suicide, fear of suicide, gesture of committing suicide, attribution of wanting to commit suicide, promise of preventing suicide, claim of having successfully prevented suicide, each of these fears, threats, and promises stokes the furnaces of the madhouse industry, especially of its children's division.[65]

Why Is Suicide among Children Increasing?

If the frequency with which adolescents and young adults kill themselves is a measure of the difficulty they experience growing up, then we have convincing evidence that growing up in the United States is becoming steadily more difficult. In 1957, 4 persons in 100,000 aged 15 to 24 killed themselves. In 1977, the figure was 13.6 in 100,000, an increase of more than 300 percent. Today, suicide is the second leading cause of death (after accident) in that age group.[66] Since many accidents are covert suicides, these are startling statistics, indeed. What do they mean?

To the psychiatrically enlightened, the escalating frequency of youthful suicide proves that mental illness is a real disease, that it causes suicide, that suicide is a public health problem that has reached epidemic proportions, and that the nation needs more child psychiatrists, more children's mental health facilities, and more government funding for programs dedicated to preventing adolescent suicide. The literature of child psychiatry is replete with assertions supporting these psychiatrically self-serving clichés. Cynthia Pfeffer, a prominent suicidologist, declares: "Studies are beginning to indicate that suicidal tendencies in children are not the result of normal developmental turmoil, but are the outcome of a psychopathological process. . . . [A]ll children who consult a psychiatrist should be evaluated for suicidal impulses."[67] Child psychiatrists Emmett Kenney and Kenneth Krajewski assert: "Hospitalization is mandated whenever a suicidal gesture or attempt is made."[68]

Child psychiatrists systematically ignore the possibility that mental health professionals, with a vested interest in diagnosing children as mentally sick, might magnify or even manufacture the risk of suicide. At the same time, they deny the deleterious consequences intrinsic to psychiatric diagnosis and hospitalization. "When in doubt," Howard Sudak and his colleagues counsel, "it is preferable to err on the conservative side. Obviously, less harm is done by a relatively unnecessary admission than by a needless death."[69] The authors offer no evidence to support this claim. Instead, they distort and disparage my critique of psychiatric coercion: "Freedom [in Szasz's books] becomes equated with 'freedoom' [sic]." As for my view that mental illness is a metaphor, for Sudak and his colleagues that translates into: "Therapists can evade their professional responsibilities."[70]

No one has demonstrated that mental illness *causes* suicide. Instead of engaging the moral problem of suicide and the practical problems of suicide prevention, Sudak and his colleagues criticize my views: "Such a view [as Szasz's] totally ignores the fact that a majority of suicidal individuals suffer from depressions of one sort or another and these are among the most treatable illnesses—often, even without the patient's cooperation."[71] Then, without further explanation, they reasserts the psychiatrist's social mandate to coerce: "Since it is clear that for children and adolescents, whether or not one believes in mental illness per se, therapists and 'the state' have the responsibility to prevent them from self-harm, the issue of 'don't hospitalize them against their will' is not nearly so evident. Dealing with minors who can be signed into hospitals by their parents also, of course, helps to obviate this issue."[72] However, even the most ardent supporters of psychiatric coercions admit that the confinement of allegedly suicidal adolescents does not help to prevent their suicide, a fact that Sudak and his co-workers acknowledge: "There are no satisfactory objective data to tell us which therapies are best . . . there are little objective data to confirm our biases."[73]

Although I have written very little about child psychiatry, child psychiatrists seem even more antagonized by my work than psychiatrists who deal with adults. Kenney and Krajewski also base their support for confining crazy children in mental hospitals on inveighing against my baneful influence on the psychiatric scene. They write: "[According to Szasz,] adults have a right to suicide if they are not suffering from a major psychiatric illness. This complicates the decision-making ability of certain treatment personnel who extend Szaz's [sic] concern to patients of the adolescent years."[74] Kenney and Krajewski are unable or unwilling to grasp that I oppose psychiatric coercion, period.

I have commented at length on the child psychiatrists' enthusiasm for coercing the allegedly suicidal adolescent only to demonstrate that the troubled youngster and his therapist are hopelessly mismatched. The former is hypersensitive to cant, hypocrisy, deceit, and betrayal. The latter's professional status depends on the conscientious cultivation of precisely such duplicitous speech and behavior, epitomized by his claim that he is an agent of the child-patient's "best interests." Overestimating the danger of suicide, and underestimating the danger of psychiatric coercion, serve the economic and professional interests of the psychiatrist, not the existential needs of the (adolescent) patient. That is why I contend that coercive psychiatric interventions are more likely to promote, than prevent, suicide.

CHILD PSYCHIATRY AND THE JUVENILE COURT SYSTEM

The empire of child psychiatry was erected on a moral fault line, namely, the assumption that "juvenile delinquency" is a disease that the child psychiatrist is especially qualified to diagnose and treat. But delinquency is not a disease, like diabetes. It is not even a disposition, like compulsivity. It is simply an invidious, incapacitating status ascribed to a misbehaving minor. The misconduct justifying the diagnosis varies: It may be an act that, if committed by an adult, would constitute a felony, for example, assault or murder; or it may be an act that would constitute only a misdemeanor, for example, making an obscene telephone call; or it may be an act that would not constitute a crime at all, for example, truancy.

Although the term *juvenile delinquency* implies that the child so diagnosed is guilty of a misconduct, the diagnosis is often made in the absence of any proof that the accused child actually disobeyed authority or broke the law. In fact, psychiatrists regularly label youngsters as delinquents merely on the basis of an accusation, to enable juvenile court judges to sentence them to psychiatric incarceration until they reach maturity. For decades, American medical and legal authorities regarded this form of child abuse as the most enlightened and benevolent method the world has ever known for managing problem children. Finally, in 1964, the United States Supreme Court agreed to hear a case that, albeit only for a brief moment, exposed the injustice done to children in the name of "psychiatric justice."[75]

In re Gault

In June 1964, Gerald Gault, an Arizona resident aged 15 years, was accused of having made a lewd telephone call and taken into custody by the police. Diagnosed as a juvenile delinquent, he was committed to the State Industrial School until the age of 21. After Arizona courts dismissed petitions for habeas corpus, the Supreme Court agreed to hear the case.[76]

The facts of the case are briefly as follows. When Gerald appeared in court, his accuser, a Mrs. Cook, was not there. No one gave sworn testimony. There was no record of the proceedings. The evidence against

Gerald was conflicting. Nevertheless, he was found guilty and was, in effect, sentenced to a 6-year prison term. Had an adult been convicted of the same offense, the maximum penalty would have been a fine of $50 or imprisonment for not more than two months.

Such severe punishment, meted out on such flimsy grounds without judicial safeguards—on a defenseless child, on the pretext of protecting his own best interests—offends our sense of justice. However, as I noted, the system under which Gault was "tried" has long been regarded as the proper—constitutionally and psychiatrically sanctioned—procedure for managing unruly children. Although Gault's story is in no way unique, in this case the Justices declared: "Juvenile proceedings to determine 'delinquency,' which may lead to commitment to a state institution, must be regarded as 'criminal' for purposes of the privilege against self-incrimination. To hold otherwise would be to disregard substance be-cause of the feeble enticement for the 'civil' label-of-convenience which has attached to juvenile proceedings."[77] Concurring with the majority's opinion, Justice Hugo Black pressed the attack against psychiatric injustice for the child deeper still:

> Thus, in a juvenile system designed to lighten or avoid punishment for crim-inality, he [Gault] was ordered by the State to six years' confinement in what is in all but name a penitentiary or jail. Where a person, infant or adult, can be seized by the State, charged, and convicted for violating a state criminal law, and then ordered by the State to be confined for six years, I think the Constitution requires that he be tried in accordance with the guarantees of all the provisions of the bill of Rights made applicable to the States by the Fourteenth Amendment.[78]

Although hailed as a landmark Supreme Court decision, the ruling, not surprisingly, had virtually no effect on the practice of child psychiatry. The Court has always upheld the rights of parents to authorize the psychiatric imprisonment of their child and the fiction that psychiatric imprisonment (civil commitment) is a civil law procedure. The practice of child psychiatric slavery has flourished more luxuriantly than ever since *Gault*.

CHILD PSYCHIATRY *IS* CHILD ABUSE

The Gault decision was a classic case of sound and fury signifying noth-ing. Following *Gault*, lower courts handed down one psychiatric *Dred Scott* decision after another, judges consistently upholding the rights of parents to consign their unwanted children to madhouses. It seems to me obvious that so long as psychiatrists, courts, and the public endorse the medical model of mental hospitalization, they will consider the practice of madhousing persons, especially children, reasonable and proper. After all, a parent has the right, indeed the duty, to hospitalize his minor child (against his wishes) for medical and surgical treatment, say for meningitis or appendicitis. Mutatis mutandis, he also has the right, and the duty, to hospitalize him for psychiatric treatment of mental illness.

Consistent with this medical-scientific conception of mental illness and mental hospitalization, courts regularly rule that parents are permitted "to hospitalize their child if they wish, as long as the admitting psychiatrist agrees."[79] Then, with shocked surprise, the media reports that "we are increasingly seeing cases of parents going to the state judicial system once their insurance runs out and asking the judge to make their children wards of the state, thus qualifying them for Medicaid."[80] The United States loves to dispose of its unwanted children by means of psychiatric storage, as the following vignette illustrates:

> A Florida court has ordered a 14-year-old Pensacola boy quarantined in a hospital psychiatric ward after state health officials said the boy had been exposed to AIDS, was sexually active, and represented a danger to public health. . . . Judge [William] Frye . . . noted that the confinement order was for an indefinite period until the public health risk could be eliminated.[81]

This case is only the visible tip of the proverbial iceberg. Out of sight are the countless catastrophic consequences of child psychiatry, such as the wholesale psychopathologizing of child misbehavior and the mass poisoning of "hyperactive" children with Ritalin and other neuroleptic drugs.

Power Corrupts: The Bettelheim Scandal

Everyone interested in the problem of power is familiar with Lord Acton's famous maxim, "Power tends to corrupt; absolute power corrupts absolutely." If a person is offered unlimited power over another and decides to seize it, his intelligence and good intentions are all for naught. Bruno Bettelheim, the most celebrated child therapist in the United States after World War II, fell into this trap of power. Or perhaps he eagerly rushed into it.

Although not trained or credentialed as a psychoanalyst, Bettelheim, a survivor of Nazi concentration camps, was a respected analyst and director of the famed Orthogenic School for "disturbed children" in Chicago.

While Bettelheim was alive, no one dared to challenge the grand image of his persona, inquired into the inner working of the Orthogenic School, or questioned the Lourdes-like cures he and his supporters claimed for it.[82] There were many reasons for this suspension of critical scrutiny. Bettelheim's patients were children categorized as crazy, and hence devoid of credibility. The patients' parents were devout Freudians who firmly believed in Bettelheim's powers to cure crazy children. And Bettelheim himself was a charismatic figure, a gifted writer, and a successful self-promoter. After Bettelheim committed suicide in a nursing home in the spring of 1990, survivors of his (mis)treatment came forward to set the record straight.

The first crack in Bettelheim's image occurred when Charles Pekow, a professional writer, published a critical essay about the Orthogenic School and its despotic director.[83] Pekow, who had spent 10 years as a patient at Bettelheim's school in the 1960s, was bitterly unhappy about his sojourn there. But he had kept his silence, until now. As he compellingly revealed, it would have been futile, or worse, had he tried to complain while he was imprisoned. He was defined as a crazy child. Bettelheim was accredited as a sainted savior of mentally sick children. Pekow's own grandfather "had gotten Bettelheim his job and had backed him financially for years." The gist of Pekow's thesis was that Bettelheim lied and abused the children: "While publicly condemning violence, [he] physically abused children. . . . [He] had standard lines he gave us all: we were considered hopelessly crazy by the outside world and only he could save us." Bettelheim also terrorized the children by threatening to send them to an insane asylum: "'You get better here or you go to a nut house.'"

After Pekow broke the ice, other former patients of Bettelheim came forward to support his charges. Alida Jatich, a computer programmer, stated: "Those who were going through normal adolescent growing pains were labeled as psychotic. He didn't cure autistic or extremely disturbed children." Roberta Redford, another survivor, reported that Bettelheim "called us 'crippled in the mind.' . . . [He] used all-school assemblies to tear people down."[84]

As the Bettelheim affair illustrates, the child psychiatrist's authority is altogether beyond the reach of his denominated patients. This elementary fact makes the child psychiatrist one of the most dangerous enemies not only of children, but also of adults who care for the two most precious and most vulnerable things in life—children and liberty. Psychiatric slavery cannot be reformed. It must be abolished.

5

THE HOMELESS

The myth of Eden records the first trauma of homelessness. Home, after that expulsion, is what we make, what we build.
                                                        —*Lance Murrow* [1]

In the United States today, homelessness, mental illness, and the combination of the two are recognized psychiatric categories and the daily subjects of journalism. Defined as an identifiable subgroup of the population, the homeless and the homeless-mentally ill are viewed as victims with distinct sociological characteristics, psychiatric problems, legal rights, and organizations that represent their interests.

IDENTIFYING THE PROBLEM OF HOMELESSNESS

Like the concept of mind, the concept of home is closely related to our idea of the self, a connection reflected in our language. We have many words for a homeless person, such as beggar, bum, derelict, drifter, floater, gypsy, hobo, rambler, tramp, vagabond, vagrant, wanderer, wino; but we have not a single word for a nonhomeless person. However, just as the concept of disease does not tell us what health is, so the concept of homelessness does not tell us what a home is.

The Idea of Home

Sir Edward Coke's famous phrase, "A man's house is his castle," alludes to a crucial connection between the possessive individualism of capitalism and the possession of a home. A group home is a euphemism. An institutional home is not a home at all. Only individuals and families can have homes. In this connection, we must keep in mind that the idea of the worth of the person qua individual is a modern Western invention. "Taking a world view," writes Colin Morris, "one might almost regard it [individualism] as an eccentricity among cultures."[2] Soviet satirist Mikhail Zoloshchenko's mocking remark underscores these observations: "Of course, to occupy one's own, separate apartment is philistinism. One must live all together, as one big family, and not lock oneself away in one's own castle home."[3]

Not only is individualism a modern Western value, but so too is our idea of home. "Domesticity, privacy, comfort, the concept of the home," writes John Lukacs, are "the principal achievements of the Bourgeois Age."[4] Witold Rybczynski agrees: "What places the bourgeois in the center of any discussion of domestic comfort is that unlike the aristocrat, who lived in a fortified castle, or the cleric, who lived in a monastery, or the serf, who lived in a hovel, the bourgeois lived in a house. Our examination of the home begins here."[5]

Although both home and mental illness are complex, modern ideas, we have fallen into the habit of using phrases such as "housing the homeless" and "treating the mentally ill" as if we knew what counts as housing a homeless person or what it means to treat mental illness. But we do not. We have deceived ourselves that having a home and being mentally healthy are our natural conditions, and that we become homeless or mentally ill as a result of "losing" our homes and minds. The opposite is the case. We are born without a home and without reason, and have to exert ourselves and are fortunate if we succeed in building a secure home and a sound mind.

Homemaking as a Learned Skill

We come into the world homeless and mindless. As fetuses, we develop in our mother's womb. Without that elemental shelter, there would be no human (or mammalian) life. As infants, children, and adolescents, we develop and grow in homes tended or neglected by parents. Without such homes, our bodies can grow, but our souls shrivel.

The ability to make a home—to function as a homemaker, a term that has become almost unpopular—is a learned skill. Its rudiments, like the rudiments of speaking our mother tongue, are acquired by imitation. However, to master this skill we must exert ourselves and need practice. Many people cannot form a grammatically correct sentence. Similarly, many people cannot make a home for themselves.* If they are wealthy, they can pay others to make a home for them. If they are not, they are likely to be housed by relatives, or the welfare, prison, or mental health systems.

Like any learned skill, competence to make a home develops gradually. The young child, provided with a home tailored more or less to his needs and his parents' means, rarely displays much interest in homemaking. His home is where his mother (or mother-substitute) is. Forced to leave home to attend school, the child becomes "homesick." What he misses is not so much his familiar space as the familiar faces in it. Nevertheless, the school-age child begins to show interest in his home. Before long, he becomes possessive of his own space, a trait manifested by transforming his room or a part of it into a private sphere, marked off from the spaces of parents and siblings. Finally, the young adult acquires the economic and social skills necessary for renting, owning, and maintaining his own home.

We must keep in mind, however, that until recent times, living alone was a deviant form of behavior, characteristic of eccentrics and hermits. Unmarried adults lived with their married relatives or in boarding houses. Priests and nuns, who formed no families of their own, lived communally. In contrast, single persons now constitute a third of all households in the United States, a situation due to the destigmatization of divorce, the disappearance of the extended family, longevity, advances in housing and food technology, and a rising standard of living.

Men and women who live alone must make homes for themselves. Although many such persons own expensive condominiums or houses, sometimes their places are barely furnished and are more like lodgings than homes. Although homemaking has nothing to do with sex (in the biological sense of the term), by tradition, women have been the homemakers. Precisely for that reason, the rejection of domesticity stands high on the list of the sacred values of feminism. In 1992, Gloria Steinem told the *New York Times* that "she is finally making her house a home after living in the same apartment for 25 years. 'I had lived in the apartment for at least four or five years before I found out that the oven didn't work. I don't know why it took me so long to realize you need to have a home.'"[6] Male conservatives are not necessarily any more interested in homemaking.

---

* These observations are not intended to minimize the tragic consequences of these disabling deficiencies.

Rush Limbaugh "doesn't even have a dining room table on which to plunk his Chinese takeout."[7] Compare Steinem's and Limbaugh's homemaking styles with Mencken's observations about the meaning of a home:

> A home is not a mere transient shelter: its essence lies in its permanence, in its capacity for accretion and solidification, in its quality of representing, in all its details, the personalities of the people who live in it. In the course of years it becomes a sort of museum of those people; they give it its indefinable air, separating it from all other homes, as one human face is separated from all others. It is at once, a refuge from the world, a treasure-house, a castle, and a shrine of a whole hierarchy of peculiarly private and potent gods.[8]

The process of acquiring homemaking skills is often reversed in old age. If we live long enough, the chances are that we will become unable to care for ourselves and our home. Some old people feel at home in their children's homes or even in nursing homes. Most do not. Home is partly a state of mind. "When the ways of friends converge," wrote Hermann Hesse, "the whole world looks like home for an hour."[9] More often, for many people, the whole world looks like an inhospitable shelter.

Nearly everything I have said about having a home applies to having reason. We come into the world without possessing any reason, and many of us leave it in the same condition—paraphrasing Shakespeare, *sans* speech, *sans* understanding, *sans* anything at all that we associate with the idea of sanity or mental health. This is why it is absurd to speak of a newborn baby as mentally ill, but it is not absurd to speak of it as bodily ill. Mental health—as reasonableness or the ability to interpret and cope with our environment—is a capacity we acquire gradually and, if we live long enough, are almost sure to lose.

I have tried to show that the terms *home* and *mental health* refer to complex, personal traits-as-possessions, which must be acquired, cultivated, and maintained by ceaseless effort. To have a home, a person must be able and willing to make a home for himself or arrange to have another person make a home for him on some basis of mutuality. Sometimes, some people lack the ability or the will (or both) to make a home for themselves and are unable or unwilling to be domiciled by others in their private capacities; and some people lack these capacities all the time. Although the dispensations of the welfare state combined with disability payments for mental illness have severed the traditional linkage between indigence and vagabondage, we think of every person called "homeless" as poor. When we discover that he is not, we call him mentally ill, and his deviant exploits are featured prominently in the newspapers.[10] The simple truth is that some people choose not to use their funds to house themselves (using their funds to purchase drugs instead), reject living with family members willing to take them in, and prefer a life of mental illness, crime, and vagabondage.

A House Is Not a Home

The nuanced distinctions between the terms *home* and *house* illustrate the strikingly personal nature of the former concept. Home is where the heart is. It is not merely a lodging, but a locus of affection, specifically domestic affection. The term *home* implies attachment, as in homeland or homesickness. In contrast, a house is merely a shelter or storage place. The term *house* implies impersonality or formality, as in house of prostitution, madhouse, poorhouse, workhouse, courthouse, White House.*

Prior to the industrial revolution, the household was the basic social unit of economic production and consumption, socialization, moral support, and mutual help.[11] The word *economy* comes from the Greek *oikos,* meaning house or home, and *nomos,* manager; and the word *nostalgia* comes from the Greek *nostos algos,* which means the agonized longing to return home. Recognizing homesickness as a metaphoric illness that signifies the vital role of the home in our lives, we do not mistake the term for the name of a real illness.

Other linguistic clues further illuminate the subtle meanings of the term *home.* We have many words to identify a place where a person could live but where he could hardly be said to be "at home," for example, asylum, flophouse, hospital, institution, or shelter. The essential homelessness of the chronic mental hospital patient and of the shelter resident is underscored by the fact that such a person is allowed to occupy his bed only during the night.

The emotional connotations of the words *home* and *homeless* are perhaps better appreciated by a person whose mother tongue is not English and who is familiar with the different feel of lexically corresponding terms in other languages. Albeit in another context (apropos of the problem of translation), George Steiner chooses the German word for *home* to make this point. He writes: "There are no translations. . . . *Home* is not *Heim;* the German has covert echoes of refuge, asylum, workhouse, yet it shades into the strong excitement of *Heimat, Heimatland,* the homeplace of national consciousness, the hearth of political exaltation. English has no exact equivalent."[12]

---

* There are some exceptions to this rule. The term *home* may be used euphemistically, to make a dwelling seem more intimate and personal than it truly is, as in terms such as foster home, nursing home, and home for sale.

The lack of equivalence between English and German is equally striking with respect to the word *homeless*. In German, a homeless person is not *heimlos* (there is no such word), nor *heimatlos* (which means being without a country), but *obdachlos* (without a roof [over his head]). *Dach* means roof, *Obdach*, shelter. The English word *homeless* misleadingly implies that home is something one can give another, rather than something a person must create for himself. The German word *obdachlos* makes it clear that one can give a person an *Obdach*, but one cannot give him a *Heim*, and that a person to whom we have given shelter is still home-less.*

HOMELESSNESS AS PHENOMENON AND AS SOCIAL PROBLEM

Why do some Americans have homes, and others do not? Some answers come quickly to mind. A person may be homeless because he is too poor to purchase housing and no one else is willing to take him into his home; because he lacks the psychological and social competence necessary to create and maintain a home; because he rejects a responsible, settled style of life in favor of a life of vagabondage; or because he knows that if he can successfully define himself as homeless, he can obtain housing at the taxpayer's expense.† Many New Yorkers living with friends or relatives define themselves as homeless, so they can benefit from the city's right-to-shelter policies. "More than 70% of the families seeking shelter in New York City come directly from the homes of relatives and friends . . . . Given the chance to get a subsidized apartment within a few months, many view temporary 'homelessness' as a rational decision."[13]

---

* The Hungarian word for homeless is *hajléktalan*. *Hajlék* is shelter, not home; *talan* means without. An older word for the homeless is *ágyrajáró*, *ágy* meaning bed, and *jár*, to go or walk. This is an exquisitely visual term, conjuring up the gloomy image of a person who, literally, goes to a bed he rents for the night, much as we might go to a restaurant for dinner, the difference between the two "goings" being that after a meal at a restaurant we go home, whereas after a night in a rented bed, the *ágyrajáró* must leave and has no place to go to. The French term for flophouse, *asile de nuit*, implies a similarly depressing image.

† I do not consider here those rendered temporarily homeless by natural or social catastrophes, such as earthquakes, hurricanes, revolutions, and wars.

Defining Homelessness and Identifying the Homeless

What do we mean when we classify a person as homeless? If we mean that he has no home *of his own,* then the majority of mankind must be counted as homeless. Children, women in many parts of the world, persons living in mental, military, monastic, and other institutions, and people in Communist societies do not reside in dwellings that belong to them. On the other hand, if we mean that the person has no place to live that *we* consider to be an adequate lodging, then society's standards determine who is homeless, just as its standards determine who is mentally ill. For example, a poor person living in a tent in a public park might consider his domicile a home, but a social worker might not; whereas a social worker might consider a public shelter into which she wants to place such a person a home, but the person so housed probably would not.[14]

Like poverty and mental illness, homelessness is a culturally constructed concept. In Asia and Latin America, millions of people live on the streets or in shanties under appalling conditions. They are considered neither homeless nor mentally ill, only poor. In the former Soviet Union, "The living space of many millions [of people was] . . . less than the *minimum,* according to law, allowed in [American] federal *prisons.* "[15] One-third of all Soviet hospitals had no running water or indoor toilets, and half of the schools had no central heating, running water, or sewage system.[16] In the United States, such buildings would not be considered hospitals or schools.

By conjoining homelessness and mental illness, as if they went together like love and marriage in sentimental lyrics, we have obscured the fact that chronic mental hospital patients have always been (latently) homeless.[17] Unlike the person hospitalized for a heart attack who has a home to which he can return when he is discharged, the person hospitalized for schizophrenia typically has no such home. The experts who now make confident pronouncements about the "homeless mentally ill" are actually addressing the age-old problem of the "indigent insane," who are homeless because they are indigent, not because they are insane.[18]

The chronic mental patient is not the only person whose latent homelessness is obscured by his living in an institution. Russian military personnel and aged Americans in prison are in a similar situation. Tens of thousands of Russian soldiers on German soil cannot be sent home because there is no place for them to live. Thousands of American geriatric prisoners cannot be released because "they have no homes, no job skills, no savings or medical insurance."[19] The prison is their home.

More than 20,000 men in American prisons are older than 55, with 400 older than 85. The number of old prisoners is doubling every four years, and the cost of maintaining them is about three times the norm.

Homelessness and the Politics of Housing

Economists have long warned that government-mandated housing policies, epitomized by rent control, cause rather than cure housing problems. The mechanism is fairly straightforward. Rent control legislation scapegoats landlords. They abandon the housing market and invest their surplus funds elsewhere.[20] Years before homelessness became the officially denominated problem it is today, Hayek warned about the consequences of rent control:

> Thus [by rent control] house property was in effect expropriated. Probably more than any other measure of this kind, it worsened in the long run the evil it was meant to cure . . . . It also contributed much toward weakening the respect for property and the sense of individual responsibility . . . . [Whoever has seen the effects of rent control] will appreciate the deadly effect that this one measure can have on the whole character of an economy—and even of a people.[21]

Unfortunately, when economists assert that rent control "does not work," they are missing something important. Providing people with affordable housing is only the avowed purpose of rent control. Its real purpose is to help politicians get elected, which rent control does very well indeed.

During most of its history, the United States had no housing policy. With the passing of the Housing and Urban Development Act of 1968, the federal government assumed the task of providing "a decent home and suitable living environment for every American family."[22] Probably because of this promise, there are now more homeless persons and more unsold and unoccupied housing units in the United States than at any time in our history. On top of it, the taxpayer has been saddled with a bill for more than $300 billion for bailing out the failed savings and loan associations, which, aided and abetted by the federal government, are partly responsible for this debacle.[23]

After the 1960s, the problems created by rent control were further aggravated by the process called "gentrification," which consisted of razing single-room-occupancy hotels (SROs), other low-cost housing complexes, and slum dwellings, and replacing them with office towers and expensive condominium developments. Between 1974 and 1983, almost one million housing units renting for less than $200 a month were lost to conversion or demolition. "In New York City, the number of people living in SRO units declined from about 100,000 in 1965, to less than 20,000 in 1986."[24]

The rich having displaced the poor, the latter were left with the choice of living in mental hospitals, shelters, prisons, or the streets. De-institutionalization virtually eliminated the option of long-term residence in mental hospitals. The number of persons housed, and the cost of housing them, in prisons, shelters, and on the streets, exploded.[25]

HOMELESSNESS AS A BUSINESS

Victimology is big business. Caring for the poor, the homeless, the physically sick, the mentally sick, the drug addict, the sexually abused child, the battered wife, and so forth gives employment to mental health professionals, physicians, lawyers, judges, law enforcement personnel, and journalists, virtually all of whom have a vested interest in inflating the number of persons considered to be the victims of one or another of our fashionable crowd madnesses. In 1988, NBC news anchor Tom Brokaw asserted that "65 million American children live in poverty."[26] Sixty-five million was then the total number of children in the United States.

People who address the subject of homelessness with the aim of playing benefactor with the taxpayers' money have a vested interest in inflating the number of homeless persons and attributing their predicament to a condition in the relief of which they claim to possess special expertise. Who counts as homeless thus depends more on who is doing the counting than on the condition or needs of those counted. According to the National Coalition for the Homeless, there are 3 million homeless persons in the United States. This number was invented by the late Mitch Snyder, a leading homelessness activist, who told Congress: "The figure is meaningless. We have tried to satisfy your gnawing curiosity for numbers because we are Americans with Western little minds that have to quantify everything in sight, whether we can or not."[27] A 1988 study by the Urban Institute, set the total number of American homeless at 600,000.[28]

The Turf War for the Homeless

Psychiatrists have, and always had, a vested interest in classifying social deviants as mentally ill. In the past, they defined the masturbator, the homosexual, and the epileptic as mentally ill and hence their fiduciary property. Now it is the homeless person's turn. "The homeless mentally ill," declares Neal L. Cohen, director of psychiatry at Gouverneur Diagnostic and Treatment Center in New York, "represent a clinically distinct psychiatric subpopulation who frequently have both positive and negative symptoms of schizophrenia."[29]

Although psychiatrists like to claim that they treat patients with brain diseases, actually they impose their unwanted "help" on the most helpless members of society, ensuring the preservation and enlargement of their turf. A report in *Psychiatric News,* the APA's official newspaper, tells about psychiatric residents in Washington, DC, "trying to serve their patients *about whom the physicians know little* . . . in a shelter environment [that] one of the residents said resembled nothing so much as a battlefield."[30] If these young doctors know so little about the persons they supposedly serve, it would seem to behoove them to learn more about their patients before they prescribe drugs for them. And if the shelters are like battlefields, they ought to help the imperiled persons leave their dangerous domicile, instead of making sure that they stay put. Explains Robert Kiesling, chief of Washington, DC's Emergency Psychiatric Response Division: "We think we'll be able to bring a lot more people into treatment by providing the services on site."[31]

Another claimant on the homeless is the drug abuse specialist whose favorite victim is the "mentally ill chemical abuser" (MICA). Treating these involuntary patients is portrayed as a combination of hard science and a soft heart, giving the experts engaged in this heroic effort virtually unlimited access to government funds. Irving Shandler, director of the Diagnostic and Rehabilitation Center in Philadelphia, claims that 75 to 80 percent of homeless men and women are addicts and asserts: "Substance abuse is one of the major issues causing people to be homeless and keeping them homeless."[32] The *New York Times* agrees: "Drugs and alcohol abuse have emerged as a major reason for the homelessness of men, women, and families."[33] Yet housing the homeless has only aggravated this problem. According to a 1992 survey of New York City shelters, "80 percent of the men had drugs in their system, mostly cocaine." In Washington, DC, shelter residents reported that their facility "was a crack haven . . . [where] 80 percent of the shelter population and 50 percent of the staff were doing drugs."[34]

Veterans' organizations, a third group with a vested interest in the homeless, claim that from one-third to one-half of the homeless are veterans, implicitly attributing their homelessness to military service.[35] This is a very odd claim. War is not a new phenomenon. Hundreds of millions of men, from dozens of countries, saw military service in this century alone. Yet, only after the war in Vietnam, and only in the

United States, did veterans' groups claim that military service—or the memory of it, or even faking the memory of it—causes homelessness.

Hospital administrators constitute still another group with a stake in the homeless. If an indigent patient is admitted to a hospital, the hospital is stuck with his bill, but if he is defined as homeless, Medicaid pays the bill. In 1988, the federal Medicaid program disbursed $5.5 billion in New York State, more than 60 percent of it in New York City. An anonymous bureaucrat explains: "The temptation of that money evidently influences the number of persons in New York City who are counted as homeless."[36] Workers at Bellevue Hospital documented that by declaring patients homeless and using contrived accounts of their lives as rootless panhandlers, hospital personnel "were not only increasing the numbers of patients eligible for Medicaid at the hospital but also diminishing the likelihood that their stories could ever be followed up by investigators." After these allegations were published, workers at the city's 15 municipal hospitals, and at many private hospitals, came forward and testified that "similar activities are common at their hospitals."[37]

Increasingly, the medical profession as a whole is also claiming the homeless. Until the 1960s, when the economic basis of medical practice rested firmly in the private sector, physicians were happy to leave the care and coercion of unwanted persons to the ministrations of the psychiatric and penal systems. As medical practice became economically dependent on the government, supplying medical services to destitute and deviant persons became a lucrative enterprise, and physicians began to cast a covetous eye on them as potential sources of income.

It was bad enough that psychiatrists attributed homelessness to mental illness. However, the danger in that tactic was limited, as psychiatrists were known to attribute badness to madness. Attributing homelessness to real illness poses a more serious threat, to the homeless and the taxpayer alike. A special article in the *Journal of the American Medical Association* illustrates this ominous trend. The author builds his case for claiming the homeless for medicine by asserting that there are "9.2 medical problems per homeless person," that "the rate of substance abuse (chiefly alcohol) among men [is] 85%," and that "much of it [is] preventable."[38] This is medicine? To me it looks more like economic and existential cannibalism, an interpretation supported by the author's final recommendation: "The tragedy of substance abuse among the very poor cannot be underestimated . . . these reports document the terrible need for *public mental health and substance abuse programs* that are simply not available."[39] We do not need medical jargon to know that a destitute person, alone in the world, is not likely to be healthy, in body or spirit. Calling such a person's drug use "preventable" is a cruel lie. The truth is that several of our recent First Ladies, and would-be First Ladies, have been unable to cope with their lives without alcohol, amphetamines, and Valium. Yet the American Medical Association expects our Last Ladies and Men to cope with their miserable existence without drugs.

No survey of proprietors of the homeless would be complete without mentioning the traditional protectors of the poor, the clergy. In 1988, perhaps fearing the loss of its market share, the Vatican reasserted its time-honored claim on these victims, declaring: "Adequate shelter [is] a universal right . . . any person or family that, without any direct fault on his or her part, does not have suitable housing is the victim of injustice."[40] Pope John Paul II supported this combination of anticapitalist cant and envy mongering by citing the United Nations' definition of the homeless as "those lacking adequate shelter." The disintegration of the Soviet Union has made the Vatican Commission's language and conclusions the more remarkable: "[O]ne-fifth of the world's population currently lacks decent housing. . . . Homelessness is a human rights issue . . . . Housing is a basic social good, and not simply a market commodity."[41]

HOMELESSNESS, HOUSING, AND DRUGS

Twenty years ago, when I asserted that schizophrenia is a housing problem rather than a medical problem, psychiatrists scoffed at the idea as absurd.[42] Now they busy themselves with providing housing for so-called homeless mental patients, and insist that doing so is a therapeutic intervention. Indeed, the proposition that a mental patient's homelessness is a psychiatric problem has become a part of our culture's conventional wisdom. Public interest lawyers, instead of protecting persons from involuntary mental hospitalization, have joined the mental health lobby as would-be housing agents. The Mental Health Law Project proudly proclaims that it "will provide national leadership in efforts to secure adequate housing for mentally ill people who are homeless."[43] Sociologist David Mechanic declares: "Homelessness is an acute problem among mentally ill persons; [hence] housing is an integral part of the therapeutic plan."[44] Since mental patients also lack money and sexual partners, would supplying these needs also constitute "an integral part of the therapeutic plan"?

It is easy enough to see why most people think that the homeless are mentally ill and that psychiatrists ought to provide housing for them.

Poor, desocialized people living on the streets do not look normal. Psychiatrists keep telling the public that the homeless are insane. Many have a history of mental hospitalization. These facts are enough to convince people that the subjects are mentally ill.

Examining the relationship between homelessness and mental illness undermines this facile explanation. Mental illness is undefined, undefinable, and, in my opinion, nonexistent. As there is no objective test for mental illness, it is impossible to be certain whether a person is or is not mentally ill. Even official statistics fail to support the view that most homeless persons are mentally ill. A 1992 survey of persons housed in New York City shelters found that only about 10 to 12 percent "had a record of mental hospitalization."[45] Not surprisingly, homeless persons who had been in mental hospitals are determined to avoid further contacts with psychiatrists. Psychiatrists have found, "Homeless persons who had a previous psychiatric hospitalization were the least likely to sleep in an emergency shelter . . . and were the most involved in criminal activities. The majority had not made an outpatient mental health visit in 5 years."[46] It is ironic that, to provide secure shelter for themselves, in their *homes*, psychiatrists must diagnose the homeless as mentally ill and claim them for psychiatry; whereas to provide secure shelter for themselves, on the *streets*, the homeless must avoid psychiatrists and reaffirm their self-ownership.

The War on Drugs as a War on Housing

The principal causes of homelessness in the United States today are rent control, gentrification, and the repeal of antivagrancy laws. The War on Drugs is a contributory factor that deserves brief mention.

Street-level drug trade, as the term implies, is a street-corner business. Higher level drug dealers, preferring a location that offers protection from detection and robbery, operate from so-called crack houses. Antieviction laws, motivated by the desire to protect tenants in rent-controlled buildings, make it virtually impossible for landlords to get rid of undesirable tenants, such as drug dealers. As a result, the government of the city of New York has become a drug landlord. A spokeswoman for the city's Bureau of Housing Preservation and Development explains: "We don't evict anyone unless we catch them dealing drugs and convict them twice in the same year."[47] Superintendents who try to drive drug dealers from city-owned buildings run a good chance of being murdered.

The War on Drugs and the War on Homelessness are on a collision course that no one in the media or in public life is willing to acknowledge. Ostensibly aimed at decreasing the use of illegal drugs, the War on

Drugs succeeds only in increasing homelessness. A few examples must suffice.

During the 1980s, Father Bruce Ritter—the founder of New York's famed Covenant House and a decorated hero in the War on Drugs—was venerated for his selfless struggle to save "kids" from drugs. The stunt that made Father Ritter a celebrity was his method of securing housing for his wards. He stole the apartments of alleged drug abusers and bragged about it: "To get the space I needed was simple. I just kept taking over more and more of the apartments in my tenement. Most of them . . . were occupied by junkies, dealers, and speed freaks . . . . It was kind of, if you will, muscular Christianity. The Holy Spirit made me do it."[48]

Father Ritter's efforts to increase homelessness were amateurish compared with those of the U.S. government. After a drug raid in Harlem, Andrew Maloney, United States Attorney for the Eastern District of New York, declared: "The object of the seizure is not to catch drug violators . . . [but] to lock up the premises."[49] And not merely to lock them up but to destroy them:

> In the 11 months since the Federal Government began seizing properties in an accelerated program of weekly drug raids in New York City, almost 100 apartment buildings and other residences have been barricaded or bulldozed . . . . But while scores of suspects have been taken off to jail, other occupants of these buildings—guilty only of having criminals for neighbors—have been abruptly forced to flee their homes and seek shelter elsewhere . . . . Neither the agency nor Federal authorities can say how many people are now homeless as a result of these building seizures.[50]

Similar stories abound. In Rochester, New York, Maxine LaPiana, a single parent, was helping her 14-year-old daughter to get ready for school when "nine agents from the U.S. Marshall Service, with guns slung across their shoulders, showed up and presented LaPiana with a forfeiture warrant." She was considered guilty of using her house for selling illegal drugs and "would have to prove in federal court that she didn't know about her son's alleged drug transaction to keep her house."[51] By 1989, federal authorities were holding more than 25,000 properties confiscated in the course of the War on Drugs.[52]

Some government agencies spend millions to house homeless persons. Others spend millions to evict innocent citizens from their homes, turning them into homeless persons or the guests of the government's prison system. The scenario is familiar. To save the Vietnamese from the Vietcong, we burned down their villages. To save poor inner-city Americans (mostly blacks and Hispanics) from drugs, we bulldoze their homes.

PART TWO

THE POLITICAL ECONOMY OF PSYCHIATRY

6

THE ORIGIN
OF PSYCHIATRY

*Once . . . insane asylums exist, there must be someone to sit in
them. If not you—then I; if not I—then some third person.*
—*Anton Chekhov*[1]

At the beginning of the seventeenth century, there were no mental hospitals, as we now know them. To be sure, there were a few facilities—
such as Bethlehem Hospital, better known as Bedlam—in which a
small number, usually less than a dozen, of pauper insane were confined. By the end of the century, however, there was a flourishing new
industry, called the "trade in lunacy."[2]

To understand the modern concept of mental illness, it is necessary
to focus on the radically different origins of the medical and psychiatric professions. Medicine began with sick persons seeking relief from
their suffering. Psychiatry began with the relatives of troublesome persons seeking relief from the suffering the (mis)behavior of their kin
caused them. Unlike the regular doctor, the early psychiatrist, called
mad-doctor, treated persons who did not want to be his patients, and
whose ailments manifested themselves by exciting the resentment of
their relatives. These are critical issues never to be lost sight of.[3]

Unconventional behavior must have existed for as long as human beings have lived together in society. Psychiatry begins when people stop

interpreting such behavior in religious and existential terms, and begin to interpret it in medical terms. The fatal weakness of most psychiatric historiographies lies in the historians' failure to give sufficient weight to the role of coercion in psychiatry and to acknowledge that mad-doctoring had nothing to do with healing.

THE ORIGIN OF THE MADHOUSE

Higher mammals, especially humans, remain dependent on their parents for some time after birth. Because only women can bear children and because caring for infants is a time-consuming job, societies have adopted the familiar gender-based job differentiation, females caring for the young and tending the shelter, males providing food and protection for the family.

Once a society advances beyond the stage of subsistence economy, mother surrogates often replace the nurturing role of the biological mother. For centuries, parents who could afford household help delegated the task of child care to servants—governesses for infants and young children, tutors for older ones.

The belief that every parent passionately loves his child and would like nothing better than be able to take care of him is a modern fiction and self-delusion. Taking care of children, day in and day out, is not a very interesting activity. Many adults dislike being merely in the company of a small child. Most people feel similarly disinclined to care for an insane adult, that is, for a person who is selfish and self-absorbed, demanding and dependent, intemperately happy or unhappy, perhaps even threatening and violent. Stripped of three hundred years of psychiatric-semantic embellishments, the fact is that a mad person appears to his relatives as an unpleasant individual whose company they would rather avoid. To deny their embarrassing lack of love for their lunatic kin, people burdened by a crazy relative now call him their "loved one," especially when they enlist a psychiatrist to dispose of him.

Delegating the care of an insane adult to hired help, especially if he resists being cared for, presents a very different problem than delegating the care of a child. A young child has neither the physical strength nor the political power to resist being controlled by his parents and their deputies who have lawful authority over him. Adults have no such rights vis-à-vis their adult relatives or other grown-ups. Before an adult deemed to be insane can be treated as a madman, he must therefore first be divested of his rights.[4] Reframing the political status of the insane adult as similar to that of a child accomplishes this task.

Insanity as an Infantilizing Illness

Historically, the first order of business in psychiatry was to establish insanity as a genuine disease, that is, as neither malingering nor an (immoral or illegal) act carried out by a responsible adult.[5] The next business was to distinguish insanity from other diseases and assign to it the singular characteristic of having the power to deprive the patient of his higher mental faculties, rendering him childlike, and justifying controlling and caring for him against his will.* This whole package was required by the political character of seventeenth-century English society, where, for the first time in history, a people dedicated themselves to honoring the values of liberty and property. It is not by accident that the ideas of limited government, the rule of law, and insanity as an infantilizing illness all arose and developed in England. Both the medicalization of madness and the infantilization of the insane were, and are, needed to reconcile a society's devotion to the ideals of individual liberty and responsibility with its desire to relieve itself of certain troublesome individuals by means other than those provided by the criminal law.

The idea of insanity as a condition requiring the madhousing of the insane was invented by those who needed it, the members of the dominant classes of seventeenth-century English society. It was they who had to carry the burden of being responsible for their mad relatives by having to provide for their needs and who, at the same time, had to conform their behavior to the requirements of a social order that placed a high value on the liberty of persons and the ownership of property. What was a man to do with his spouse, adult child, or elderly parent who flaunted convention and perhaps neglected his own health, but who was considered to possess a basic right to liberty and property? The time was past when such a troublesome individual could treated as a clan member, responsible to the group, devoid of individual rights in the modern sense. The rule of law liquidated the autocratic prerogatives of elders regarding deviant adults. From the seventeenth century onward, the adult members of families were held together more by cooperation and compromise, and less or not at all by direct coercion. Regrettably, cooperation and compromise are useless with persons who are unable or unwilling to cooperate and compromise.

These political and legal developments placed family members faced with a disturbing relative in a difficult situation. Though embarrassed

---

* Hence the close association between severe head injury, brain disease (neurosyphilis), and insanity.

and victimized by their (mad) kinfolk, the (sane) relatives could not control him by means of the informal, interpersonal mechanisms normally used to harmonize relations in the family. They had only two options, both useless. One was to set the engine of the criminal law against the offending family member (provided he broke the law), a course that would have led to the social or physical death of the mad relative and the abject humiliation of the family. The other was to expel him from his home, a course that would have required them to possess more power than the party they wanted to expel and would therefore have been most impractical when it was (felt to be) most necessary. It was an intolerable impasse. Sane (or perhaps merely scheming) family members had to come up with a socially acceptable arrangement to enable them to control, by means of a noncriminal legal procedure, the unwanted adult relative (who was senile, incompetent, troublesome, or perhaps simply in the way). That was the need that generated the concept of mental illness and that is the reason the concept of mental illness differs so radically from the concept of bodily illness. The point is that the physically ill person can be cared for without requiring that he first be subjected to coercive social control, but the so-called mentally ill person cannot be cared for in this way, because he (rightly) rejects the patient role.[6]

In what way did a property-owning madman in England in, say 1650, endanger his relatives? He did so in one or all of the following ways: Personally, by embarrassing them; economically, by dissipating his assets; and physically, by attacking his relatives. In this connection, it is necessary to acknowledge that a person who spurns our core values—that life, liberty, and property are goods worth preserving—endangers not only himself and his relatives but, symbolically, society and the social fabric itself. The madman's embarrassing behavior gave his family impetus for hiding him; his improvidence, which provided an important conceptual bridge between the old notion of incompetence and the new idea of insanity, gave them an impetus for dealing with him as if he were incompetent. The law had long recognized mental retardation as a justification for placing the mentally deficient person under guardianship. Now the law was asked to do the same for the mentally deranged person. Medieval English guardianship procedures lent powerful support to the emerging practice of madhousing. Both procedures grew from the soil of English political-economic and legal tradition, grounded in the value of preserving landed wealth and ensuring its stable transmission in the family. As far back as the thirteenth century, common law recognized two classes of incompetents: Idiots, mentally subnormal from birth, who were considered to be permanently impaired; and lunatics, normal persons who went mad, who were considered to be capable of recovery. The procedure for declaring a person a lunatic was similar to that of declaring him incompetent: "Commissions examined such persons before a jury that ruled on their sanity . . . Physicians played essentially no role in the certification process itself."[7] Before pauper lunatics were exiled to madhouses, propertied persons considered to be mad were managed in a manner that presaged the practice of mad-doctoring:

> Physical supervision and care of the disabled party was commonly handled by retaining a live-in servant, the so-called "lunatics keeper," a person usually of the same gender as the disabled individual. . . . Boarding out the lunatic or idiot at a private dwelling, in the company of a servant, was also commonplace; this practice in some respects anticipated the development of private madhouses in the eighteenth century.[8]

MADNESS AND THE METAPHOR OF WAR WITHIN THE SELF

Although some special facilities for housing lunatics existed before the seventeenth century, for example, in ancient Greece, in medieval England, and in Islamic societies, these were isolated arrangements for looking after a few unwanted persons. They were not instances of an institutional arrangement serving the explicit purpose of incarcerating persons categorized as insane. The history of mental hospitalization, as we know it, began in seventeenth-century England, when and where, for the first time in history, the care of the insane was systematically delegated to persons outside the family. Forcibly removed from his home, the mad person was forcibly rehoused in the home of a surrogate caretaker.

The Self Divided against Itself

Who wants to deprive us of life, liberty, and property? Enemies abroad, criminals at home, and the state to which we entrust the power to protect us from them. These threats are external to our selves. Our lives, liberties, and properties may also be threatened (metaphorically speaking) from within, by the self acting in opposition to its conventionally defined interests. In fact, the metaphor of the self divided against itself is as central to psychiatry as the metaphor of the Trinity is to Christianity. The "split personality" of schizophrenia is only the most familiar example. Psychiatrists have managed to infect the Western mind with many other examples of "divided selves," such as the true versus the false self, the authentic versus the inauthentic self, the sane or healthy versus the insane or sick self, and so forth.* To be sure, we all harbor diverse desires, some at odds with others, but we have only one self per person. The force of the maxim, "Actions speak louder than words," lies largely in its power to prevent the disuniting of actor and action. However, it is precisely the "reality" of that disunion that we desire to legitimize when we assert that a person who neglects himself or his property, whose economic behavior is injudicious, or who harms or kills himself is "not himself." People have always engaged in such behaviors. In religious societies, they were viewed as martyrs, sinners, or persons possessed by demons. In the West since the Enlightenment, they have been viewed as mentally ill.

To see through the confusions embodied in the image of the mentally ill person as "not himself" we must be clear about the connection between behavior and disease. Every part of our body influences our behavior. If we have arthritis, we cannot move normally. If we have glaucoma, we cannot see normally. The organ affecting behavior most directly is the brain. If it is seriously damaged, we die; if less seriously damaged, we lose a wide range of bodily functions, such as the ability to see or speak. The question we must keep in mind is: When and why do we attribute a person's behavior to brain disease, and when and why do we not do so? Briefly, the answer is that we often attribute bad behavior to disease (to excuse the agent); never attribute good behavior to disease (lest we deprive the agent of credit); and typically attribute good behavior to free will and insist that bad behavior called mental illness is a "no fault" act of nature.[9]

Madness, Malady, and Morality

The disease model of derangement is soundly based in the illness now known as neurosyphilis or paresis. In seventeenth-century England, syphilis caused many people to become mad. But many mad people did not have syphilis. The paucity of medical knowledge at the time made it virtually impossible for people to know whether a particular person's abnormal behavior was or was not due to brain disease. However, even then, there was a simple and reliable method for distinguishing

---

* This pseudoscientific, quasi-medical imagery is a modern version of the old theological split between the erroneous or disloyal self of the heretic and the true or loyal self of the faithful.

persons whose brains were being destroyed by syphilis from those who went mad for other reasons. The syphilitic madmen died, usually within a year or two after admission to hospital, whereas the healthy madmen often outlived their sane mad-doctors.

Although a person may behave abnormally because he has a brain disease, the typical madman behaves the way he does because of his particular adaptation to the events that make up his life. Examples abound in Shakespeare's tragedies. King Lear goes mad because of his poor choice for retirement. Lady Macbeth is driven mad by guilt and remorse over a criminal career. Hamlet breaks down under the stress of discovering that his mother and uncle murdered his father. Yet, none of these persons is relocated in a madhouse. Why? Because there are no madhouses. A century later, the practice of resolving such family conflicts by letting the stronger party psychiatrically dispose of the weaker one was well on its way of becoming accepted in principle, established in practice, ratified by law, and embraced by the public.

Some people have always found it difficult to grow up and assume the responsibilities of adulthood. Formerly, the person who failed to meet this universal challenge—who remained unskilled, unmarried, unemployed, and unemployable—was cared for in the family, or became a vagrant, leading a marginal existence. His relatives, if they were educated, might have called him a "tatterdemalion." Now they call him mentally ill, usually schizophrenic. Regardless of such a person's medical condition, there is a clear and critical connection between the *value* we attach to life, liberty, and property and the *idea* of insanity or mental disease. The "misbehavior" of a prostate is not a moral issue, but the misbehavior of a person is. The distinction is important for the observer-respondent: If he accepts the moral dimension of insanity, he is faced with an ethical-political problem, whereas if he rejects it, he is faced with a medical-technical problem.

Finally, I want to acknowledge the rationale, though not the validity, of bracketing the insane with infants. There are similarities between the behavior of an adult who does not eat or sleep properly, neglects his possessions, perhaps even attacks his relatives, and the behavior of an unruly child.[10] That analogy forms the basis for the legal-psychological strategy of treating the insane as if they were (like) infants. Correlatively, the relatives of a misbehaving adult (madman) feel compelled to protect him as well as themselves from his embarrassing and destructive behavior. That similarity forms the basis for the legal-psychological strategy of letting psychiatrists act as the guardians of their mental patients, as if they were parents and the patients were (like) children.[11]

THE MADHOUSE AS SURROGATE HOME

When the trade in lunacy began, the individuals incarcerated as insane were members of the propertied classes who posed a problem to their families. The sane relatives' problem was not finding a home for a homeless person, but finding a justification for removing the lawful occupant of a home from his residence and relocating him in someone else's home. Although the historical record is clear, Michel Foucault constructed a history of psychiatry that has confused the matter. Influenced by his Marxist bias, he traced the origin of the practice of incarcerating madmen to the segregation of lepers and, more specifically, to the large-scale confinement of urban indigents in France in the seventeenth century.[12] Some of what Foucault described happened. But it was not the way the systematic confinement of persons diagnosed as mad came into being. Individual rights were virtually nonexistent in seventeenth-century France. They were assuredly nonexistent for the propertyless French masses. Hence, imprisoning the rabble in "general hospitals" did not require the pretext of insanity as an illness. Moreover, it is simply not true that institutional psychiatry represented the beginning of a new mode of warfare between the haves and have-nots, the former resorting to the tactic of labeling the latter as insane in order to remove them to the madhouse. The incarceration of rich persons in private madhouses came first and was followed, considerably later, by the incarceration of poor persons in public insane asylums. Roy Porter emphasizes that early psychiatry was *not:*

> a discipline for controlling the rabble. . . . Provision of public asylums did not become mandatory until 1845 . . . . Even at the close of the eighteenth century, the tally of the confined mad poor in Bristol, a town of some 30,000, was only twenty. . . . [Whereas] about 400 people a year were being admitted to *private* asylums.[13]

The Clergyman as Mad-Doctor

Except for some historians of psychiatry, few people realize that the early madhouses were not hospitals, but were simply the homes of the keepers, who took a few, often only one or two, madmen or madwomen as involuntary boarders or houseguests; or that the keepers, who owned and operated these private madhouses, were laypersons, principally clergymen; and that the connection between religion (the cure of souls) and mad-doctoring (the cure of minds) made good historical sense.

The practice of healing began as an undifferentiated religious-medical enterprise. Later, as the social world split into sacred and profane parts, the practice of healing also split, one part remaining a sacred, religious activity, the other becoming the secular profession of medicine. In the West, this separation occurred twice: First, with respect to the body, in Greece, two and a half millennia ago; second, with respect to the mind, in England, less than four hundred years ago. Since the Enlightenment, spiritual and scientific healing have become, and have been perceived as, distinct and separate enterprises.

There is a long Western tradition of interpreting insanity in religious terms, as a manifestation of demonic possession, treatable with exorcism; and, most importantly, viewing clerical coercion as morally laudable and politically legitimate. When people believed that eternal life in the hereafter was more important than a brief sojourn on earth, torturing the possessed person to improve the quality of his life after death was regarded as an act of beneficence. Hence the long history of lawful clerical coercion.

In contrast, before the seventeenth century, there was no historical tradition justifying the use of force by physicians. Unlike the doctor of divinity, the doctor of medicine had no right (as yet) to imprison and torture his patients. In fact, when Englishmen first tried to enlist the doctor in the service of diagnosing and disposing of their problematic relatives, the physician, as Shakespeare showed in *Macbeth*, declined the invitation. This rejection was consistent with the physician's historical mandate. From ancient times, his help was sought by suffering persons on their own behalf, or by healthy persons on behalf of relatives too disabled to seek help for themselves. The clergyman labored under no such tradition, which explains his role as pioneer mad-doctor and madhouse keeper. Subsequently, as the clergyman's power diminished, the mad-doctor's increased, and theological coercion was replaced by psychiatric coercion.[14]

The Private Madhouse: A "Home" for Paying Guests

The trade in lunatics must be understood in economic and social terms. The enterprise satisfied the existential needs of the lunatics' relatives, and the economic needs of the entrepreneurs who supplied the demanded service.[15] The madhouse keeper's retainers were wealthy—able and willing to pay him to relieve them of the company of their unwanted relative. The keepers were relatively impecunious, eager to please their paymasters. Contemporary observers recognized what was happening.

Thomas Bakewell, himself the proprietor of a madhouse, observed: "The pecuniary interest of the proprietor and the secret wishes of the lunatics' relatives, led not only to the neglect of all means of cure, but also to the prevention and delay of recovery."[16] Another madhouse keeper wrote: "If a man comes in here mad, we'll keep him so; if he is in his senses, we'll soon drive him out of them."[17] The practice of involuntary mental hospitalization thus began as a private, capitalist enterprise. Like chattel slavery, psychiatric slavery had to be sanctioned by the state.

Because madhousing was soon transformed into a largely statist program of confining troublesome poor people, the entrepreneurial origin of psychiatry as a form of private imprisonment merits reemphasis. In the seventeenth century, England was essentially a two-class society, consisting of those who owned property and those who did not. Because wealth, especially land, generated income, members of the propertied classes did not have to work to procure a livelihood for themselves and their families. The poor, whose only property was their labor, had to work or face destitution. Because they had no "real" property other than their daily labor, their relatives had nothing to gain, and much to lose, by having them declared mad. The very poverty of the poor thus protected them from the ministrations of the early mad-doctors.

Ironically, long before the misery of poorly paid factory workers generated denunciations of private profit, the early critics of madhouses blamed the abuses of the trade in lunacy on the profit motive. It was an important factor, to be sure, but it was merely a symptom. Forbes B. Winslow, the proprietor of two private asylums, denounced the practice of patients being "brought into the market and offered for sale, like a flock of sheep, to the highest bidder."[18] He was referring to the practice of madhouse keepers advertising for "guests." A typical advertisement ran as follows: "Insanity. Twenty per cent. annually on the receipts will be guaranteed to any medical man recommending a quiet patient of either sex, to a first class asylum, with highest testimonials."[19] *Plus ça change* . . . . Today, private mental hospitals not only advertise their services but encourage their staff to double as psychiatric bounty hunters. It hardly needs adding that the madhouse keepers hawk their wares not to the so-called patients but to their relatives who are eager to get rid of them. Since government and insurance programs now pick up the tab, this tactic has become more tempting and more popular than ever.[20]

Unfortunately, the early critics of the madhouse business aimed their fire at the wrong target. The root problem was not profit but power, the mad-doctor's power to lawfully transform a sovereign British subject from person into mental patient and thus deprive him of liberty.

Madness: An "English Malady"?

My thesis is that, like limited government, the free market, and the workhouse, mad-doctoring was also an English invention. This interpretation is supported by the writings of seventeenth- and eighteenth-century English physicians, who maintained that mental illness was a peculiarly English malady.

In 1672, Gideon Harvey, physician to King Charles II, wrote a treatise titled, *Morbus Anglicus,* a term he used for "hypochondriacal melancholy."[21] Fifty-one years later, George Cheyne popularized this notion in his classic, *The English Malady.* That antique work remains of considerable interest because it already exemplifies the confusion, still characteristic of psychiatry, of metaphorical maladies of the soul with literal diseases of the body.[22] "The Spirit of a Man," wrote Cheyne, "can bear his Infirmities, but a wounded Spirit who can bear? saith a Prophet. As this is a great Truth in the Intellectual World, so it may allude to the *Human machin*. . . ."[23] To what "conditions" did Cheyne refer when he categorized them as instances of the "English Malady"? They were "Spleen," "Vapours," "Lowness of Spirits," "Hysterical Distemper," and other similar "ailments." Despite naming "it" "Lowness of Spirits," he explicitly identified that "condition" as a bodily disease, and recommended treating it with mercury, antimony, and other arcane compounds and concoctions, as well as dietary regimens and purgatives.[24] However, Cheyne's effort to medicalize problems of living was premature, as he himself realized. He wrote:

> [O]ften when I had been consulted in a Case . . . and found it what is commonly called Nervous, I had been in the utmost Difficulty, when desir'd to define or name the Distemper, for fear of affronting them, or fixing a Reproach on a Family or Person . . . . If I said it was Vapours, Hysterick or Hypochondriacal Disorders, they thought I call'd them Mad . . . [and] was in hazard of a Drubbing for seeming to impeach their Courage; . . . I myself was thought a Fool, a weak and ignoble Cox-comb, and perhaps dismiss'd in Scorn.[25]

PIONEER CRITICS OF THE PRACTICE OF MADHOUSING

Madhousing the unwanted family member was a novel method for coping with age-old familial and social problems. Since every solution of a human problem creates a new set of problems, protests against the novel practice typically arise in the same cultural milieu as the reforms.

The Industrial Revolution and the Luddite revolt against the machine both began in England. And so did the protests against what we now term "psychiatric abuses."

False Commitment: The Wrong Target

Insofar as insanity is accepted as a justification for depriving a person of liberty, the basic risk inherent in involuntary mental hospitalization becomes analogous to the risk inherent in imprisoning criminals. In each case, a person might be wrongfully identified as suffering from insanity or being guilty of a crime, and wrongfully deprived of liberty.

Preoccupation with the wrongful confinement of sane persons in insane asylums, called "false commitment," is a leitmotiv that runs through the entire history of psychiatry. The history of this protest movement is characterized by the stereotypical claims of incarcerated mental patients that they are sane and have been misdiagnosed as insane, while at the same time enthusiastically supporting the diagnoses of their fellow victims as insane and applauding their incarceration as just and proper. Evidently it never occurred to the protestors to challenge the legitimacy of psychiatric slavery itself. The mad, no less than the sane, accepted the principle that the illness called insanity justifies incarcerating the patient.

However, madmen and madwomen claiming to be sane were not the only critics of the madhouse system. Their impeached pleas were amplified and supported by the unimpeachable voices of journalists and men of letters. These critics alerted the public to the fact that individuals were often committed not because they were insane but because they were the victims of scheming relatives and greedy madhouse keepers. These accusations were supported by anecdotes of philandering husbands committing their innocent wives, and greedy children confining their harmless elderly parents. Obsession with false commitment thus obscured the fundamental issue of the freedom and responsibility of the so-called mad person, and reinforced the belief that incarcerating the truly insane was in the best interests of both the patient and society.

Daniel Defoe

Daniel Defoe (1660–1731), famous as the author of *Robinson Crusoe*, was what we would now call an investigative journalist. As such, he was also a pioneer critic of the business of mad-doctoring. Like other madhouse reformers, Defoe objected only to the confining of sane persons, an abuse he attributed partly to the selfishness of the relatives initiating the commitment process, and partly to the rapacity of the madhouse keepers. He wrote:

> This leads me to exclaim against the vile Practice now so much in vogue among the better Sort, as they are called, but the worst sort in fact, namely, the sending their Wives to Mad-Houses at every Whim or Dislike, that they may be more secure and undisturb'd in their Debaucheries. . . . This is the height of Barbarity and Injustice in a Christian Country, it is a clandestine Inquisition, nay worse . . . . Is it not enough to make any one mad to be suddenly clap'd up, stripp'd, whipp'd, ill fed, and worse us'd? To have no Reason assign'd for such Treatment, no Crime alledg'd or accusers to confront? . . . In my humble Opinion all private Mad-Houses should be suppress'd at once.[26]

Note that Defoe speaks only of the practice of locking up persons of "the better Sort," as he called members of the propertied class. The large-scale commitment of the poor in public madhouses lay still in the future.

Because they never questioned the idea of mental illness or the legitimacy of incarcerating persons diagnosed as insane, the critics of false commitment accomplished less than nothing. By shaming the madhouse keepers and society into prettifying the psychiatric plantations, they preserved and strengthened the system of psychiatric slavery.[27] Psychiatrists became more sophisticated, concealing incarceration as hospitalization and torture as treatment. Since 1800, the persistence of psychiatric abuses has been attributed to a succession of fashionable scapegoats, such as untrained or sadistic doctors, inadequate government funding, the severity of the patients' diseases, the inadequacy of available treatments, and, in the present day, the overuse or underuse of psychiatric drugs.

Anton Chekhov

One of the most moving criticisms of involuntary mental hospitalization is Anton Chekhov's novella, "Ward No. 6." Written in 1892, it is a veiled, but nonetheless powerful, attack on the entire system of psychiatric incarceration. The gist of the story is this.

Andrew Ephimich Raghin, an aimless young doctor, takes a job at a provincial mental hospital. After he assumes his post, it is made clear to him that he is expected to play the part of a feudal master, leaving the care of the patients to the brutal hospital attendants. Although warned against mingling with the inmates, to relieve his boredom he drifts into engaging one of the patients in conversation. Soon, the patient appears to be quite sane to him, and he, the doctor, appears to be increasingly more mad to his acquaintances. As the story nears its climax, Ephimich is declared insane and is imprisoned in the same cell as Ivan Dmitrich, the patient he befriended. This appalling scene follows:

> "But suppose I were to go out of here, what harm would that do anybody?" asked Andrew Ephimich . . . "I can't understand this! Nikita, I must go out!" . . .
>
> "Don't start any disorders, it's not right!" Nikita [the attendant] admonished him.
>
> "This is the devil and all!" Ivan Dmitrich suddenly cried out and sprang up. "What right has he got not to let us out? How dare they keep us here? The law, it seems, says plainly that no man may be deprived of liberty without a trial! This is oppression! Tyranny!"
>
> "Of course it's tyranny!" said Andrew Ephimich, heartened by Ivan Dmitrich's outcry." "I've got to, I must go out! He has no right to do this! Let me out, I tell you!"
>
> "Do you hear, you stupid brute?" Ivan Dmitrich shouted, and pounded on the door with his fist. "Open up, or else I'll break the door down! You butcher!"
>
> "Open up!" Andrew Ephimich shouted, his whole body quivering. "I demand it!"
>
> "Just keep on talking a little more!" Nikita answered from the other side of the door. "Keep it up!"
>
> "They'll never let us out!" Ivan Dmitrich went on. . . . "They'll make us rot here! . . . Open up, you scoundrel, I'm suffocating!" he cried out in a hoarse voice and threw his weight against the door. "I'll smash my head! You murderers!"
>
> Nikita flung the door open, shoved Andrew Ephimich aside roughly, using both his hands and one knee, then swung back and smashed his fist into the doctor's face.
>
> Ivan Dmitrich let out a yell. Probably he, too, was being beaten. . . .
> Toward evening Andrew Ephimich died from an apoplectic stroke.[28]

And so the story ends. Chekhov, himself a physician, knew whereof he spoke.

ENGLISH LITERATURE AND THE ORIGIN OF MAD-DOCTORING

When Shakespeare wrote his great plays, there were no private madhouses in England. One hundred years later, the trade in lunacy was a flourishing industry. Shakespeare's tragedies thus provide a superb, and surprisingly neglected, source for tracing the origin of mad-doctoring.[29]

Are Shakespeare's Tragic Heroes Mad?

The longer I have pondered Shakespeare's portrayal of madness, the more impressed I have become with how psychiatrists, psychoanalysts, historians of psychiatry, and literary critics alike have distorted Shakespeare's depiction of madness. They have done so by concentrating on the behaviors of the persons denominated as mad, ignoring the behaviors of the persons who so denominate them, and imposing psychoanalytic interpretations on the *dramatis personae* instead of letting the playwright have the last word.

From among a multitude of psychiatric studies of Shakespeare, I shall comment on one only, Sir John Bucknill's (1817–1897) *The Mad Folk of Shakespeare,* first published in 1859 as *The Psychology of Shakespeare.*[30] Bucknill, one of the founders of British psychiatry, took for granted that Shakespeare's tragic heroes were ill, in the literal, medical sense of the term. The psychiatrist's task, as he saw it, was to identify precisely what ailed them. To Bucknill, who knew that there were no insane asylums in England in 1600, this meant only that there was an unmet need for such institutions. He wrote:

> In his [Shakespeare's] time the insane members of society were not secluded from the world as they are now. If their symptoms were prominent and dangerous, they were, indeed, thrust out of sight very harshly and effectually; but if their liberty was in any degree tolerable, it was tolerated, and they were permitted to live in the family circle, or to wander the country.[31]

Bucknill acknowledged that the absence of mental hospitals in Shakespeare's time might signify that there was more tolerance for personal eccentricity in Elizabethan than in Victorian England, but failed to pursue this lead. Instead, he continued:

> That abnormal states of mind were a favourite study of Shakespeare would be evident from the mere number of characters to which he has attributed them, and the extent alone to which he has written on the subject . . . The consistency of Shakespeare is in no characters more close and true, than in those most difficult ones wherein he portrays the development of mental unsoundness, as in Hamlet, Macbeth, and Lear; . . . It is on the development of insanity . . . that the great dramatist delights to dwell.[32]

In Bucknill's view, then, Shakespeare described the development of mental diseases. In my view, Shakespeare painted imperishable literary portraits of life as tragedy. Let us briefly reconsider, without psychiatric prejudgments, some of Shakespeare's mad/tragic heroes and heroines.

Aided and abetted by his loyal wife, Macbeth destroys his rivals and reaches the pinnacle of political power. Unable to relish the role she so hungrily coveted, Lady Macbeth becomes unhinged by guilt. She is tormented by anguish, cannot rest or sleep, and hallucinates blood on her hands that she cannot wash away. Macbeth summons a doctor to cure her. He does not ask the doctor to discover what ails Lady Macbeth; he just wants him to restore her to her "premorbid" condition. However, the doctor quickly grasps the meaning of Lady Macbeth's madness and her husband's reasons for wanting to deny its meaning. He tells Macbeth that his wife is "Not so sick, my lord / As she is troubled with thick-coming fancies / That keep her from her rest."[33] Macbeth is not satisfied. He presses the doctor with these immortal words:

> Cure her of that:
> Canst thou not minister to a mind disease'd,
> Pluck from the memory a rooted sorrow,
> Raze out the written troubles of the brain,
> and with some sweet oblivious antidote
> Cleanse the stuff'd bosom of that perilous stuff
> Which weighs upon her heart?"[34]

The doctor, conscientious and wise, remains unmoved. His exemplary reply is: "Therein the patient / Must minister to himself."[35] This answer leaves the disturbed and disturbing persons to their own devices, to cope with their problematic lives as best they can. With neither divorce nor commitment being available to Macbeth, both his and Lady Macbeth's options were limited—to murder and suicide.

In my reading of this play, part of its message is that personal misconduct is not a disease; that the troubling consequences of moral failure do not constitute a treatable medical condition; that the mad person needs moral, not medical, guidance; and, in the final analysis, that the patient must "cure" himself. When this formula is inverted—when madness is accepted as a disease over which the patient has no control, and when the (mad)doctor is empowered to control him by force and fraud—then, and *only* then, can mad-doctoring as a profession arise and coercion begin to masquerade as cure.

While in *Macbeth*, Shakespeare presents a "nervous breakdown" as morally merited punishment for the actor's evil deeds, in *Hamlet*, he exhibits the duplicity intrinsic to mad-doctoring. After Polonius realizes that Hamlet's erstwhile friends, Rosencranz and Guildenstern, have been enlisted as agents by Gertrude and Claudius, Polonius ponders aloud:

'Tis too much proved, that with devotion's visage
And pious action we do sugar o'er
The devil himself.[36]

The metaphor of the "devil sugared over" alludes to the pretense that foe is friend, that the effort to silence a person who suspects crimes in high places is an attempt to protect a madman from his madness. Hearing Polonius' words, Claudius acknowledges that his concern is not for Hamlet's mind but for his own soul:

(Aside) O, 'tis too true.
How smart a lash that speech doth give my conscience!
The harlot's cheek, beautied with plast'ring art,
Is not more ugly to the thing that helps it
Than is my deed to my most painted word.
O heavy burthen![37]

The scenarios of both *Macbeth* and *Hamlet* point to a powerful, albeit latent, demand for alternative housing for certain upper-class persons, a demand generated not by those to be rehoused, but by their relatives seeking to rehouse them.* Because no such service existed, the would-be buyers turned to physicians, in effect asking them to expand their professional repertoire by providing madhousing. It was a reasonable proposal. Physicians were in the business of helping healthy people care for their sick, and therefore problematic, relatives. Lady Macbeth was a problem to her husband. He called for the doctor to help him. This triangular relationship—comprising a disturbing man or woman, his or her dissatisfied spouse, and a doctor—remains the main engine of psychiatry.

For Shakespeare and his contemporaries, it must have still seemed self-evident that the individuals who act madly as well those who define

---

* We touch here on some similarities between madhouses and prisons on the one hand, and homes and hotels on the other. In the former domiciles, individuals are rehoused involuntarily; in the latter, individuals rehouse themselves voluntarily.

them as mad are responsible for their behavior. No one's (mis)behavior is excused as due to demonic possession, mental disease, or any other duress. Lady Macbeth is responsible for her crimes and her guilty conscience; Macbeth, for denying the meaning of his wife's dis-eased mind and trying to enlist a doctor in an immoral collusion; Claudius and Gertrude, for covering up their villainous deeds and trying to incriminate Hamlet as mad. Perhaps most interestingly, Othello is responsible for becoming and being mad. Here is Shakespeare's affirmation of the central role of personal responsibility for our character and conduct:

> *Iago.* . . . 'tis in ourselves that we
> are thus, or thus. Our bodies are our gardens,
> to which our wills are gardeners; so that if
> we will plant nettles or sow lettuce, set hyssop
> and weed up thyme, supply it with one gender of
> herbs or distract it with many, either to have it
> sterile with idleness or manured with industry,
> why the power and corrigible authority of this lies
> in our wills.[38]

At the very moment when the idea of insanity as non-responsibility is developing in its mother's womb, Shakespeare presciently declares it a monster unworthy of life. Hamlet, Lear, Lady Macbeth, Othello, none is mad when he or she first enters the stage. They go mad before our very eyes. For Shakespeare, madness is the consequence of a person's freely chosen conduct, fated perhaps (in the classic Greek sense), but neither an excuse for evil nor an illness that requires medical attention. On the contrary, everything connected with madness is motivated action: Claudius and Gertrude attribute madness to Hamlet as a weapon of aggression; Hamlet feigns madness as a defensive ruse; Lear and Othello go mad because they have trusted imprudently or were immoderately jealous.

Jonathan Swift: "A House for Fools and Mad"

Barely a hundred years after Shakespeare, the English people were as engrossed with the abuse of reason as madness as we are with the abuse of drugs as addiction. I have remarked earlier on some of the cultural and economic reasons for this development. There were other, more subtle stimuli at work as well. Michael DePorte, for example, attributes the growing interest in insanity in the seventeenth century "to the policy at Bethlehem Hospital of allowing visitors to come and go freely, a practice which not only gave writers a chance to observe madmen at first hand, but which also gave them an audience familiar with the behavior of the insane."[39] This is a perceptive and persuasive observation. Indeed, visiting Bedlam as if it were a zoo not only gave artists a chance to observe madmen, it also gave madmen an opportunity to address a more sympathetic audience than their fellow victims, disdainful keepers, and hostile relatives.

Swift made many references to madness, almost all satirical. Like Shakespeare, he also took for granted that there is method in it. Specifically, he viewed madness as a tactic the madman chooses to enhance his self-esteem. In *A Tale in a Tub*, for example, he describes a madman as "a *tailor* run mad with pride,"[40] echoing Hobbes's interpretation a half century earlier: "The passion, whose violence, or continuance, maketh madness, is either great vainglory which is commonly called *pride*, and self-conceit; or great *dejection* of mind. . . ."[41] In the same essay, Swift satirizes the view that geniuses are insane and the sadistic practices that pass as mad-doctoring: ". . . *Epicurus, Diogenes, Appolonius, Lucretius, Paracelsus, Des Cartes*, and others, who if they were now in the world . . . would in this our undistinguishing age incur manifest danger of *phlebotomy*, and *whips*, and *chains*, and *dark chambers*, and *straw*."[42]

In his magisterial biography of Swift, Irvin Ehrenpreis writes:

> The theme of madness which runs through Swift's work normally carries the motif of power without responsibility. In Irish affairs it grows into the concept of a nation gone mad: Parliament as Bedlam populated by lunatics who think themselves statesmen, the kingdom as a land of absurdities . . . the machinery of government in Ireland has for its true function that of farcical entertainment, diverting people from their real problems.[43]

Shakespeare always, and Swift most of the time, view madness as a moral and political matter, not a medical malady. Both use the term *madness* as a figure of speech, an evocation of the turmoil and tragedy of human existence, not as the diagnosis of a disease requiring medical intervention. However, Swift's conduct toward allegedly mad persons, himself included, was inconsistent with some of his writings. Although he characterized Bedlam as a place of "phlebotomy, whips, chains, dark chambers, and straw," yet he joined the hospital's governing board and tried to commit one of his friends to it, who, Swift believed, "went mad from thinking too long about the problems of calculating longitude."[44] At the same time, he suggested that since "incurable fools, incurable rogues, incurable liars, [and] the incurably vain or envious" qualified for admission to Bethlehem Hospital . . . a certificate as an 'incurable scribbler' would elect him [Swift] a patient at the foundation."[45] Said in jest but meant in earnest?

The most interesting evidence of Swift's concern with madness is his last will, in which he bequeathed his estate for the construction of an insane asylum in Dublin, which as yet had none. His poem, "Verses on the Death of Dr. Swift," written in 1732, ends with this grand double-entendre:

> He gave the little Wealth he had,
> To build a House for Fools and Mad:
> And shew'd by one satyric Touch,
> No Nation wanted it so much.[46]

To his bequest of about eleven thousand pounds, a substantial sum at that time, other gifts were added, enabling the city of Dublin in 1757, 12 years after Swift's death, to open St. Patrick's Hospital, better known as Swift's Hospital.

For Swift, the immortal artist, madness was largely a metaphor for hypocrisy, perversity, and stupidity. However, for Swift, the modern hypochondriac afraid of illness, madness was a disease that might even render the patient dangerous and hence justify his segregation. It must be recalled that during much of his adult life Swift suffered from Ménière's disease, or labyrinthine vertigo, which was then a mysterious ailment that made him fear for his own sanity.[47] In the poem in which he recorded his bequest, he described his condition thus:

> That old vertigo in his head
> Will never leave him till he's dead:
> Besides, his memory decays,
> He recollects not what he says;
> He cannot call his friends to mind;
> Forgets the place where he last din'd.[48]

Swift's fear of going mad might signify a growing appreciation of the relationship between brain disease and the sorts of behaviors that were becoming understood as the symptoms of insanity.

7

ECONOMICS
AND PSYCHIATRY

*Nobody but a beggar chooses to depend chiefly upon the benevolence
of his fellow-citizens. And even a beggar does not depend upon it
entirely . . . . The greater part of his occasional wants are supplied*
in the same manner as those of other people, by treaty, by
barter, by purchase.

—*Adam Smith*[1]

Although economists and psychiatrists address essentially the same subject, human behavior, they work in virtual isolation from one another. On
the rare occasions when they cross boundaries, they tend to embrace each
other's fashionable fictions as if they were scientific truths.

ECONOMICS, PSYCHIATRY, AND HUMAN BEHAVIOR*

Around the turn of the century, as one group of Austrians was developing
an approach to the cure of souls that became known as psychoanalysis,

---

* I use the word *psychiatry* as shorthand for all the mental health professions.

another was developing an approach to economics that later became known as the Austrian school.[2] Friedrich von Wieser, one of its founders, began his pioneering work, *Social Economics,* as follows:

> This investigation uses the methods recently designated as "psychological." The name is applied because the theory takes its point of departure from within, from the mind of economic man. I myself once spoke of economic theory in this sense as applied psychology.[3]

Wieser's most distinguished pupil, Ludwig von Mises, identified the scope of economics in almost the same terms that might be used to identify the scope of psychiatry. He wrote:

> Nothing that men aim at or want to avoid remains outside [the scope of economics as] . . . the general theory of human action. . . . Human action is purposeful behavior. . . . to do nothing and to be idle are also actions, they too determine the course of events.[4]

Nevertheless, the ideas of economists and psychiatrists have remained isolated from one another, and for good reason. The economist views man as a *rational actor,* choosing both ends and the means to attain them. The psychiatrist views him as an *irrational patient,* that is, as a (mad)man who is not an actor at all, but a puppet propelled by impulses or the victim of mental illness.[5] This difference is a human artifact that reflects two different ways of constructing social reality and seeking to control behavior.

Gary Becker has tried to reconcile these two approaches, applying so-called rational choice analysis to such ostensibly noneconomic behaviors as addiction, gambling, and family relations.[6] According to him, the economic approach "is not restricted to material goods and wants or to markets with monetary transactions, and *conceptually* does not distinguish between major and minor decisions or between 'emotional' and other decisions."[7] Becker uses the word "emotional" to describe decisions psychiatrists would call "irrational," noting that "the objections by many non-economists that theory of choice assumes rationality is not well founded [because] it is difficult to distinguish operationally between irrational choices and poorly informed ones . . ."[8] Economic theory, he concluded, "is much more compatible with irrational behavior than had been previously suspected."[9] Since the distinction between rational and irrational behavior is in no meaningful sense scientific, this conclusion should not surprise us.[10]

Controlling Behavior: Coercion and Cooperation

As soon as man formed an idea of ownership, he must have realized that if Peter wanted something that Paul had, he could get it either by plunder or by exchange. Cooperation among persons and groups requires control of man's predatory impulses. Thus did the family, religion, and the state come into being, each assuming the task of controlling personal conduct.

As social beings, we must coordinate our behavior with the behavior of others, and vice versa. Such coordination is ensured by two means, self-control and external coercion.* Some moral codes and political-economic systems rank internal controls more highly than external coercions, for example, Stoicism, the Protestant ethic, and the market economy. Others rank dependence on benevolent authorities and external coercions more highly than self-discipline, for example, theocracies, dictatorships, and the Therapeutic State.

Adam Smith—who taught moral philosophy, not economics—is remembered and revered as the prophet of the self-disciplined, cooperative lifestyle.[11] For associations among adults, Smith advocated voluntary relations exemplified by trade, because "When two men trade between themselves it is undoubtedly for the advantage of both."[12] Since the person "who is not disposed to respect the law and obey the civil magistrate" does not deserve the privileges of citizenship, Smith based his faith in cooperation on the premise that society will ensure that it will consist of self-disciplined citizens.[13]

To enable us to respect and obey the civil magistrate, we must first learn to respect and obey our parents. Because the family has proved to be the most effective social arrangement for transforming irresponsible children into responsible adults, it is our most enduring and most important institution. It is not an accident that hostility to the family has been the hallmark of the promoters of dependency on authority. The Jacobin, the Communist, the psychoanalyst, the Laingian, and the feminist—each in his or her way—has been bitterly critical of the family and has opposed the development of personal autonomy, usually under the guise of promoting it. Smith felt so strongly about the importance of the family that he deplored people having too many children, because "where there are many children, they cannot all have the affection of the parent, and it is only by this means that any of them can establish themselves."[14]

---

* I construct this dichotomy to emphasize that persuasion and other forms of noncoercive influence are effective only insofar as they succeed in altering the subject's choices.

Schools of Economics and Psychiatry

In economics, we distinguish between experts who support the interventionist state, such as Gunnar Myrdal and John Kenneth Galbraith, and those who support the minimalist state, such as Friedrich von Hayek and Milton Friedman.[15] In psychiatry, we similarly distinguish among various schools, but the distinctions are based on expediency rather than principle and are in constant flux. Mainstream psychiatry has always been based on the proposition that mental illnesses are brain diseases, that mental patients are dangerous to themselves or others, and that they are therefore rightfully incarcerated. The Freudian revolution, based on the proposition that mental symptoms have meaning and that the psychoanalyst's patient must be an independent person who cooperates with his therapist, arose in dialectical opposition to this classic psychiatric perspective. However, the members of both groups embraced the dogma of the literal existence of psychopathology (abnormal behavior as illness), and psychoanalysts supported the psychiatrists' authority to coerce and excuse their patients (civil commitment and the insanity defense).

During World War II and the immediate postwar period, when psychoanalysis became absorbed into psychiatry, the opposing factions became redefined as the medical and psychological perspectives on abnormal behavior. United under the banner of "dynamic psychiatry," both schools escalated their endorsement of coercing the (seriously ill) mental patient. The distinction between the supporters of the biological (medical) and nonbiological (existential, psychological, social) schools of psychiatry thus do not correspond to the distinction between the supporters and opponents of command economies.*

PSYCHIATRY, PARENS PATRIAE, AND STATISM

In modern, capitalist societies, most goods and services are manufactured and distributed by individual entrepreneurs. Psychiatry has been and continues to be an exception to this rule.[16] Curiously, although free market economists have criticized virtually every tax-supported institution, advocating their abolition or privatization, they have refrained from challenging the legitimacy of statist-coercive psychiatry.[17]

---

* Today, the psychiatric situation in the United States and other advanced societies resembles the economic situation that prevailed in the Soviet Union. In Communist societies, there was no room for free-market economists whose values were incompatible with those of the state. Similarly, in therapeutic societies, there is no room for contractual psychiatrists whose values are antagonistic to those of officially sanctioned psychiatry.

The Contradiction between the
Market and Psychiatry

In societies called "free," it is unfashionable to oppose freedom openly. Still, not everyone loves liberty. Many people value health and security more highly. Hence, the enemies of liberty need not attack freedom directly. Instead, they can conceal their opposition to it as the protection of health, especially mental health. In the United States today, state interference with the liberty of the (noncriminal) citizen is typically justified on the ground that it is necessary for the protection of his own health and safety or the health and safety of the community. Today's Trojan horse is the clinic or hospital, concealing antifreedom fighters called "health professionals."

The political-economic backbone of psychiatry has always been the *state* mental hospital system, which supplied both its legitimacy for the use of force and the funds necessary for its operation. This historical association between the state and psychiatry accounts for psychiatry's habitual hostility to liberty and the market. When psychoanalysis and psychotherapy were more sharply demarcated from psychiatry than they are now, there was, for a relatively brief period, a genuine market in those services. Today, however, the market in mental health services has, in effect, been abolished. The reason is simple. Market relations imply the renunciation of the use of force. But unless the psychiatrist is willing to run the risk of being sued for malpractice, he can no longer assume this posture. Today, psychiatric practice, both in the office and the hospital, rests on the premise that it is the therapist's duty to protect the patient from killing himself or others, by force if necessary. The result is that the patient, his relatives, and the psychiatrist are enmeshed in a relationship that is, actually or potentially, coercive. Specifically, the therapist coerces the patient he deems to be "dangerous to himself or others," by incarcerating him in a mental hospital; reciprocally, the patient who "threatens" to kill himself or others coerces the therapist, because, if he carries out his threat, his relatives or his victims can sue the psychiatrist for malpractice. The milieu for market relations has thus been destroyed.

The reality of this state of affairs has, so far, remained unappreciated by psychiatrists and the public alike. Mental health professionals and their supporters view themselves as an enlightened elite who must struggle ceaselessly against hostile forces to protect the cooperative relationship that they regard as the milieu necessary for psychotherapy. But in this struggle, psychiatrists and psychoanalysts have become their own adversaries. For the human context necessary for psychotherapy is identical to the political context necessary for the market, which, as Milton Friedman cogently emphasized, "is simply a meeting of people . . . for the purpose of making deals." The crucial issue in such relations is: "Who are the participants in the market and on whose behalf are they operating?"[18] But whether the patient or a third party pays the psychiatrist, he can no longer be operating, to use Friedman's felicitous phrase, on behalf of the patient. Private, confidential therapy—aimed at helping the client increase his autonomy and responsibility, regardless of how he might use his expanded powers—is an anachronism.

The psychiatrically correct attitude toward mental health care has become thoroughly socialist. Prominent psychiatrists univocally advocate that the mental health care system be a government monopoly. "My view," declares Leon Eisenberg, a professor of psychiatry at Harvard, "is simply this: whereas the profit motive may be more or less effective for producing automobiles or steel, . . . it has no place in the provision of health care."[19]

Private Property and Individual Liberty

Since the publication of Smith's *Wealth of Nations* in 1776, it has become commonplace, especially among free-marketeers, to regard private property and individual liberty as two sides of the same coin. Mises developed this theme so fully that little needs to be added to it. "If one abolishes man's freedom to determine his own consumption," he wrote, "one has taken all freedom away."[20]

It was also clear, already in Smith's day, that the peaceful market offers a more effective means for raising people's material well-being than do other economic arrangements based on the use of force by a centralized source of political power (such as theocratic rulers, feudal lords, the state). However, if the market is so effective in protecting us from pain and securing us pleasure, why has it not become the universal method for conducting human affairs? Smith offered the following answer: "To expect . . . that the freedom of trade should ever be entirely restored in Great Britain, is as absurd as to expect that an Oceana or Utopia should ever be established in it. Not only the prejudices of the public, but what is much more unconquerable, the private interests of many individuals, irresistibly oppose it."[21]

In addition to people's private economic interests, the market is opposed also by people's personal existential interests, specifically, their efforts to combat the experience—universal in childhood and often persisting into adulthood—of feeling lost in a strange and threatening world. That experience generates a yearning for dependence on a benevolent authority—God, great leaders, doctors, the state. Moreover, it is the lot of mankind to feel not only insecure but also bored. To combat that experience, people long to be passively entertained, which requires less effort than assuming responsibility for self-improvement.

Smith's view of human nature was overly optimistic. He assumed that people want peace and prosperity to pursue their private, productive activities, working, marrying, raising families, and improving their own and their families' well-being. Unfortunately, that is only a part of the story. People are also lazy and bored and want "bread and circuses." Since it is easier to destroy than build, people find the spectacle of the destruction of life, liberty, and property endlessly entertaining, a truism in the light of the history of the species and its present use of television. Honoring the value of competence and steadfastness requires a generosity of spirit and curbing the passion for envy, traits that few people value and fewer still cultivate and acquire. Not until there is more of Smith and less of Hobbes in the human heart, will the majority of people prefer peaceful and boring market relations to the violent and exciting relations between coercer and coerced, predator and victim.*

LIBERTY, POLITICAL PHILOSOPHY, AND PSYCHIATRY

In the English-speaking world, the word *freedom* has traditionally meant the right to life, liberty, and property, the first two elements resting squarely on the last. More than any other single principle, this idea informed and animated the Framers of the Constitution. "If the United States mean to obtain and deserve the full praise due to wise and just governments," wrote James Madison in 1792, "they will equally respect the rights of property and the property in rights."[22]

The essential feature of capitalism, as a political-economic system, is the security of private property and the free market, that is, the right of competent adults to trade in goods and services. To ensure such a free social order, the state must protect people from force and fraud and external aggression, and abstain from participating in the production and distribution of goods and services. Of course, no such perfect capitalist order, guarded by a minimalist state, has ever existed or, perhaps, could exist.

---

* In psychiatric jargon, such relationships are called sado-masochistic and are categorized as pathological or sick.

In ancient Athens, slaves and women were excluded from the class of full-fledged persons. Two thousand years later, the Constitution of the United States legitimized Negro slavery and excluded women from the franchise. Such direct disfranchisement of specific groups is no longer popular. Instead, adults are disfranchised indirectly, by treating them as if they were children or mental patients who need to be protected from themselves. In the United States, this trend began in earnest with Franklin Roosevelt's socialist revolution. "In these twenty years," wrote Garet Garrett in 1953, "a revolution took place in the relationship between government and people. Formerly government was the responsibility of people; now people were the responsibility of government."[23] The current formula for this therapeutic dehumanization by infantilization may be summarized as follows:

> Anyone may be a victim of mental illness. The mentally ill are incompetent, like children, and hence must be protected from themselves; they are also dangerous, like criminals, and hence society must be protected from them. If properly treated, the mentally ill are expected to recover; hence, the involuntary detention of persons denominated as mental patients is not a deprivation of liberty, but rather a method of therapy and a legal protection ensuring political liberation (from the shackles of psychosis).

The term *victim of mental illness* in this formula may be replaced by several other cliches, such as *victim of addiction, parental deprivation, child abuse,* and so forth. For each of these attributions, a person may be relieved of his responsibility. Thus, we are relentlessly reminded of our growing list of rights, while our most basic self-regarding acts—exemplified by self-medication and suicide—are treated as offenses against the criminal and mental health laws.[24] At the same time, our basic obligations to ourselves and others as adults—exemplified by being held responsible for contracts—are abrogated by tort litigations undreamed of a mere half century ago.[25]

Who Is Fit for the Market and Freedom?

Long ago, political philosophers recognized that the game of market relations requires players who *understand* the rules, *have the capacity* to adhere to them, and *can be held accountable* for violating them, by subjecting them to criminal and civil law penalties. Prima facie, these specifications exclude children under the age of consent. Does this mean that all chronological adults are fit to play? And if not, how do we separate those who are, from those who are not? For a long time, this question has been disposed of by recourse to a formula that Thomas Hobbes (1651) already took for granted and articulated as follows: "Children, fools, and madmen that have no use of reason, maybe personated by guardians, or curators; but can be no authors, during that time, of any action done by them. . . ."[26] And again: "Over natural fools, children, or madmen, there is no law, no more than over brute beasts . . . because they had never power to make any covenant, or to understand the consequences thereof."[27]

Even before Hobbes, English law treated infants, idiots, and the insane as if they comprised a homogeneous group, characterized by the absence of the capacity for reasoning and self-control, rendering them unfit for participation in political society. Accordingly, they were deprived of the benefits of liberty, and the burdens of responsibility were lifted from their shoulders. In *Two Treatises on Government* (1690), Locke put it thus:

> And so, Lunaticks and Ideots are never set free from the Government of their Parents; Children, who are as yet not come unto those years whereat they may have; and Innocents which are excluded by a natural defect from ever having; Thirdly, Madmen, which for the present cannot possibly have the use of right Reason to guide themselves, have for their Guide, the Reason that guideth other Men which are Tutors over them.[28]

To this day, this cliché is trotted out when needed, as if it solved the dilemma of the rights and responsibilities of mental patients. Actually, the problem of adult dependency, especially of the type exhibited by mental patients, has so perplexed modern economists and political theorists, that most of them have simply ignored it. There are no children, disabled persons, or chronic mental patients in Ayn Rand's novels. Mises, Hayek, and Friedman are either silent about the problem of dependency posed by the mentally ill or casually bracket the insane with infants, as if the legitimacy of the mental patient's dependency-and-disfranchisement were not considerably more problematic than that of the child's.

John Stuart Mill and Sir James Fitzjames Stephen

In the Middle Ages, only persons whose behavior resembled that of the proverbial "wild beast" were categorized as insane. After the trade in lunacy became established, the category of insanity was greatly expanded. Nevertheless, the bracketing of the insane with infants remained the operative justification for the legal control of the mentally ill. The first political philosopher to assail this extrapolation in legal theory from infancy to insanity was John Stuart Mill. He wrote:

> Over himself, over his own body and mind, the individual is sovereign. It is, perhaps, hardly necessary to say that this doctrine is meant to apply only to human beings in the maturity of their faculties. We are not speaking of children. . . . Those who are still in a state to require being taken care of by others, must be protected against their own actions as well as against external injury. For the same reason, we must leave out of consideration those backward states of society in which the race itself may be considered as in its nonage. . . . Despotism is a legitimate mode of government in dealing with barbarians, provided the end be their improvement, and the means justified by actually effecting that end.[29]

Mill's list of those unfit for political freedom did not include the insane. Indeed, he added this memorable caveat: "Each [person] is the proper guardian of his own health, whether bodily, *or* mental and spiritual."[30] Few people then shared this view, and even fewer share it today. According to contemporary conventional wisdom, a person authoritatively diagnosed as mentally ill is sick until proven otherwise and hence ceases to be the proper guardian of his own health. Mill's following remarks are especially pertinent in this connection:

> But the man, and still more the woman, who can be accused either of doing "what nobody does," or of not doing "what everybody does," is the subject of as much depreciatory remark as if he or she had committed some grave moral delinquency. . . . [F]or whoever allow themselves much of that indulgence, incur the risk of something worse than disparaging speeches— they are in peril of a commission *de lunatico,* and of having their property taken from them and given to their relatives.[31]

In a long footnote, Mill then launched into this denunciation of psychiatric interventions to deprive people of liberty and property:

> There is something both contemptible and frightful in the sort of evidence on which, of late years, *any person* can be declared judicially unfit for the management of his affairs; and after his death, his disposal of his property can be set aside, if there is enough of it to pay the expenses of litigation. . . . These trials speak volumes as to the state of feeling and opinion among the vulgar with regard to human liberty. . . . In former days, when it was proposed to burn atheists, charitable people used to suggest putting them in a madhouse instead; it would be nothing surprising now-a-days were we to see this done.[32]

Unfortunately, by acknowledging that members of "backward races" may legitimately be coerced in their own interest, Mill seriously weakened his argument about mental patients. If it was proper to coerce the "immature" members of backward races, why was it not also proper to coerce "immature" mental patients? In his celebrated critique of Mill's *On Liberty*, Sir James Fitzjames Stephen recognized the Achilles heel in Mill's remarks and properly attacked him on that vulnerable point. He wrote:

> You admit that children and human beings in "backward states of society" may be coerced for their own good. . . . Why then may not educated men coerce the ignorant? . . . It seems to me quite impossible to stop short of this principle if compulsion in the case of children and "backward" races is admitted to be justifiable; for, after all, maturity and civilisation are matters of degree. One person may be more mature at fifteen than another at thirty.[33]

Stephen's rejoinder is unassailable. The problem lies in the assumption or conclusion—it does not matter which—that insane adults are so much like infants that it is politically legitimate to treat them also as irresponsible. As I showed, this facile equation has long governed the views of professionals and laypersons alike. "Freedom," writes Milton Friedman, "is a tenable objective only for responsible individuals. We do not believe in freedom for madmen or children."[34] It is time now to examine in what ways madmen are like, and unlike, children.

ARE INSANE ADULTS LIKE INFANTS?

The dissimilarities between infants and the insane could hardly be more glaring. They range from *their* respective repertoires of coping skills to *our* methods of identifying infancy and insanity. To distinguish between a child and an adult, we rely on the person's physical appearance. If we are in doubt about a youngster's age, we ask for his birth certificate or other proof of his age. To distinguish between an insane and a sane person, obviously we cannot rely on the subject's physical appearance. Instead, we ask the subject where he lives and whether he has a "psychiatric history" (especially a history of mental hospitalization). We also "examine" him for evidence of mental illness. None of this information, however, constitutes proof of mental illness, much less evidence of similarity between infancy and insanity. Finally, let us not overlook the obvious: Infants never, and young children rarely, commit crimes or suicide; whereas mental patients often do both. The bracketing of infancy and insanity is not based on evidence. It is an a priori judgment, serving important social interests.[35]

Infancy, Insanity, and Incompetence

Children are small, weak, ignorant, and cannot fend for themselves. Before they can participate in social life, they must undergo a period of training to enable them to control their impulses and acquire adult skills. Accordingly, in all cultures children are subjected to special controls by parents and relieved of certain responsibilities by the state.

Children undisciplined at home and in school by parents and teachers whom they love and respect are likely to become unruly youths. For the past several decades, American society has embraced the policy of constraining children less and adults more, with the result that children have become more disorderly, and adults more childish. This is probably the main reason more children now commit crimes and suicide than in former times. None of this proves that adults called "mentally ill" resemble children, unless we use the term *mental illness* as a synonym for immaturity. I do not deny that such a connection often exists. Freud and Jung liked to emphasize the "infantilism" of the "neurotic." However, the more seriously we take that similarity, the less ground we have for treating mental illness as an illness. Immaturity is surely not a brain disease curable with chemicals. A childish adult needs to grow up, not to be treated with drugs. Moreover, it is one thing to say that a five-year-old who wets his pants is immature, and quite another to say that a twenty-five-year-old who joins a cult and spends his time worshipping his guru is immature. One man's immaturity is another man religiosity, and vice versa. The issue on which I touch here is fundamental to our conception of the very nature of man and society. I am rearticulating and defending an old-fashioned view, namely that the criteria for the misbehaviors of children are laid down and enforced by their parents and teachers, whereas the criteria for the misbehaviors of adults (crimes) are laid down by legislators, and guilt for violating the criminal law is determined by juries and punished by judges (by means of sanctions specified by law). Another way to phrase this fundamental distinction is to assert that it is morally proper and necessary that parents discipline their children; but it is morally improper and indeed impermissible that the state discipline adults. To be sure, adults ought to be punished for crimes against others; but they should not be disciplined (although punishment may well have the effect of disciplining them).[36] The aim as well as the effect of psychiatrizing misbehavior and its control is to obscure and abolish these fundamental distinctions.

Finally, the boundary between childhood and adulthood is defined objectively, by age, not subjectively, by judging behavior. Although the age at which minority ends is a social convention, the term *childhood* refers to a period of time that is the same for everyone. In short, ascertaining whether a person is a child requires legal proof, not medical opinion.

None of this is true for mental illness. A young adult "accused" of being, or mistaken for, a minor can easily prove that he is not a child. An adult "diagnosed" as mad or mistaken for a mentally ill person cannot prove that he is sane. The status of being a child ends after a fixed period. The status of being a mental patient often never ends. We determine that a person is mentally ill partly by the diagnosis attributed to him by medical authority, and partly by his previous psychiatric record, each criterion reinforcing the other. Lastly, it is impossible for a normal adult to successfully impersonate a child, whereas nothing is easier than for a sane person to successfully impersonate a madman.[37]

The obvious differences between the coping skills of infants and the insane become apparent during periods of great social upheaval, such as war and revolution. Deprived by death or abandonment of their caretakers, infants quickly perish, while most of the insane survive and, indeed, become indistinguishable from the sane. It is precisely the coping skills infants lack but mental patients possess that enable the latter to survive on the streets and disturb the social order.

TWO THREATS TO LIBERTY: TYRANNY AND THERAPY

The threat therapeutic zealotry poses to liberty is intrinsic to the dual nature of the state, as a source of both danger and protection. For the libertarian, the state is a guardian entrusted with a monopoly on the legitimate use of force, and hence a permanent threat to individual liberty. Whereas for the (modern) liberal, the state is a social apparatus for protecting people from destitution, discrimination, and disease. Those who distrust the state, believe the government should provide only those services that individuals or informal groups cannot provide for themselves. Those who trust it, believe the government should provide as many services as people in need require. Actually, all modern governments provide numerous services unrelated to protecting people from aggressors, such as delivering the mail, disposing of sewage, providing potable water, educating children, licensing professionals, controlling so-called dangerous drugs, and so forth.

The Blind Spot of Classical Liberalism: Psychiatry

Although political philosophers have long recognized the threat of the state as despot, they have failed to recognize the danger of the state as therapist. For example, qua economist, Mises rejected categorizing people as abnormal. "The notions of abnormality or perversity," he declared, "therefore have no place in economics. It does not say that a man is perverse because he prefers the disagreeable, the detrimental, and the painful to the agreeable, the beneficial, and the pleasant. It says only that he is different from other people.[38]

Nevertheless, Mises accepted the traditional view that insane adults are like infants and ought to be treated as such. He wrote: "Even if we admit that every sane adult is endowed with the faculty of realizing the good of social cooperation and of acting accordingly, there still remains the problem of infants, the aged, and the insane. *We may agree that he who acts antisocially should be considered mentally sick and in need of care.*"[39] It was not that Mises was unaware of the imperfections of psychiatry. On the contrary. Echoing Mill, he wrote: "No better [than religion or Marxism] is the propensity, very popular nowadays, to brand supporters of other ideologies as lunatics. Psychiatrists are vague in drawing a line between sanity and insanity."[40] However, in the next breath, von Mises continued: *"It would be preposterous for laymen to interfere with this fundamental issue of psychiatry."*[41] But precisely because the psychiatrists' authority to "draw[ing] a line between sanity and insanity" forms the basis of their power to deprive persons of liberty, and because laymen bear the ultimate responsibility for delegating that power to psychiatrists, laymen *must* address the twin issues of insanity and psychiatric power.

Toward the end of *Human Action*, Mises returned to the subject of psychiatry and put his foot even deeper into his mouth: "If a man imagines himself to be the king of Siam, the first thing which the psychiatrist has to establish is whether or not he really is what he believes himself to be. Only if this question is answered in the negative can the man be considered insane."[42] Here, Mises confuses a person's claims (which we know because he asserts them) with his thoughts (which we cannot know, but can only infer or imagine). Since advancing false claims about themselves is the stock in trade of religious and political leaders, it is difficult to see how doing so can justify annulling the personhood of an individual labeled "mentally ill."

Ascribing Nonresponsibility as a Threat to Liberty

Throughout most of history, people were deprived of liberty directly, rulers despotically robbing, imprisoning, and killing them. This fact framed the context of Mill's classic, *On Liberty*, and many treatises on the subject before and after it. Modern Western democracies no longer engage in such despotic assaults on freedom. Instead, they deprive people of liberty indirectly, by relieving them of responsibility for their own (allegedly self-injurious) actions and calling the intervention "treatment."

Prior to the twentieth century, only individuals classified as insane were treated in this way. Today, the members of countless groups, especially drug users and gamblers, are treated this way, and many of them perceive such coercive state interventions as helpful.[43] Moreover, a great deal of contemporary tort litigation is premised on a similar assumption, namely, that the consumer is incompetent to enter into a binding contract with the vendor. The result is the destruction of the principle of *caveat emptor* and loss of access to goods and services previously available in the free market, such as the intrauterine loop.[44] The resulting loss of liberty is not due to despotic action by agents of the state, but is the consequence of an insidious destruction of responsible adult-to-adult relationships.*

This perspective controls popular and political attitudes toward both legal and illegal drugs. That smoking tobacco is harmful to health has been known for centuries. Yet, only a few decades ago, it would have been absurd for a smoker to sue a tobacco manufacturer for addicting him to cigarettes and causing his lung cancer, or a gambling casino for making him wager and lose money. Today, smokers and gamblers routinely engage in such litigation and courts let their suits go forward, in effect shielding legally competent adults from the unhappy consequences of their freely chosen actions.

The Competent Adult: Client, Patient, or Citizen?

Minors, the mad (however defined), and other dependents are human beings and belong in and to society. It is wicked to devalue, diminish, or destroy them. But it is absurd to value them more highly than the productive members of society. The legal and political framework of a free society, fit for adults, cannot be based on the needs of dependents and nonproducers and on extrapolating from their proper relations to the state to the proper relations of independent adults to the state. Kenneth Minogue makes this point eloquently. He writes:

---

* The person who would now maintain that, say, blacks, women, and mental patients do not deserve liberty and should be deprived of it would be dismissed, as he ought to be, as a despicable foe of human decency. However, the person who claims that members of these groups deserve to be protected and excused from the consequences of their self-injurious behavior is regarded as the compassionate champion of true freedom.

The state is essentially an association of independent and resourceful individuals living under law and, from a political point of view, the poor and the needy are nothing less than a threat to our freedom. They are, for example, the materials of the demagogue, who tries to gain power by promising to use the coercive power of the state to redistribute benefits.[45]

Minogue is right. The state is not, and cannot be, an association of dependent individuals, unable to live under law because they cannot be held responsible for violating legal prohibitions. Minogue rightly emphasizes that the nonproductive members of society pose a threat to liberty by virtue of their dependency and seducibility. Nor is that all. They threaten liberty also because the productive members of society have to take care of them as well of their guardians. "None of this," Minogue cautions, "is to deny that we have moral and perhaps political duties toward the poor. . . . [T]he essential point is that to take one's bearings on the nature of the state from the condition of the poor is to start off on the wrong foot. Citizens are categorically different from pensioners."[46] Citizens are also categorically different from dependents.

These reflections explain why, as the state increasingly treats adults as patients, the language of traditional political philosophy atrophies, and instead we adopt the language of diagnosis and treatment for analyzing the relations of the citizen to the state. In turn, the abandonment of the language and perspective of political philosophy explains the pernicious disjoining of the mental patient's rights and responsibilities that has been the hallmark of modern mental health reforms. Illustrative of this phenomenon is that the law treats institutionalized and deinstitutionalized mental patients alike as competent to retain their right to vote, but not competent to be held responsible for violating the criminal law. "The abuse of greatness," Shakespeare remarked, "is when it disjoins remorse from power."[47] Similarly, a characteristic modern abuse of power is that it disjoins responsibility from liberty.*

A certain level of dependency is intrinsic to the family and society. The young, the old, the sick, the poor, and the unemployable we shall always have with us. These persons are our responsibility. If the dependent is a member of our family or an intimate friend, we must take care of him because he is our *personal responsibility.* It is what I, as a person, *owe* him, as a person. If the dependent is a member of our congregation, we must take

---

* I touch here on some similarities between the economic and political consequences of deinstitutionalization and decolonization, each process "liberating" large numbers of persons unable to support themselves and rendering them dependent on their liberators.

care of him because he is our *religious responsibility*. It is what I, as his "brother," *owe* him, as my "brother in God."

It is regrettable enough that we must delegate to the state the care of individuals without family supports. It is folly to deliberately enlarge the scope of the Therapeutic State by adding to it fresh categories of claimants on its services, such as sexually active teenagers (who might get pregnant or acquire AIDS), or gainfully employed adults (who use legal or illegal drugs or gamble). Such individuals neither need nor deserve the services of the state, in the sense in which, say, an orphaned child or destitute old person needs and deserves them.

I focus here on the distinction between what we might call "market-work" and "command-work." I use the former term to designate the performance of such labor for which the Other is willing to pay the worker; and the latter term to refer to bureaucratic meddling or services, euphemistically called "working with people," for which the government pays the worker. Regardless of whether command work is morally noble or ignoble, it is fallacious to treat a bureaucratic "service" as similar to work that satisfies the needs of a paying consumer. Nevertheless, economists calculate the gross domestic product as the sum of the goods and services produced each year, regardless of what the services are or who pays for them. Whether we produce and sell more cars and corn, or create and service more mental patients (schizophrenics) and prisoners (drug offenders), the GDP goes up either way. This is one of the reasons contemporary American society excels in creating helping professions that, under the guise of enabling handicapped persons, disable them.[48]

8

ADULT DEPENDENCY: IDLENESS AS ILLNESS

[Paul] applies the appellation of disorderly persons, *not to those that are of a dissolute life, or to those whose characters are stained by flagrant crimes, but to* indolent and worthless persons, who employ themselves in no honorable and useful occupations.

—*John Calvin*[1]

Higher mammals care for their offspring until they reach biological maturity. The young adult must then fend for himself or perish. Early man probably behaved much the same way. As Hobbes noted, the life of man in nature, if there was such a man, must have been nasty, brutish, and short. Civilization, a product of social cooperation, is the source of both our creature comforts and social discomforts.

SOCIETY AND DEPENDENCY

The two-faced character of civilization in general, and of the market in particular, is reflected in the views of two of the giants of British political economy, Adam Smith and Thomas Malthus. Focusing on providers, Smith saw the market as a vast reservoir of productivity, capable of

140

supplying the wants of an ever-growing population. Focusing on dependents, especially children, Malthus saw it as a manufactory of a parasitism that threatens to drown producers and dependents alike. Both were right. One saw the proverbial glass half full, the other, half empty.

The more productive the society, the larger the number of dependents it can support. From the political-economic point of view, one of the most important features of the class composed of dependents called "mentally ill" is that, more than any other class of dependents, it is elastic. There are several reasons for this: The criteria for determining who is mentally ill are vague, subjective, and politicized; and mental health professionals make exaggerated claims about the (high or low) incidence of mental illness as if they were scientific facts, which the media and the public then accept as truths. Typically, modern American mental health experts claim that "more than one in ten adults suffers a mental disorder each year . . . and [yet] few get help."[2] Stalinist Soviet mental health experts claimed that there was virtually no mental illness in the Soviet Union, a "fact" that was regularly cited by leftist American mental health propagandists.[3]

Disease, Disability, Dependency, and Productivity

I have long maintained that we cannot understand the problems that chronic mental patients pose to their families, their society, and themselves without critically scrutinizing the connections between disease, disability, dependency, and productivity. Let me therefore first define some of the key words I use.

I use the word *producer* to designate a person who earns his own living by working or risking (investing) his capital; the word *nonproducer,* to refer to a person who does neither, and is therefore economically dependent on others (family or society); and the word *dependent,* to describe a person unable or unwilling to physically or socially care for himself. A dependent may or may not be a producer, and vice versa. For example, an infant is a nonproducer and a dependent; a factory worker temporarily laid off because of a downturn in the economy is a nonproducer, but not necessarily a dependent; a wealthy, physically disabled person living off his investments is a producer and a dependent. The connections between disease and disability, disability and dependence, and disability and productivity are empirical, not logical. Churchill said it well when he observed, "Most of the world's work is done by people who don't feel very well."[4] Although both Helen Keller and Franklin Roosevelt were seriously disabled, they were producers. Whereas the typical schizophrenic, though able-bodied, is a nonproducer; he is also likely to be a dependent, because even with economic support he is unlikely to manage his life in a socially acceptable manner. Simply put, the person who has diabetes or hypertension is not necessarily unproductive or inclined to commit crimes, whereas the person who is said to have schizophrenia or antisocial personality disorder is typically unproductive and likely to engage in conduct defined as antisocial or criminal. That is why persons diagnosed with nonpsychiatric diseases are almost never incarcerated in hospitals and treated against their will,* whereas persons diagnosed with mental diseases are.

People may become, or choose to become, nonproducers for many reasons other than mental illness. Economists have long recognized that, as James Dale Davidson and Lord William Rees-Mogg noted, "An increase in the repertoire of skills required to earn income in the market automatically increases the relative attractiveness of seeking what one wants by violence. Crime is easier than calculus."[5] Schizophrenia is also easier than calculus.

The emotionally charged associations we bring to concepts and terms such as disease, disability, dependence, producer, nonproducer, and parasite make it imperative that we use them with care and precision.[6] For example, it would be patently false and foolish to assume that every producer is a good person engaging in a morally praiseworthy activity; or that every nonproducer is a bad person engaging in immoral behavior. I use the terms *producer* and *nonproducer* in a purely existential-economic sense. A producer is a person who, regardless of the nature of his work, is economically self-supporting: He may be a farmer growing wheat or a judge sending a marijuana grower to prison. Similarly, a nonproducer is a person who, regardless of the reasons for his being a nonproducer, is economically dependent on others: He may be the cherished baby of loving parents, an able-bodied, professional welfare recipient, or Vincent van Gogh supported by his brother. If we attribute a person's nonproductivity to his character, we might call him a parasite (a term now so politically incorrect as to be taboo). Because disease (bodily or mental) does not automatically annul the ability to be productive, distinguishing a healthy nonproducer from a genuinely disabled person is a daunting task. For our present purposes, there will be no need to make the distinction. It will be enough to identify people as productive or not, economically self-supporting or not, dependent or not.

---

* Today, virtually the only persons so managed are a few individuals with infectious tuberculosis who refuse to complete their prescribed course of antibiotic therapy.

Davidson and Rees-Mogg call attention to another factor in contemporary American society that fosters nonproductivity, namely lawyering. They write: "America's elite education today is . . . more adept at training persons to redistribute income than to produce it. Ten lawyers graduate in America for every engineer. . . . In 1990, there were more lawyers in the United States than all the rest of the world combined."[7] Lawyers and politicians (most of whom are lawyers) are largely income redistributors. Mental patients and criminals, and those charged with confining and caring for them, are income redistributees. It should not surprise us, then, that, per capita, the United States has the most lawyers, the most criminals, and the most mental patients in the world.

In sum, there are three ways a person can obtain the necessities of life: (1) As a dependent, receiving food and shelter from donors (parents, family, church, state); (2) as a producer, providing for his own needs; or (3) as a predator, using force or the threat of force to rob others of the goods and services he needs and wants. An individual who does not want to be, or cannot be, a producer, must become a dependent or a predator or perish. Anything that discourages or prevents peaceful market relations among productive adults—regardless of whether it is due to biological, cultural, economic, or political factors—thus encourages dependency or predation or both. The fact that both are adaptive—that both parasitism and crime "pay"—accounts for the increased frequency of both behavior patterns during times of social upheaval and among members of the underclass. Finally, because many of the people we call mentally ill engage in de facto predatory behavior, and because many others use their dependency coercively in a quasi-predatory fashion, the supposedly mysterious connection between crime and mental illness turns out to be no mystery at all. It is simply the result of our penchant for attributing many predatory activities to mental illness.

THE LIFE CYCLE, DEPENDENCY, AND PSYCHIATRY

According to Calvin, God created man to "be a creature of fellowship." Division of labor and the exchange of goods and services were thus the very essence of fellowship: "*Those who employ usefully whatever God has committed to them are said to be engaged in trading. The life of the godly, is justly compared to trading*, for they ought naturally to exchange and barter with each other, in order to maintain intercourse."[8] Calvin therefore condemned idleness as a sin.[9]

Whether or not we believe our lives have a divinely ordained purpose, we must form an opinion about the minimal personal competence and behavioral standards a modern society must expect of adults implicitly endowed with the rights of citizenship—in particular, with the rights to vote and make contracts. For the sake of pursuing this inquiry, let us agree that the principal task of youth is to develop self-discipline and acquire marketable skills—that is, the ability to maintain onseself by doing something useful for others, as others define usefulness. Acquiring that level of competence does not guarantee success or sanity; but failing to acquire it is a virtual guarantee of dependency and insanity. Although the ostensible aim of economic regulations, such as minimum wage laws, is to improve the conditions of the least productive members of the labor force, their effect is the severing of the bottom rungs of the economic ladder, enlarging the pool of persons without marketable skills, many of whom are then treated (supported) as mental patients.

I submit that the task of personal self-development between the ages of, say, 5 and 25 is of paramount importance for the fate of both the individual and the society of which he is a member. Nevertheless, this subject is utterly neglected in the psychiatric literature. Instead, it is replete with accounts that exaggerate the significance of the individual's experiences during early childhood, to which it attributes a determining role in his life as an adult. By fetishizing the first 5 years of life, Freud managed to mislead everyone who absorbed his message. Undoubtedly, the early years are important. But I believe the remaining years of childhood and youth are probably even more important. It is during that period when the young person—nurtured or neglected by family, church, school, and society—must design, build, perfect, and test himself as a future adult.

Although children are dependents, they are tolerated, supported, and usually loved by their parents. However, notwithstanding the contemporary American delusion that a good parent loves his child unconditionally, such tolerance has limits and imposes deadlines. The limits depend largely on the parents' expectations. The deadlines, for the most part, are set by society and comprise the various stages of the passage from childhood to adulthood. The passage begins with the child's expulsion from home to attend school; continues with his development from childhood to adolescence; and is completed with his transition from adolescence to adulthood. The entire process is expected to end during the third decade, at the latest. In short, between his teens and twenties, the young person must learn to become useful to others and stand on his own feet. If he fails to accomplish this task, he and his family are destined to face serious difficulties, nowadays often conceptualized in psychiatric terms, typically as the manifestations of schizophrenia.

The Useless Young Adult: Schizophrenia

People instinctively realize that doing useful work is as important for the worker as for those who depend on his labor. Thorstein Veblen even suggested that workmanship is an instinct, related to the "parental bent."[10] Chekhov declared: "What is needed is work; everything else can go to the devil."[11]

The young person who fails to engage in some activity others value, and for which they show admiration and appreciation, in effect opts to become a dependent, exploitative, or predatory person.[12] As the reality of his uselessness dawns on him, the young adult begins to feel inferior to siblings and friends and to envy their competence and success. To avert the painful realization of his justified lack of self-esteem, he protects himself by means of a dangerous psychological defense. He tells himself he is better than others, becomes arrogant and conceited (psychiatrists call it "narcissistic"), and embraces the logic of hostile entitlement: "I am not a useless person. Others are unworthy of my doing anything for them. They have more than I do and ought to feel guilty and help me." Or worse still: "Everything the producers have, they have gained by exploiting others. I have a right to rob them of their possessions."* When such behavior is indulged, it results in the young adult's becoming a sort of "adult-baby prima donna," playing the role of the most useless and yet most important member of the family.†

This process of desocialization usually starts during adolescence. Parents and peers often respond it by treating the youngster as an individual with "special problems." Gradually, others expect less and less of him, and he does less and less for them and himself. Once past adolescence, such a young adult is likely to slide into continued dependence—on parents, as long as they support him, then on relatives or social and welfare agencies. Somewhere down this path, he commits or threatens to commit a violent act, against himself or others, which the representatives of the adult world can no longer ignore. Then, he is brought into the presence of a psychiatrist who is likely to diagnose him as schizophrenic and launch him on the career of the chronic mental patient. My point is that becoming socialized *and* desocialized both require practice. An adolescent is not

---

* Herein lie the similarities between the antiproductive mentality of the chronic mental patient and the anticapitalist mentality of the socialist/communist.

† I realize that psychiatrists sometimes attach the terms *mental illness* and *schizophrenia* also to productive persons, who are not poor, are not on the psychiatric dole, and whose only "offense" is that their conduct falls outside the range of what psychiatrists define as normal behavior. The psychiatric defamations of prominent persons—such as Abraham Lincoln, James Joyce, and Ludwig Wittgenstein—come quickly to mind. I have addressed this aspect of the idea of insanity elsewhere.

yet a functioning member of adult society. It is an error, therefore, to speak of his "dropping out." First, he must "drop in," and that requires much effort. The adolescent who fails to accomplish this by his late teens or early twenties will discover that his family, psychiatry, and society are likely to make it increasingly difficult for him to accomplish it later. It is this predicament, characteristic of modern youth, that J. D. Salinger portrayed so masterfully in *The Catcher in the Rye*.

Although psychiatrists deny it, their own accounts amply document that the condition they call schizophrenia refers to a young person's idleness, not his illness. Here are two typical vignettes from a treatise on schizophrenia. "John, a young, working-class unemployed schizophrenic, recently discharged from hospital, sat at home all day, brewing tea and smoking, and playing records, and proving himself a great aggravation to his mother."[13] The language is misleading but revealing. John did not sit "at home." He sat in a house that was another person's home, to the maintenance of which he did not contribute, and where he was not welcome. In another case, a mother describes her schizophrenic daughter's presence in the parental home thus: "Whenever Ruth is at home, he [her father] feels continually irritated by her lack of purpose and idleness."[14]

Broadcast and print media alike now inundate the public with case histories intended as morality tales to bring home the message that the mental patient is not responsible for being unproductive. The story headlined, "The 100 faces of John," is typical. We learn that John, age 50, has spent most of his adult life in mental hospitals, having been psychiatrically confined on 23 different occasions. For the past several years, John has lived in a fashionable apartment building where he "spends most of his time painting acrylic portraits, ocean scenes, and images with Oriental hummingbirds. . . . [He] takes long walks around the city, attends Chief [baseball] games, and borrows mysteries from the main library."[15]

The results of a NAMI (National Alliance for the Mentally Ill) survey of their membership support my foregoing remarks. Asked, "What does your mentally ill relative do during the day?," respondents described 59 percent of the patients as completely non-self-supporting, 45 percent as engaging in "no productive activity at all," and 14 percent as spending their days "in a structured day-treatment program."[16]

If this road map to the destination of a schizophrenic career is accurate, then it is clear why psychiatric treatments cannot help such persons. By conceptualizing the young adult's uselessness as an illness, psychiatric interventions can only harm him because they render his chances of becoming a useful, self-respecting person ever slimmer.

The Useless Old Person: Depression

The second great life transformation, reversing the first, is from useful adulthood to useless old age. It is a relatively recent cultural development. In 1776, the human life span was about 35 years, an age we now regard as barely midlife. Prior to the nineteenth century, few people survived past 50 or 60, and, those who did continued to work or were cared for in an extended family. Today, in advanced industrial societies, persons over 55 comprise the largest and fastest growing segment of the population.

Unlike young children, most elderly people can care for themselves, both economically and physically, at least for a while. They have savings, receive pensions and Social Security benefits, own their homes, and possess a store of competence and self-esteem accumulated during a lifetime of productive work. However, with the relentless advance of age, these assets gradually erode. Unless the old person receives continued stimulation and support through human contacts at work or in the family, he becomes idle and lonely, often ending up in a nursing home, drugged into mindless passivity. If he remains alert, he may become depressed and tell himself something like this: "No one needs me any more. I am of no use to others. I cannot even take care of myself. I am worthless. I would be better off dead."

The human life cycle thus comes full circle and is complete: From nothingness to incompetence to competence, and back again.* It should not surprise us, then, that psychiatrists claim that old persons who refuse to remain cheerful in the face of their progressive loneliness, uselessness, and helplessness suffer from "clinical depression" and represent a "psychiatric challenge." The following case report is illustrative. Four years after being hospitalized for a dissecting aneurysm of the aorta, a 76-year-old man is readmitted with a diagnosis of depression. The psychiatrists describe him thus: "He knew his wife had died yet he continued to talk to her and felt persecuted by her. He had lost 20 lbs., was anhedonic, slept poorly, had diminished self-esteem, and wished to die." To me, this man's behavior does not appear to be an unreasonable reaction to his situation. However, the authors viewed it as a treatable mental illness and gave him a series of electric shock treatments. "After the sixth

---

* This understanding of the life cycle was the solution to the riddle of the mythological Sphinx of Thebes. Passersby had to answer the question: What is it that has one voice yet becomes four-footed and two-footed and three-footed? Those who failed to give the right answer were devoured by the Sphinx. Oedipus solved the riddle, whereupon the Sphinx killed herself.

treatment, with no improvement, treatment was stopped. [The patient] continued to decline and was placed in a nursing home; he died 3 months after the last treatment."[17]

Averting our eyes from the tragedy of life, we define the young person unable to make the transition from uselessness to usefulness as schizophrenic; the old person, unable to make the return trip, as depressed; and claim that both "conditions" are "treatable illnesses." *Cui bono?*

THE REWARDS AND RISKS OF PRODUCTIVITY

The simplest type of economic organization is called a "subsistence economy," to denote that its members produce only enough to sustain their own lives. As societies progress culturally and technologically, they advance economically. People produce more than they consume, enabling them to trade with others, save for the proverbial rainy days, and support increasing numbers of dependents. These advantages are partially offset by the fact that the producers' achievements make them inviting targets for predatory humans who prefer looting to laboring.

Envy, Equality, and the State

The primary source of wealth is work. But it is not its only source. There is also marriage, inheritance, fraud, force, and luck. Because it is better to be rich than poor, poverty has always excited compassion, and riches the suspicion of wrongdoing. The inchoate belief that being wealthy is somehow shameful or sinful has a long history, probably originating from a primitive fear of jealous gods. In the fourth century B.C., the philosopher Isocrates complained: "One must now apologize for any success in business, as if it were a violation of the moral law, so that today it is worse to prosper than to be a criminal."[18] Lord Bauer, the economist, has dubbed social policies based on pandering to this passion "the economics of resentment," while the sociologist Helmut Schoeck attributed them to the role of envy in human affairs.[19] Mental health professionals, blissfully unaware of such works, seem to believe that politically correct claims about "poverty" and "exploitation" articulate perennial truths about "greed" that must be constrained by the benevolent state, aided by selfless intellectuals specializing in the business of human betterment.

In the nineteenth century, politicians began to lure people into placing increasing reliance on the government in matters that most intimately affect their welfare, especially education and health. They quickly succeeded and the welfare state was born. Since then, throughout the West (as well as in Communist countries), people have steadily exchanged personal liberty-and-responsibility for various government services. According to economist Allan Carlson, this process began in Sweden "in the 1840s, with the passage of a mandatory school attendance law."[20] Since then, responsibility for the care of children, old people, and the sick was gradually transferred from the family to the state. Sociologist David Poponoe calls the result a "client society . . . in which citizens are for the most part clients of a large group of public employees who take care of them throughout their lives."[21] Since the end of World War II, American governments have shown an increasing tendency to treat dependents as if they were sick and required treatments. I therefore proposed to call such a polity the "Therapeutic State."[22]

Carlson's analysis is correct in principle, but not in detail. The divestiture of individual and family responsibility for kinfolk did not begin in Sweden, in the nineteenth century, with the transfer of the dependency needs of children from the family to the state. Instead, it began in England, during the seventeenth century, with the transfer of the dependency needs of adult dependents from the family and the parish to the state.[23] This process has developed farthest in the contemporary American mental health movement, a fact that makes psychiatry of special importance for economics and political philosophy.

The Greeks viewed finding the truth as an act of discovery that required removing "the veil that covers or hides a thing."[24] The veil that we use to hide the truth of the human condition is psychiatry. If we lift it, we rediscover the familiar fundamentals of existence, namely, that some people work and others do not, and that the business of psychiatry is distributing poor relief (concealed as medical care) to adult dependents (whose indolence and incontinence are concealed as illness).

9

THE NEW
PSYCHIATRIC DEAL

Today, when the doctor has succeeded the priest, and can do practically what he likes with parliament and the press through the blind faith in him which has succeeded to the far more critical faith in the parson, legal compulsion to take the doctor's prescription, however poisonous, is carried to an extent that would have horrified the Inquisition and staggered Archbishop Laud. Our credulity is grosser than that of the Middle Ages, because the priest had no such direct pecuniary interest in our sins as the doctor has in our diseases.
—*George Bernard Shaw*[1]

In 1950, the population of the United States was about 150 million and there were nearly one million patients in public mental hospitals. Today the population is more than 250 million, and there are fewer than 150,000 patients in public mental hospitals. This dramatic decrease is attributed to antipsychotic drugs* and deinstitutionalization.

---

* There are several names for the drugs said to be effective for treating severe mental illnesses. I shall use the adjectives "antipsychotic," "neuroleptic," "psychiatric," "psychotropic," and "tranquilizing" (drug) interchangeably, unless there is a reason for preferring a particular term.

LAYING THE GROUND FOR DEINSTITUTIONALIZATION

In the seventeenth century, the edifice of psychiatry was built on a solid foundation, sunk deep into the bedrock of developing Western society, namely, on the incarceration of insane individuals in madhouses. In a free society, only the state has the authority to deprive an individual of liberty, and only if he has been convicted of a felony. Hence, a new principle was needed to justify denying liberty to persons innocent of lawbreaking. The new science of mad-doctoring or psychiatry provided the justification: Insanity.[2] As only persons convicted of a criminal offense could be lawfully confined in prison, so only persons diagnosed as mentally ill could be lawfully confined in an insane asylum. The state assumed the dual obligation of protecting itself from the madman and the madman from himself, and authorized the mad-doctor to implement and enforce this principle. Thus did the systematic, forcible incarceration of unwanted persons, qua dangerous mental patients, become the social policy, called "mental hospitalization."

In the 1950s, the principle and practice of involuntarily hospitalizing the mental patient was supplemented by the principle and practice of involuntarily dehospitalizing him, called "deinstitutionalization." The term refers to the policy of medicating mental hospital patients with psychotropic drugs, evicting them from public mental hospitals, transferring (many of) them to other public facilities, and refusing them readmission, especially if that is what they want. Like institutionalization, deinstitutionalization also required the use of state-sanctioned coercion.* Moreover, this policy ran counter to the traditional practice of confining crazy people for long periods, and thus also needed to be justified. This was accomplished by means of the interlocking claims that psychotropic drugs offered an effective treatment for mental illness and that the mental patient's best interests required that he be discharged from the hospital "to the least restrictive setting in the community."

In 1955, Daniel Blain, the medical director of the American Psychiatric Association, promised that "the 750,000 patients now in this country's mental hospitals" would soon be returned to the community, *"cured."*[3] The truth is that after treatment with neuroleptic drugs, mental patients tend to be sicker and more disabled than before. Many exhibit the toxic

---

* This remark requires qualification. State mental hospitals belong to the state, not to the patients who live there. Once a patient loses the owner's permission to occupy the premises, he becomes a kind of squatter, whom the police have the right to remove, by force if necessary.

effects of the drugs, suffering from a disfiguring neurological disturbance called "tardive dyskinesia." Virtually all of them continue to depend on family or society for food and shelter. The contrast drawn
between the mental hospital and the community is a lie. The domiciles
now housing chronic mental patients are neither more nor less a part of
the community than the state hospital.

Before deinstitutionalization, psychiatrists claimed that the best
treatment for seriously ill mental patients was long-term hospitalization, combined with insulin shock or electric shock. Now they claim that
the best treatment for them is short-term hospitalization, combined with
antipsychotic medication and deinstitutionalization. Both claims are
pseudoscientific fables, concealing heartless bureaucratic-psychiatric
policies of storing unwanted persons.[4] A British report on American
mental health policies makes precisely this point:

> In New York State, for example, a large number of psychiatric patients were re-
> cently thrown out of large institutions, almost literally overnight, and left to
> wander the city streets . . . . Yet when winter comes, those very people are
> rounded up and herded into huge warehouses, not much different from the
> workhouses of old, where they are "kept" for the winter.[5]

I maintain that neither long-term mental hospitalization nor deinstitutionalization has anything to do with illness, treatment, or medicine.
Both are legal and socioeconomic policies, using medical rhetoric as jus-
tificatory pretexts.

World War II: Psychiatry Gains Medical Legitimacy

For centuries, psychotics and psychiatrists alike were banished to madhouses, located on the outskirts of cities or in the countryside. The typical psychiatrist worked in a public insane asylum, overseeing desolate
scenes of human misery. Between roughly 1935 and 1955, two events radically transformed both the image and the reality of American psychiatry. One was the influx of European psychoanalysts; the other was the
introduction of psychiatric drugs.

Most of the European psychoanalysts who managed to escape from
Nazism emigrated to the United States. London, where Freud died, became the shrine of the Freudian cult. The United States, especially New
York City, where the influential analysts and their wealthy backers settled, became the movement's new power base.

Psychoanalysts were generally better educated and more cultured
than psychiatrists. Thrown together in the armed forces during World

War II, the analysts outshone the psychiatrists. Furthermore, General William Menninger, the highest ranking and most influential psychiatrist in the armed forces and the younger brother of famed Karl Menninger, was an accredited psychoanalyst. Both Menningers were talented promoters of what, in fact, was traditional, hospital-based psychiatry cloaked in the beguiling mantle of psychoanalysis. For young psychiatrists in the late 1940s, the psychoanalyst—with cigar, or at least cigarette or pipe, perpetually between his lips—became an irresistible role model. As a result of American psychiatry's war experience, the profession became seemingly psychoanalytic. I say seemingly because the influence of psychoanalysis on psychiatry was purely cosmetic, imparting to it its pretentious jargon and bogus therapeutic claims, but not its authentic spirit.

Drafted into the armed forces, psychiatrists left their hospitals and offices, donned uniforms, mingled with other physicians and, presto, became accepted as real doctors, on equal footing with other physicians. The military mad-doctor did not need to display any genuine medical skills. His status as a medical officer was enough to legitimize him as a regular physician. Also, a crucial fact of military life lent support to the psychiatrist's becoming recognized as a real doctor. Being tired of the war was defined as a bona fide disease, "battle fatigue"; servicemen exhibiting symptoms of it were diagnosed as "neuropsychiatric casualties"; and, *mirabile dictu,* many of these patients were easily cured. Since the illnesses were nonexistent, this should not have surprised anyone. For the serviceman, psychiatric disability was an honorable escape from the dangers of war. For the military bureaucracy, it was a convenient method of getting rid of unwanted personnel.* Naturally, this was not the way military psychiatrists interpreted their patients' behavior, which they regarded as genuine diseases; or their own ministrations, which they regarded as genuine treatments.†

When the war ended, the victorious psychiatrists returned to civilian life, determined to conquer the United States for psychiatry. *Deutschland über Alles* lost. Psychiatry über Alles won, and was let loose on the American population.

---

* Neither the German nor the Soviet military authorities recognized battle fatigue as an illness.

† Performing a caricature of a psychoanalysis accelerated by a short-acting barbiturate (usually sodium amytal). Military psychiatrists called their quackery "narco-analysis."

Meanwhile Psychiatry Loses Medical Legitimacy on the Home Front

Ensconced behind the war zone, military psychiatrists thrived on malingerers, defined as neuropsychiatric casualties. Meanwhile, back on the home front, the prisoners of America's snake pits languished in the wretchedness to which they and their keepers had become accustomed. The returning psychiatric veterans, who had spent their formative years in military service, found state mental hospital conditions appalling, reminiscent of the horrors of concentration camps. Even makeshift psychiatric wards in military hospitals provided a far more humane environment than did the best civilian state hospitals. The perennial complaints of mental patients, together with a fresh spate of exposés in the press, suddenly acquired credibility. Phrases such as *snake pit* and *shame of the states,* lifted from the titles of best-selling books, quickly gained popularity. The medical legitimacy of psychiatry, qua state hospital psychiatry, reached its nadir. The word was out that psychiatrists were merely warehousing people. Like the picture of Dorian Grey, the portrait of the American state hospital underwent a sudden transformation, from hero to villain. The following two statements—excerpted from the addresses of presidents of the American Psychiatric Association separated by 30 years—tell the whole story:

> *William A. White* (1925): The state hospital, as it stands today, is the very foundation of psychiatry.[6]
>
> *Harry C. Solomon* (1958): The large mental hospital is antiquated, outmoded, and rapidly becoming obsolete. . . . [It is] bankrupt beyond remedy . . . and should be liquidated as rapidly as possible.[7]

Unfortunately, both the psychiatrists' blind support of the state mental hospital as a therapeutic institution and their righteous rejection of it as an antitherapeutic institution were insincere and wholly self-serving.

THE PSYCHOANALYTIC INTERLUDE

The advent of psychoanalysis and office-based psychotherapy in the early decades of the twentieth century introduced a new element into the established socioeconomic order of psychiatry. Traditionally, being a psychiatrist meant being an employee of a state hospital. In most of Europe, Jewish doctors could therefore not become psychiatrists.

However, they could become general practitioners and neurologists, or so-called nerve doctors, listen to and talk to their patients, call it "psychotherapy" or "psychoanalysis," and sell their services to fee-paying customers. Psychoanalysis thus came into being as part of the private practice of medicine, then one of the so-called free professions.[8] The psychoanalytic patient, like the customer of any service supplied by entrepreneurs in the free market, sought out the analyst, went to his office, received a service, and paid a fee for it. The client was on top, the therapist on tap.

The practice of psychoanalysis sprouted in the soil of the free market and depended on it for its integrity and survival.[9] But Freud and the early analysts neither understood the market nor supported its values. They only took advantage of it, like spoiled children taking advantage of wealthy parents. No sooner did Freud get on his feet, economically and professionally, than he embraced the style of the conquering hero, to which he always aspired. In 1900, he wrote: "I am not at all a man of science, not an observer, not an experimenter, not a thinker. I am by temperament nothing but a conquistador—an adventurer, if you want it translated. . . ."[10] Four years later, he added: "I have never doubted [my] posthumous victory."[11] To Jung he announced that psychoanalysis must "conquer the whole field of mythology."[12] Freud's self-image as a "conquistador" thus meshed perfectly with his ambition to conquer psychiatry for psychoanalysis. Neither Freud nor the Freudians had any intention of honoring the promises implicit in the psychoanalytic contract.

Freud and his expansionist followers were not satisfied with limiting themselves to their contractually defined role, aspiring instead to be magical healers in the grandiose tradition of medical-messianic quacks. They claimed, and themselves came to believe, that they were treating real diseases and that their treatment was more scientific and more efficacious than that offered by other medical specialists. Few European or British psychiatrist bought this boast. However, many influential American psychiatrists did. This is the reason psychoanalysis was so readily integrated into American psychiatry. Fifteen years after visiting the United States, Freud reminisced: "As I stepped on to the platform at Worcester to deliver my Five Lectures on Psycho-Analysis, it seemed like the realization of some incredible daydream: psycho-analysis . . . is recognized by a number of official psychiatrists as an important element in medical training."[13] After World War I, American state hospital psychiatrists embraced psychoanalysis, and the analysts gratefully reciprocated by embracing coercive-statist psychiatry.[14]

Psychoanalysis Has Its Moment of Glory

Unlike in Europe, psychoanalysis was well received in the United States. However, this friendly reception, as I noted, rested on the totally mistaken belief that psychoanalysis was an effective method for treating mental illness. During World War II, the status of psychoanalysis was elevated, while its integrity was utterly destroyed, by the analysts' uncritical acceptance of their role as agents of the armed forces.

Long ago, civilian society delegated to the psychiatrist the task of separating the sane from the insane. In the military, he was assigned the analogous task of separating those fit and willing to fight and die for their country from those unfit and unwilling to do so. This job required fabricating appropriate pseudomedical explanations for why people are unwilling to die in battle. Psychoanalysts, adept at explaining why anyone did anything, took to their military role like the proverbial duck to water. Many were recent refugees from Nazism. Grateful to their adopted country, they were happy to do the bidding of the military authorities: They found "neuropsychiatric casualties" by the millions. The pragmatic necessities of the military thus found a loyal ally in psychoanalytic theory. This was an utterly phony, albeit expedient, use of psychoanalysis. The upshot was that psychiatrists spouting psychoanalytic jargon enjoyed a brief moment of glory as professionals valued for their arcane knowledge and ardent patriotism.

During the war, psychoanalysis and psychiatry were joined together, much as a veneer of fine mahogany may be bonded to the body of a common pine cabinet. For a brief period, the glamor and prestige of this superficially psychoanalyticized psychiatry carried over into civilian life. But it was all show, devoid of substance. Chairmen of psychiatry departments in medical schools, directors of state hospitals, and psychiatrists in private practice who used ECT (electroconvulsive therapy) on their patients all displayed psychoanalytic credentials and spoke in psychoanalytic jargon. In the process, the tiny nucleus of truth in psychoanalysis vanished, and "psychoanalysis" became a corrupt cult that had forsaken and forgotten its core values.[15]

The Incompatibility of Psychiatry and Psychoanalysis

Like the core elements of the classic concept of liberty, the core elements of psychoanalysis are best stated as negatives, that is, as the absence of factors antagonistic to its aims and values. Political liberty is the absence of the coercions characteristic of the traditional relations between rulers and ruled. Similarly, psychoanalysis is the absence of the coercions characteristic of traditional relations between psychiatrists and mental patients.* Consider the contrasts. The psychiatrist controls and coerces, the psychoanalyst contracts and cooperates. The former wields power, the latter has authority.

Political liberty is contingent on the state's respect for private property and its noninterference with acts between consenting adults. Psychoanalysis is contingent on the therapist's respect for the client's autonomy and his noninterference with the client's life.† This (ideal) psychoanalytic situation represented a new development in the lunacy trade, introducing into psychiatry and society a new form of "therapy," in which the expert eschewed coercing deviants and housing dependents, and confined himself to conducting a particular kind of confidential dialogue. In the psychoanalytic situation, there is, in the medical and psychiatric sense, neither patient nor doctor, neither disease nor treatment. The dialogue between analyst and patient is therapeutic in a metaphorical sense only. Purged of jargon, the psychoanalytic "procedure" consists only of listening and talking. So conceived, psychoanalysis undermined rather than supported psychiatry as a medical specialty and extralegal system of social control.

When Freud remarked "that analysis fits the American as a white shirt the raven,"[16] he would have been closer to the mark if, instead of "American," he had said "psychiatrist" or "psychiatry." Psychiatry did not acquire, and could not possibly have acquired, any of the real substance of psychoanalysis. The two enterprises rested on completely different premises and entailed mutually incompatible practices. The typical psychiatrist was a state-employed physician who worked in a mental institution; the typical psychoanalyst (often not a physician) was a self-employed provider of a personal service who worked in his private office. The typical psychiatric patient was poor, was cast in the patient role against his will, and was housed in a public mental hospital. The typical psychoanalytic patient was rich (usually wealthier than his analyst), chose to be a patient, and lived in his own home (or a hotel). The marriage between the psychiatrist and the psychoanalyst

---

* I refer here to the ideal form of psychoanalysis, which excludes such aberrations as training analysis and child analysis. The reader must judge for himself whether this conception of the core value of psychoanalysis was Freud's, or whether it is my idiosyncratic interpretation of it. Be that as it may, Freud must have been familiar with Goethe's famous, and fitting, adage: "Whoever wants something great, must be able to limit himself."

† Simply put, this means that the therapist must limit his interaction with his client to listening and talking to him and abstain from interfering, in any way whatever, in the client's life outside the four walls of the therapist's office.

was a misalliance from the start, each party disdaining and taking advantage of his partner. Psychiatry acquired the worst features of psychoanalysis—a preoccupation with sex and the past, an elastic vocabulary of stigmatizations, and a readiness for fabricating pseudo-explanations. Psychoanalysis acquired the worst features of psychiatry—coercion, mental hospitalization, and disloyalty to the patient. Bereft of professional integrity, postwar American psychiatry relapsed into its old habit of embracing prevailing medical fashions, which, as it happened, was more-drugs-and-less-discourse. The curtain was now ready to go up on the next act in the drama of modern psychiatry, the tragicomic episode called "deinstitutionalization."

THE ECONOMIC AND LEGAL BASIS OF DEINSTITUTIONALIZATION

There is scarcely any human activity uninfluenced by economic incentives. In the case of basic science and its applications, economic incentives often play a minor role. For example, when penicillin replaced arsenic in the treatment of syphilis, it was not because drug companies or physicians made more money using one treatment than another. It was because penicillin was a more effective treatment. In the case of psychiatry, this is not true. Mental health propaganda to the contrary notwithstanding, replacing institutionalization with deinstitutionalization had nothing to do with science and therapeutic efficacy.

Psychiatry between the End of the War and 1960

After victory in war, the United States needed a new Good War against an Evil Enemy. For a while, the Cold War did the job. But the Soviets acquired nuclear weapons and the conflict became an emotionally unsatisfying stalemate. Luckily, there were many helpless enemies at home. The first to be attacked was mental illness. Poverty, drugs, and homelessness soon followed.[17]*

Psychiatrists have always been hostile to the free market and ignorant about its role in creating the economic and political blessings of an open society. The psychiatrist's statist bias is inherent in the nature of his profession. As the name of his employer, "state hospital," implies, the

---

* There are some obvious similarities among these wars. The greater the danger, the more federal funds required to protect the nation from it, and the more intractable the problem becomes.

institution in which he worked was a state agency, supported by state funds. Before deinstitutionalization, the cost of operating state mental hygiene departments was one of the largest items in state budgets, often amounting to a third or more of all expenditures. The reason for this situation, which has since become an anachronism, was that until the advent of Medicare and Medicaid, no one challenged the tradition of states' rights, according to which financial support of insane asylums, as well as of schools and welfare programs, was a responsibility of the states. Except for operating Veterans Administration Hospitals and a few drug addiction facilities—and, in 1950, establishing the modestly funded National Institute of Mental Health (NIMH) to promote psychiatric research—the federal government played no role in caring for mental patients. It is worth noting here that the initial appropriation for NIMH was a minuscule $870,000. Ten years later, NIMH cost the taxpayer $68 million, and in 1992 more than $1 billion.[18] Let that be a lesson to those who cling to the belief that Reagan and Bush were trying to get the government off the backs of the American people.

A Camelot for Psychiatric Quackery

The election of John F. Kennedy to the presidency put psychiatrists in a mood of celebration unparalleled in the history of mad-doctoring. Finally, a President of the United States took up the cudgels for curing mental illness.* The scene was set for a veritable Camelot of Quackery.

In January 1963, for the first time in American history, the President devoted a part of his State of the Union Message to lecturing the American people on mental health. With insolent hypocrisy, John F. Kennedy—whose sister, Rosemary, was involuntarily lobotomized in the 1940s and has been incarcerated ever since—hectored the nation about its callous "abandonment of the mentally ill and the mentally retarded to the grim mercies of custodial institutions."[19] A month later, Kennedy delivered a special message to Congress, entitled "Mental Illness and Mental Retardation," proposing the establishment of Community Mental Health Centers (CMHCs) and calling for "a bold new approach" in the war against mental illness. "It has been demonstrated," declared the President, "that two out of three schizophrenics—our largest category of mentally ill—can be treated and released within six months."[20] Where did Kennedy think the released schizophrenics would go? Home? But they had no

---

* The election of President Clinton and Vice President Gore promise to lead to policies that will eclipse the mistakes and surpass the costs of the Kennedy administration's psychiatric follies.

homes. Did anyone want them in his home? No. Did the Kennedys want Rosemary in their home? No.

The miracle cure Kennedy offered was simply the psychiatric profession's latest snake oil: Drugs and deinstitutionalization. As usual, psychiatrists defined their latest fad as a combination of scientific revolution and moral reform, and cast it in the rhetoric of treatment and civil liberties. Psychotropic drugs relieved the symptoms of mental illness and enabled the patients to be discharged from mental hospitals. Community Mental Health Centers provided the least restrictive setting for delivering the best available mental health services. Such were the claims of psychiatrists to justify the policy of forcibly drugging and relocating their hospitalized patients. It sounded grand. Unfortunately, it was a lie. The forces that actually propelled the change were economic and legal, specifically, the transfer of funding for psychiatric services from the states to the federal government, and the shift in legal-psychiatric fashions from long-term hospitalization to long-term drugging.

No one in authority challenged the assumptions on which this alleged reform rested. No one asked if it was it true that mental illness is like any other illness, or that psychotropic drugs made the patient mentally healthier and economically more self-sufficient. On the contrary, careers in politics, psychiatry, academia, and the media were made by *not asking* such questions, but pretending instead that we knew the answers and they were a resounding yes. The familiar psychiatric code words, such as mental illness, hospital, treatment, and schizophrenia, thus remained intact and were fortified with a set of fresh code words, such as dopamine, serotonin, antipsychotic drugs, and psychopharmacology. This lexicon of lunacy and therapy continues to do yeoman duty, concealing the fact that most people diagnosed as mentally ill have no homes, are unemployed and unemployable, and display disruptive behaviors, exemplified by threats and acts inimical to their own health and lives or to the health and lives of others.

The Government Enters the Psychiatric Scene

In 1955, Congress passed the Mental Health Study Act, mandating the appointment of a Commission to make recommendations for combating the scourge of mental illness in the United States.[21] It is impossible to exaggerate the enthusiasm with which psychiatrists greeted this legislation. Their euphoria was justifiable. In effect, the Act ratified the recasting of the very nature of the American government, changing its primary duty from protecting and promoting personal liberty and property to protecting and promoting the mental health of citizens and the community as a whole. The Act proclaimed: "It is declared to be the policy of the Congress to [undertake an] objective analysis of mental illness . . . [and] promote mental health."[22]

In the 1950s, in some states, the cost of caring for a state mental hospital patient was as little as $1 per day, the national average being $4 per day. It was clear to all well-meaning persons that, armed with enough federal dollars and new drugs, victory in the War on Mental Illness was imminent. Although mental diseases resemble heart diseases, and antipsychotics resemble antibiotics, in name only, people were not interested in scrutinizing either the illnesses or the treatments. The psychiatric future was predictable, but no one in authority was interested in it. Today, virtually every mental patient is "on drugs" and the result is that there are now more mental patients than ever, the cost of caring for them is greater than ever, and the patients are more disabled, more destructive, and more dissatisfied with psychiatry than ever. To understand how we arrived at our present situation, we must review the story of the Joint Commission on Mental Illness and Health (JC) and its role in the deinstitutionalization movement.

In 1962, the JC published its "Final Report" to Congress, entitled *Action for Mental Health*.[23] This was the document that informed President Kennedy's declaration about the dawn of a glorious new era in psychiatry and formed the basis of the Community Mental Health Centers program. Although the centerpiece of the *Report* was mental illness, the term was not defined; instead, its frequency and severity were dramatized by suitably sensational case histories, and its causes were authoritatively attributed to brain disease, bad genes, poor parenting, poverty, persecution, and racism. Henceforth, the properly compassionate and psychiatrically correct concept of mental illness was that it is a "no-fault disease." In other words, if a person succeeds in life, he deserves credit for his achievement; but if he does not, he deserves no blame for his failure, as he is the victim of mental illness.

The ideas that inspired the authors of the *Report* were the same materialist-positivist ideas that had inspired nineteenth-century psychiatrists: "Human behavior is caused."[24] This premise negates the presumption that adults are moral agents responsible for their behavior.[25] Moreover, the authors' premise contradicted one of their own major conclusions. Psychiatrists diagnose mental illness by observing the patient's behavior, not by testing his body fluids or otherwise examining his body. If behavior is caused, so is mental illness. If mental illness has a material *cause*, it can have a material *cure*. "These [antipsychotic] drugs," the *Report* declared, "have revolutionized the management of the psychotic patient . . . the drugs might be described as *moral treatment* in pill form."[26] However, material causes and chemical cures are neither moral nor immoral.

The *Report* enthusiastically endorsed the policy of mandating a reduction of the patient population of state mental hospitals, that is, relocating chronic mental patients to different domiciles. Mental patients were to be discharged not because they had improved, nor because they wanted to leave, but because the federal government ordered it. Trying to conceal this, the members of the JC were so carried away by their rhetoric that they appeared to be opposing involuntary mental hospitalization itself, declaring: "To be rejected by one's family, removed by the police, and placed behind locked doors can only be interpreted, sanely, as punishment and imprisonment, rather than hospitalization."[27] Did official American psychiatry embrace my views and reject psychiatric coercions? Not exactly. I advocated abolishing psychiatric coercions and excuses. The members of the JC advocated expanding the scope of psychiatric coercions by supplementing involuntary mental hospitalization with involuntary psychiatric drugging. And they urged that the federal government, rather than state governments, fund psychiatric services, training, and research.

I want to insert a personal note here. In 1955, when the Mental Health Study Act was passed by Congress, I was a lieutenant commander in the U.S. Naval Reserve, serving my required tour of duty at the National Naval Medical Center in Bethesda, Maryland. In 1961, when *Action for Mental Health* appeared, I was a professor of psychiatry at the SUNY Health Science Center in Syracuse, New York,* and had just published my book, *The Myth of Mental Illness.*[28] It seemed to me then—and I have had no reason to change my opinion—that there was something ominous about the Congress of the United States of America removing mental illness from the nether regions of psychiatry, law, journalism, and popular prejudice, and placing it, with the stroke of a legislative pen, in the category of genuine illness. Yet, psychiatrists, the families of mental patients, and the general public regarded, and continue to regard, using the political process to define mental illnesses as brain diseases as momentous scientific as well as moral progress. Laurie Flynn, Executive Director of the National Alliance for the Mentally Ill (NAMI), declared:

> Spurred on by the aggressive advocacy of NAMI families, the federal government has finally taken action to place the brain back into the body.

---

* The institution was then called the State University of New York, Upstate Medical Center, at Syracuse.

Congress in June [1992] approved legislation to return the National Institute of Mental Health under the umbrella of the National Institutes of Health. . . . Moving NIMH to NIH sends an important signal that mental illness is a disease, like heart and lung and kidney diseases.[29]

Two hundred years ago, to unite North and South in a political marriage of convenience, the Founding Fathers classified black slaves as a "three-fifths persons." Since the 1960s, to manage certain human tragedies and political-economic problems, the leaders of our Therapeutic State have classified millions of troubled and troublesome persons as patients, like diabetics, but yet also as unlike diabetics, their mental illnesses justifying doctors to hospitalize and treat them against their will.

Medicare, Medicaid, SSI, and Mental Health

In 1965, Congress passed and President Lyndon Johnson signed into law Title XVIII and Title XIX of the Social Security Act, better known as Medicare and Medicaid. In 1974, the Act was amended, adding the provisions of the Supplemental Security Income for the Aged, the Disabled, and the Blind (SSI) to it. These pieces of legislation had momentous psychiatric and social consequences.[30]

Although initially Medicare provided only limited reimbursement for outpatient psychiatric treatment and confinement in a private mental hospital, it authorized unlimited coverage for treatment in the psychiatric inpatient unit of a general hospital. Similarly, Medicaid did not pay for care in a facility called an "institution for mental disease" (defined as any hospital or nursing home where more than 50 percent of the patients have a psychiatric diagnosis), but provided lavish reimbursement for care in a general hospital.[31] This was a new psychiatric deal indeed: The federal government behaved as if it really believed the psychiatric cliché that "mental illness is like any other illness."

Prior to deinstitutionalization, it was generally acknowledged that real doctors did not want to treat mental patients, real hospitals did not want to admit them, and real patients did not want to associate with them. Accordingly, people with bodily diseases were treated in regular hospitals, and people with mental diseases were treated in psychiatric hospitals. The time had come to abolish psychiatric segregation. Medical patients and mental patients were "integrated" by means of the familiar combination of coercion and bribery.

For reasons with which we are familiar, the cost of medical care, especially hospital care, began to rise rapidly after World War II. Soon there was an outcry for cost controls. The quickest way to accomplish that was by limiting reimbursement for the most expensive type of medical service, namely, inhospital care. This decision led to dramatic reductions in hospital stays for medically and surgically ill patients. Many diagnostic and therapeutic procedures, previously performed on inpatients, were transferred to outpatient settings. Before long, hospitals stood half empty. Between 1965 and 1985, thanks to "Medicare's new prospective-payment system plus other cost-containment measures . . . occupancy rates at many hospitals [fell] to less than 50 percent."[32] Yet, this did not result in the creation of thousands of homeless arthritics, diabetics, and hypertensives living on the streets and assaulting people on subway platforms.*

Formerly disdained mental patients suddenly began to look attractive to the administrators of half-empty medical hospitals. Under Diagnosis Related Groups regulations (DRGs), Medicare reimbursements for medical and surgical hospitalization were rigidly limited, while reimbursements for mental hospitalization in general hospitals remained unlimited. This discrepancy, plus the fact that it costs much less to provide hospital care for mental patients than for medical or surgical patients, encouraged hospitalizing mental patients in non-mental hospitals. Moreover, Medicaid also paid for psychiatric care in general hospitals, but not in private mental hospitals. Finally, what began as the voluntary integration of medical and mental patients, soon turned into state-*mandated* regulations compelling nonpsychiatric hospitals to admit mental patients, initially voluntary patients only, then committed patients as well.

The story of the integration of medical and mental patients under one roof does not end here. Indeed, this is where the serious part of saga begins. In psychiatry, coercion is never far from center stage. Prior to 1965, most health insurance policies provided no coverage for mental diseases, just as most life insurance policies did not cover suicide. Medicare and Medicaid changed this too. State legislatures began to compel the health insurance industry to cover the cost of hospital treatment for mental illness as if it were like any other illness. Again, psychiatrists were ecstatic. A jubilant editorial in the *American Journal of Psychiatry* declared: "The 'remedicalization' of psychiatry . . . [and] the provision of psychiatric care within the mainstream of medical

---

* Although no one in an official position would admit it, deinstitutionalized mental patients became homeless not because they were discharged prematurely, nor because they stopped taking their medication, nor because they are schizophrenics, but because the hospitals were their only homes. E. Fuller Torrey's book on the homeless mentally ill, *Nowhere To Go,* is aptly titled. However, having nowhere to go is a tragedy, not a brain disease.

economics [have generated] . . . a broad movement toward the privatization of health care [that] is now a 'megatrend' in mental health economics."[33] Since psychiatric patients rarely pay for their hospital care, calling this trend "privatization" is perhaps an even more egregious misuse of language than calling misbehaviors "diseases" and madhouses "hospitals."

Mental Illness and the SSI Program

In January 1974, the Supplemental Security Income (SSI) program became effective and each "eligible person . . . [became entitled to] a monthly cash payment of $422."[34] The SSI program—whose benefits have each year been increased to keep pace with increases in the cost of living—was a veritable Economic Emancipation Proclamation for legions of chronic mental patients.

Existentially, being a hospitalized mental patient has always been an occupation.[35] Henceforth, it became an occupation economically as well. By 1980, 550,000 mentally disabled Americans were receiving monthly SS and SSI checks "for a total of some $2.25 billion for the year."[36] During that year alone, 65,000 new psychiatric recipients joined the rolls, adding more than 10 percent to total.[37] Ten years later, more than 1 million persons *under the age of 65* were receiving SS and SSI disability payments. About one-half were classified as "mentally retarded," the other half as "mentally disturbed."[38]

Since the mental patient who qualifies for disability payments is considered to be permanently unable to work, he does not have to submit to treatment, can live where he wants, spend his money as he chooses, marry, divorce, have children, and vote. If he gets arrested for a crime, he can count on being able to plead insanity. The one thing he must do to qualify for receiving the federal funds is remain crazy and unemployable.* As Ann Braden Johnson correctly observes, "SSI wound up promoting dependency and disability, by paying for it, at the same time that SSI's very existence had made it all too easy for states to get patients out of their hospitals."[39] In short, SSI freed mental patients from the ordeals of psychiatric indoor relief and enabled them to live on outdoor relief, in parks and on the streets—so long as the temperature did not drop too far below the freezing mark, when they suddenly became committable. In the American megalopolis, the severity of mental illness now depends on the weather.

---

* The operative criterion for qualifying for SSI or SSD (Social Security Disability) payment is not illness but disability preventing the patient from engaging in "substantial gainful activity."

DRUGS AND DEINSTITUTIONALIZATION

Wars have always encouraged advances in the technology of both killing and curing. During World War II, the Germans developed gas chambers and invented methadone (originally called *Dolophine,* in honor of Adolf Hitler). The Allies developed the atomic bomb and invented penicillin. After years of what might be described as better killing through chemistry (and physics), we embraced the slogan, "better living through chemistry" (originally an advertisement for the Du Pont Company). This credo dominated the postwar medical-technological atmosphere.

Better Psychiatric Living through Chemistry

Inspired by the miracles of antibiotics, psychiatrists and other experts on human betterment undertook to remedy every personal and social ill with a drug, developed in a government-directed program (called "war"), by government-financed bureaucrats and propagandists (called "scientists" and "educators"). The age of the chemical cure for chemical imbalances and chemical dependencies had arrived.

Not having any therapeutic methods of their own (save for a monopoly on coercion under medical auspices), psychiatrists, as I noted earlier, tended to imitate prevailing medical fashions. When bleeding and cupping were stylish, the alienists used bleeding and cupping. When insulin was discovered as a treatment for diabetes, psychiatrists gave their patients overdoses of insulin and called it insulin coma therapy. When electrocardiography and electroencephalography became popular medical tools, psychiatrists gave their patients electrically induced seizures, and called it electroconvulsive treatment. In the 1950s, physicians treated their patients with antacids, antibiotics, antihistamines, antihypertensives, and other drugs sporting the prefix *anti.* Antipsychotics could not be far behind. Chemists quickly found various organic compounds whose pharmacological effect was to stimulate or retard thought and movement. The stimulants became antidepressants, the retardants, antipsychotics and antianxiety agents. The insane person could now be controlled with a chemical, instead of a mechanical, straitjacket: The restraint could be put *in* him, instead of *on* him.

I well remember seeing—in 1954 or 1955, when I was in the Navy—what must have been one of the earliest films promoting chlorpromazine. Produced by Smith, Kline and French, the pharmaceutical company that patented the compound as Thorazine, the film showed aggressive monkeys being "tranquilized"—the term was new then—by the drug. This, we were told, was the new cure for schizophrenia. I did not like what I saw. In 1956, I wrote:

> The widespread acceptance and use of the so-called tranquilizing drugs constitutes one of the most noteworthy events in the recent history of psychiatry. . . . These drugs, in essence, function as chemical straitjackets . . . . When patients had to be restrained by the use of force—for example, by a straitjacket—it was difficult for those in charge of their care to convince themselves that they were acting altogether on behalf of the patient. . . . Restraint by chemical means does not make [the psychiatrist] feel guilty; herein lies the danger to the patient.[40]

The history of Thorazine is telling. First used in France as an anesthetic potentiator, the drug proved to be commercially uninteresting. It was then promoted as an antiemetic. In 1953, it was tried out on about 100 psychiatric patients, was declared to be an effective "antipsychotic," and a year later was approved for the American market.[41] It proved to be one of the biggest bonanzas in pharmaceutical history, proving, once more, that treating nondiseases is even more lucrative than treating diseases.

Once again, a new somatic psychiatric treatment proved to be the cause of serious harm to the patients. Henri Laborit, the French physician who first reported the tranquilizing properties of chlorpromazine in 1951, described its effect as "a veritable medicinal lobotomy."[42] Many persons receiving Thorazine and other antipsychotic drugs developed a severe neurological disease called "tardive dyskinesia." The magnitude of this epidemic of iatrogenic neurological disease has dwarfed the brain-damaging consequences of insulin shock, electric shock, and lobotomy combined.

With the advent antipsychotics, psychiatrists grew bolder. In the 1970s, the late Nathan Kline, then one of the most respected biological psychiatrists in the United States, seriously suggested putting antipsychotic drugs in the drinking water. He wrote: "Since we are already putting chlorine and fluorine in the water supply, maybe we should also put in a little lithium. It might make the world a little better place to live in for all of us."[43]

After declaring victory in their struggle to control schizophrenia, psychiatrists announced their next breakthrough, the discovery of a class of drugs that caused a schizophrenialike condition called "model psychosis." These alkaloids—closely related to ancient ceremonial drugs—caused altered states of consciousness or hallucinations and were called "psychotomimetics" or "hallucinogens." The effects of antipsychotics and psychotomimetics were interpreted as proof that schizophrenia is a brain disease due to a chemical imbalance. Reality was less romantic. Psychiatry's latest puffery was nothing more than a hugely successful public relations scam. Supported by politicians and journalists, psychiatrists managed to convince the public that the care of mental patients had been revolutionized by antipsychotics, much as the care of patients with infectious diseases had been revolutionized by antibiotics. This preposterous claim helped psychiatrists conceal the true nature of the problems mental patients present and the solutions psychiatrists offer to solve them—specifically, that the typical chronic mental patient is homeless and is economically dependent on his family or society; that he violates marginal (or not so marginal) social rules; and that he is restrained, during hospitalization as well as after discharge, by drugs, the threat of commitment, and involuntary mental hospitalization.

Today, the traditional functions of the madhouse are exercised by many other institutions as well, especially the public facilities of our large cities, such as libraries, bus stations, and so forth. Bedlam is now everywhere, making our streets and parks both ugly and unsafe. Ugly, because we tolerate unacceptable behavior by persons so long as, de jure, they are classified as mental patients; and unsafe, because many of these individuals engage in de facto aggression, depriving others of property, liberty, and even life.

10

RE-STORING THE MENTAL PATIENT

We're making great progress, but we're headed in the wrong direction.
—*Ogden Nash*[1]

The only incontestable fact about deinstitutionalization is that public mental hospitals have fewer inmates today than they had in the 1950s. Everything else—especially the reasons for the decrease—is a matter of interpretation and controversy.

THE MYTH OF DEINSTITUTIONALIZATION

During the early decades of the century, virtually everyone considered to be seriously mentally ill was confined in a state hospital. Psychiatry was then synonymous with hospital psychiatry. Private psychiatric practice, as we know it, did not exist. Psychiatrists and the public alike viewed the insane person as an irresponsible child and/or a dangerous criminal, who neither needed nor deserved liberty. Instead, he needed to be protected from himself, and society needed to be protected from him. The permanent confinement of the mental patient in the insane asylum was accepted as society's proper response to its double duty, to the deranged patient endangered by his disease, and to society endangered by him. In those days, psychiatrists acknowledged that the public mental hospital was a type of storage bin for society's undesirables. In 1918, a psychiatrist wrote:

> [The state mental hospital is] a lodging house for the segregation of those who, by reason of mental disorder, were unfit for ordinary social life . . . Many of the inmates will inevitably remain permanently within the institution, although not "sick," in the ordinary sense of the word at all . . . in the majority of cases no evidence of disease can be detected.[2]

Today, no psychiatrist would admit this. However, he would admit that he cannot distinguish mental health from mental illness. J. Sanbourne Bockoven, a prominent state hospital psychiatrist, stated: "Mental health workers are the first to admit their inability to give a definition of mental health or illness that has sufficient validity to be used as a test or proof of anyone's sanity."[3] And a leading text on mental health policy acknowledges: "A universally accepted and consistent definition of mental health has been elusive. . . . [There is] a long tradition of uncertainty about what constitutes mental health and illness."[4]

DIAGNOSIS BY DOMICILE

How do psychiatrists determine that an individual is a chronic mental patient? They do so, primarily, by ascertaining where he lives. A group of psychiatric researchers state: "Chronic mental patients are a subgroup characterized by institutionalization."[5] Another team defines the chronic mental patient as an individual housed in a publicly supported facility because of "mental illness" and estimates the number of such persons in the United States as ranging "from 1.7 million to 2.4 million."[6] According to these investigators, 900,000 mental patients are still "institutionalized," about 150,000 in "mental health facilities," the rest in "nursing homes." Another 800,000 "severely [mentally] disabled" and 700,000 "moderately [mentally] disabled" persons are housed "in a variety of residential settings (with families, in boarding homes, in single-occupancy hotel rooms)." A position paper by the APA supports this image of deinstitutionalization as de facto transinstitutionalization: "Deinstitutionalized patients now constitute a new class of patients [who] frequently have complex medical and psychiatric conditions that require leadership and treatment skills that only psychiatrists, by virtue of their training, can provide."[7]

In short, individuals formerly in mental hospitals have been rehoused in dwellings that are de facto psychiatric facilities, but are not called "mental" or "hospitals." Neither the patients' mental condition nor their social functioning has improved. Deinstitutionalization is simply a new fashion in mental health care, consisting of storing unwanted persons in dwellings *not* called "mental hospitals" but nevertheless treating them as if they were mental patients who required lifelong psychiatric supervision. This shift has been accomplished by replacing mechanical with chemical straitjackets, housing the patients in diverse parapsychiatric domiciles, supporting them with welfare checks, and calling the management-style "caring for the patient in the least restrictive setting in the community."[8]

RE-STORING THE DEINSTITUTIONALIZED PATIENT

Persons officially identified as mental patients are now housed in numerous locations, such as the following: state mental hospitals, Veterans Administration hospitals, community and general hospitals, private mental hospitals, children's psychiatric units, nursing homes, alcohol and drug rehabilitation centers, forensic psychiatric facilities, prisons and jails, public housing projects, community residences, adult homes, group homes, boardinghouses, single-room occupancy hotels (SROs), transitional living quarters, public and private shelters, public libraries, bus and train stations and airports, parks and streets. I shall limit my remarks here to the storage of unwanted persons in nursing homes, prisons, and private mental hospitals.

The Nursing Home as Madhouse

When I was a psychiatric resident, more than half of the inmates of state mental hospitals were unwanted old persons, called "geriatric cases." Millions of elderly people then spent their last months or years in insane asylums, just as they now spend them in nursing homes. The 1955 Mental Health Study Act singled out the psychiatric confinement of the elderly as one of the most flagrant abuses of the state hospital system.[9] During the 1960s and 70s, virtually all these persons were rehoused in nursing homes where, embalmed in neuroleptic drugs, they are stored until they can be properly buried. "What's a nursing home?" [a boy in Brooklyn asks his friend.] "That's where they keep dead people they ain't buried yet."[10]

Consider some statistics. Between 1969 and 1974, the number of aged inmates in state hospitals in California dropped by 86 percent; in Massachusetts, by 87 percent; and in Wisconsin, by a record 99 percent.[11] During the same period, the population of nursing homes exploded. By 1990, more than 1.5 million elderly persons were housed in some 20,000 such institutions.[12] Sanford I. Finkel, M.D., director of Gero-Psychiatric Services at Northwestern Memorial Hospital in Chicago, observes: "There has been a tremendous influx of psychiatric patients [into nursing homes]. . . . Nursing homes are really the psychiatric institutions of the 1990s."[13]

Although nursing home inmates are no longer counted as mental patients, they are treated as if they were. Instead of publishing exposés of snake-pit-like conditions in state mental hospitals, the popular press and even psychiatric journals publish exposés of nursing home residents overmedicated with antipsychotic drugs.[14] The quality of the inmates' lives in the new drug pits is just as bad as it was in the old snake pits, and many would-be victims know it. "Terrified of nursing homes," writes a *Wall Street Journal* reporter, "older people will do almost anything to avoid them. . . . fearing nursing homes is a major cause of suicide . . . overshadow[ing] such other factors as depression, chronic illness, and pain."[15]

The Prison as Madhouse

Many crazy persons commit crimes, and many criminals are diagnosed as mentally ill. Psychiatrists and the public alike view craziness and criminality as closely related types of deviance. The mental hospital and prison systems are close allies, each depriving its inmates of liberty and drugging them to make them more manageable. It should not surprise us that many people who might formerly have been committed to mental hospitals end up in prisons, and vice versa. A 1983 report in *JAMA (Journal of the American Medical Association)* denounced deinstitutionalization for "turning this country's 4,000 local jails into the new mental hospitals and returning care of the mentally ill to the deplorable conditions that prevailed more than 300 years ago."[16] Nine years later, a nationwide study—conducted jointly by the Public Citizen's Health Research Group and the National Alliance for the Mentally Ill, and supported by the American Psychiatric Association—revealed: "Each day, over 30,700 seriously mentally ill individuals serve time in our nation's jails . . . . [Jails] are actually the nation's largest mental institutions . . . [housing many persons held] on minor charges like disorderly conduct or vagrancy."[17]

Other studies support these claims. In 1991, the Los Angeles County Jail was described as "the largest mental institution in the nation."[18] To deal with this new problem—which many tacitly recognize as a solution—the county commissioners appointed a Task Force to make recommendations concerning "the delivery of mental health resources to jail inmates" and the allocation of "funding and resources."[19] In Arizona, "prisons and jails have become [the state's] largest mental asylums, housing inmates who receive treatments ranging from Narcotics Anonymous sessions and psychotropic drugs to isolation and leather restraints. For many disturbed people, getting arrested is the only way to get mental-health services."[20] Many state facilities have become mixtures of madhouses and prisons. An institution operated by the Arizona Department of Corrections, called the Flamenco Behavioral Health Hospital, houses "female medium-security inmates who have mental-health problems." One inmate, imprisoned for embezzlement, is described as "an alcoholic and shopping addict . . . who has been prescribed anti-anxiety and anti-psychotic medication."[21]

Prison statistics round out the story. In 1951, the prison population in New York City was 5,400, and in New York State, 17,000; in 1960, the figures were 8,800 and 19,000; and in 1990, 20,000 and 55,000.[22] The picture for California is similar. Between January 1981 and January 1991, the state's prison population grew from 24,237 to 93,781, an increase of 287 percent. California's prison system, the largest in the nation, comprises 97,000 inmates, 32,000 employees, and 20 facilities; its annual budget is more than $2.3 billion.[23] In 1960, about 100 persons per 100,000 were incarcerated in state or federal prisons in the United States; in 1991, the figure was 426 per 100,000. Today, more than 4 million persons—one of every 25 men—are under the direct control of the criminal justice system, with more than 1 million behind bars.[24] The United States has the highest criminal confinement rate in the world.[25]

The relentless increase in our prison population is due to several factors. More criminals are sentenced to serve time for offenses for which, in the past, they would have received probation; more are imprisoned for so-called drug-related (actually, drug-law-related) offenses than ever, and more are given long sentences; lastly, our society uses the prison system as an extension of the mental health and welfare systems.[26] Social observers report that unemployed inner city youths receive more social support in prison than outside of it. "Prisons provide housing that is often far better than the tenements or homeless shelters where the inmates had been living. They furnish three meals a day; decent medical care . . . remedial education and job training."[27] From an inmate's point of view, being housed in a prison is likely to be preferable not only to being housed in a mental hospital but also to being housed in a shelter.

The critics who complain about supposedly mentally ill offenders being jailed assume that the subjects would prefer being committed. There is no evidence to support this assumption. On the contrary, there is evidence that mental hospital patients often commit crimes to be transferred to prison, as the following example illustrates. On November 17, 1992, Julie Mitchell, a 23-year-old woman, "diagnosed as schizophrenic [and] a voluntary resident" at the Hutchings Psychiatric Center in Syracuse since April, stomped a fellow patient to death. "'I hate being there,'" Mitchell said in a statement to police. "'I would do anything to leave. I think that jail is a whole lot better than being in Hutchings.' Mitchell was being treated at Hutchings for chronic schizophrenia, narcissistic traits, and a history of drug abuse . . . She told patients she had been in jail six times and found the food and other services better there than at Hutchings."[28]

Psychiatric explanations of such behaviors are worthless or simply self-serving. Formerly, psychiatrists claimed that most criminals were mentally ill.[29] Now, they claim that most of them suffer from chemical dependency. The commingling of crime and disease, which began to infect the body politic in the nineteenth century, has now reached the stage of a far-advanced parasitic infestation of both the criminal justice and mental health systems.[30]

The term *deinstitutionalization* conceals some simple truths, namely, that old, unwanted persons, formerly housed in state hospitals, are now housed in nursing homes; that young, unwanted persons, formerly also housed in state hospitals, are now housed in prisons or parapsychiatric facilities; and that both groups of inmates are systematically drugged with psychiatric medications.

THE REBIRTH OF THE "PRIVATE" MADHOUSE SYSTEM

Before the 1950s, a public mental hospital was a psychiatric institution supported by public funds, whereas a private mental hospital was one supported by the fees of private patients and private donations. Today, the term *private mental hospital* denotes an institution supported by government programs and health insurance company payments. Not only does the consumer of private mental hospital care rarely pay for the services he receives, he does not even purchase his own insurance coverage for it, which he receives, instead, as an untaxed, quasi salary from his employer.* Lastly, the insurance companies that provide the coverage are also not free agents, state laws requiring them to cover treatments for fictitious ailments, such as alcoholism, drug abuse, and mental illness. Thus, employer, employee, insurance carrier, and private mental hospital are locked in an economic embrace that corrupts them all and that has encouraged an absurd growth of private psychiatric inpatient services.[31]

The General Hospital Becomes a Mental Hospital

Between 1955 and 1975, the number of patients in public mental hospitals decreased by more than 70 percent. During the same period, the number of patients in the psychiatric units of general hospitals increased by more than 400 percent and the number of psychiatric units in general hospitals increased by more than 2,000 percent.[32] Moreover, as the number of patients in public mental institutions decreased, the cost of caring for them exploded. In 1969, when there were still 21,000 patients in the Massachusetts state mental health system, the state budget for mental health was $116 million. Eight years later there were only 3,262 patients left, but the budget doubled, to $233 million.[33] The same thing occurred in all the large states. In New York, in the past three decades, the inpatient population of the state mental health system decreased by nearly 90 percent while the number of state mental hospitals increased from 18 to 22. In Gowanda, south of Buffalo, the state hospital that once housed nearly 4,000 patients remains open for only 14.[34]

The past 30 years or so have been boom times for a rapidly expanding mental health profession as well. Between 1955 and 1980, the number of psychiatrists per population doubled. Between 1970 and 1990, the number of psychologists increased from less than 30,000 to more than 191,000 (*not* counting marriage and family counselors and social workers). In 1952, the APA recognized 110 discrete mental diseases; today, it recognizes 220. In 1965, 7 million prescriptions were written for antidepressant drugs; in 1989, 32 million.[35] Not surprisingly, the cost of delivering mental health services exploded, increasing from $1.2 billion in 1955 to $20 billion in 1977.[36] When the public psychiatric system began, about two and a half centuries ago, it was a low-cost indoor relief program. Today, it is a high-cost outdoor relief plus housing plus drugging program.

---

* I venture to guess that if the average American worker were given a choice between coverage for hospitalization for mental illness and drug abuse and its cash equivalent, he would choose the latter.

Psychiatrists realize that while the number of psychiatric beds in the public sector has been decreasing, the number of psychiatric beds in the private sector has been increasing, and that this divergent trend is due to government policy. Nevertheless, psychiatrists Robert A. Dorwart and Marc Schlesinger, two experts on psychiatric policy, call the phenomenon "remarkable." They write: "In a time of private and public pressures to reduce health care costs and institutional capacity, it is somewhat remarkable to observe this growth in private psychiatric hospital care. . . . Demand has increased as insurance coverage for mental illness has continued to expand."[37]

The demand for private mental hospital beds is not driven by diseases requiring hospital-based treatment or by paying patients who seek care. Instead, it is driven much as the demand for beds in eighteenth-century private madhouses was driven, by a combination of corruption and coercion. Hospital personnel are offered bounties to bring in new patients; diagnoses are tailored to maximize insurance reimbursements; patients are seduced into admission by offers of free "programs" promising to break them of their bad habits, and are coerced by the threat of commitment for misbehavior at home or on the job; once admitted, patients are held against their will for as long as their insurance provides coverage.[38]

Writers for financial publications see the situation but fail to scrutinize the basic problems of mental illness and insurance coverage for psychiatric treatment. A reporter for *Forbes* writes: "The growth and success of psychiatric hospital chains . . . has been built largely on liberal employee benefit packages that encouraged workers to seek inpatient care for mental health and drug and alcohol abuse problems."[39] How long does an alcoholic employee or his Valium-dependent wife need to be in a hospital? For as long as the insurance company foots the bill: "Under most plans, hospitals had no incentive to release patients before their insurance benefits expired, enabling the psychiatric chains to pad their profits."[40] This racket has become so brazen that even some psychiatrists acknowledge it. One psychiatric informant tells *Forbes*: "The psychiatric chains have been doing everything they can to keep people for an unnecessarily long period for no medical reason. We think that between 40% and 70% of the people now in psychiatric hospitals don't need to be there."[41]

In 1990, the *American Journal of Psychiatry* published a remarkably candid essay on the subject, albeit cast in almost impenetrable psychiatric jargon. The authors wrote:

> Treatment in nonspecialized general hospital sites (scatter beds) is reimbursed according to diagnosis-related groups (DRGs), but treatment in

approved psychiatric units in general hospitals, as well as treatment in psychiatric hospitals, is exempt from the DRG-based prospective payment system. . . . A general hospital may even exploit the system by transferring a patient from a scatter bed to its own exempt unit.* . . . [Hospitals] have an incentive to dump as soon as possible more severely ill patients to other hospitals, particularly exempt ones, because they will still receive a full DRG payment . . . some transfers may also be motivated by an attempt to exploit the reimbursement system.[42]

In other words, psychiatrically correct mental health policy requires that mental patients be transferred from unapproved "scatter beds" in general hospitals to approved nonscatter beds.

A Critical Analysis of Psychiatric Privatization

Dorwart and Schlesinger acknowledge that the phrase "privatization of psychiatric services" actually means "the increased purchasing by public authorities of services from private agencies," and correctly note that the purchaser of mental health insurance coverage has the clout to coerce the seller: "A majority of states now [1988] have some form of *mandatory* insurance coverage . . . for mental health care."[43] The pressure to reduce health care costs is aimed *only* at the treatment of real diseases. There is no pressure to reduce the cost of treating fictitious diseases. On the contrary, there is pressure to define ever more types of undesirable behaviors as mental disorders or addictions and to spend ever more tax dollars on developing new psychiatric diagnoses and facilities for storing and treating the victims of such diseases, whose members now include alcoholics, drug abusers, smokers, overeaters, self-starvers, gamblers, etc.

Some similarities between the Social Security system and the so-called private psychiatric system deserve a brief comment in this connection. Social Security is a government-mandated program based on the seller's ability to lawfully coerce the buyer to avail himself of a "service" (he may not want)—the federal government compelling workers to pay for what is nominally a type of insurance protection and retirement program, but is actually a tax. Similarly, the private psychiatric care system is a government-mandated program based on the seller's ability to lawfully coerce the buyer to avail himself of a "service" (he does not want)—the federal government compelling employers to purchase health insurance coverage

---

* Note that the authors write as if patients were transferred by a *building,* instead of a *person.*

for mental illness for their employees, which compels insurance companies to cover the cost of mental health treatment. Employers pay for, and employees receive, what is nominally a type of insurance protection against illness, but is actually a legal-psychiatric scheme that enables physicians to involuntarily diagnose, hospitalize, and treat employees and their dependents. Ostensibly, the recipients get psychiatric treatment; actually, they are deprived of liberty and dignity. De jure, the psychiatrist functions as a physician diagnosing and treating mental illness; de facto, he is an agent of the state empowered to confine persons in mental hospitals and charge their insurance carriers for the "service." Calling this practice the "delivery of mental health services," and a "market transaction" to boot, is a debauchment of language worthy of Orwell's Newspeak.

The engine that drives the psychiatric industry today is a combination of federal and state funds, government-mandated insurance coverage, commitment laws, and the threat of involuntary mental hospitalization (together with mendacious claims about the effectiveness of neuroleptic drugs). Nevertheless, psychiatrists not only continue to pretend that mental illness is like any other illness, they maintain that mental hospitals, mental health professionals, insurance companies, and family members who commit their relatives are engaged in *free market* transactions—and complain about imperfections of the market. In an editorial in the *American Journal of Psychiatry*, Steven Sharfstein writes: "It is clear that for psychiatric care the market is a poor mechanism for efficient and fair rationing of scarce dollars. There is a need for strong government regulation and financing."[44] While it is difficult to see how government regulation of American psychiatry could be much increased, it is easy to see how government expenditures on mental health could be increased almost ad infinitum, until, like the Soviet economic system, the enterprise implodes.

From an economic point of view, our present psychiatric system is an astonishing combination of a state monopoly with a state monopsony. Monopoly means the exclusive control of the supply of a particular good or service. If the state is the monopolist, it can define competitors as lawbreakers—say, private mail delivery—with the result that there is only a single lawful supplier, the postal service. Monopsony is the mirror image of monopoly, that is, exclusive control of the purchasers of a particular good or service. If the state is the monopsonist, it can define private purchasers as lawbreakers—say, individuals buying gold or foreign currency—with the result that there is only a single lawful buyer, for example, a nationalized banking system such as prevailed in the former Soviet Union. A nationalized health care system, such as also existed in the former Soviet Union—with private medical care available in the black market—is another example of a state monopsony. This sort of political-economic rigging of the market is responsible for the current boom in the American private psychiatric hospital industry (and its economic fragility), and for the fact that its principal clients are children and old people. The young and the old are defenseless against relatives who want to get rid of them by casting them in the role of mental patient, and against psychiatrists whose livelihood depends on defining them as mentally ill.*

TREATING THE DEINSTITUTIONALIZED PATIENT

There is unanimous agreement among psychiatrists that deinstitutionalized mental patients, especially if they are homeless, need psychiatric services. One of the most prominent practitioners of, and propagandists for, the psychiatric treatment of homeless persons is E. Fuller Torrey. He has worked as a psychiatrist at St. Elizabeths Hospital, in Washington, DC, served as a special assistant to the Director of the National Institute of Mental Health, ran a clinic for mentally ill homeless women, and received the Special Friends Award in 1984 from the National Alliance for the Mentally Ill.[45] Torrey's method of managing the homeless mental patient may therefore be regarded as exemplary. He states:

> It has been clearly established in studies that approximately one-third of the homeless have "bad brains"—i.e., have mental diseases such as schizophrenia and manic-depressive psychosis (also known as bipolar disorder). . . . It should not be surprising that the majority of the people with this disease [schizophrenia] do not have insight. In order to help such people, therefore, it may be necessary to hospitalize and treat them involuntarily.[46]

To illustrate Torrey's method of treating the deinstitutionalized mental patient, I shall quote a few excerpts from his "case notes" in *Nowhere To Go*, and offer some comments on them.

A Paradigmatic Case History

> Alan P. was admitted to St. Elizabeths Hospital for the twenty-seventh time in twelve years with a diagnosis of chronic schizophrenia.[47]

Torrey does not say whether Alan P. was admitted voluntarily or involuntarily, or whether he wanted to be discharged or stay in the hospital.

---

* The poor are similarly defenseless. However, they continue to be managed as clients of the public psychiatric system.

He invariably responded well to antipsychotic medication and improved markedly on medication within three weeks.

Again, Torrey does not say whether Alan P. believed that he had responded well to the treatment, or whether this was only the psychiatrist's opinion.

He was then discharged to live in the community, given medication for two weeks, and strong admonitions to keep his outpatient appointment.

The phrase *in the community* is a psychiatric euphemism intended to conceal the fact that the patient was transferred from one psychiatric facility to another, the first called a "hospital," the second not called a "hospital." Once more, Torrey does not tell us whether Alan P. wanted or did not want the medication. The fact that he was given "strong admonitions to keep his outpatient appointment" suggests that Torrey knew that Alan P. was not motivated to keep his appointment.

He had no insight into his illness or his need for medication, however, and usually discarded the pills in a trash can en route to his boarding house. Slowly over the ensuing weeks his behavior would become increasingly bizarre as his psychosis returned.

Although Torrey knew that Alan P. usually discarded his antipsychotic medication, he nevertheless gave him medication. The relationship between Torrey and Alan P. thus resembles the relationship between a boss and his worker in a former Soviet factory, summed up in the witticism: "They pretend to pay us, and we pretend to work." Torrey pretended to treat Alan P., and Alan P. pretended to be his patient.

Psychiatrists estimate that from 50 to 90 percent of patients discharged from mental hospitals on drugs exhibit such "noncompliance." Why do they? Is it because they have no insight into their illness and need for medication? Or because they do not like the effects of the drugs and prefer being psychotic? Or because they want to relapse and be readmitted to the hospital? The explanation we choose says more about us than about the patients.

Torrey's Panacea: Coercion

If Torrey's treatment of Alan P. is a model of what constitutes the currently correct psychiatric management of the chronic mental patient, then it is understandable why so few graduates of American medical schools go into psychiatry, leaving the field—as is common knowledge in psychiatry—to the most incompetent graduates of foreign medical schools, whose ignorance of English protects them from being distressed by their patients' anguished communications. It is also understandable why Torrey, who relishes treating involuntary patients, advocates a program of national psychiatric conscription as a cure for our ailing mental health system.

Torrey first proposed conscripting psychiatrists in 1985, in a position paper published under the auspices of Ralph Nader's Public Citizen Health Research Group. After asserting, "There are now more schizophrenics on the streets of Washington and in public shelters than there are in St. Elizabeths Hospital," he went on to emphasize their need for treatment:

> It is important to stress that schizophrenia is a treatable disease in the majority of cases. And it is therefore remarkable that a situation is tolerated in which most of the approximately 1,200 persons with a treatable disease live untreated on the streets and in shelters; imagine the outcry if 1,200 untreated diabetics were living on the streets and in shelters.[48]

If schizophrenia is a treatable disease, similar to diabetes, then doctors ought to be able to treat schizophrenics, like diabetics, with their consent. Ignoring the double disanalogy between diabetes and schizophrenia and between endocrinology and psychiatry, Torrey proceeded to outline his proposal for drafting psychiatrists:

> Psychiatrists should be assigned to shelters to provide services for the homeless mentally ill. Candidates for immediate assignment include competent psychiatrists at St. Elizabeths Hospital and the National Institute of Mental Health with administrative responsibilities only. Long-term, the personnel problem could be solved by requiring two hours per week pro bono work from every physician as a condition of being licensed to practice in the District.[49]

Evidently piqued by his colleagues at St. Elizabeths Hospital for showing insufficient enthusiasm for drugging homeless people, Torrey urged targeting them for special coercion: "Leading candidates for such assignments would be ten full-time and five part-time St. Elizabeths psychiatrists who, although fully trained, currently have no patient care responsibility but only administrative assignments."[50] Because psychiatrists have been trained in part with public funds, Torrey argued that psychiatric training programs "should have mandated obligations in which the person being trained agrees to year-for-year payback in a public-sector job working with the seriously mentally ill for each year of publicly subsidized training." For psychiatrists who have already completed their training, the states should "mandate a *pro bono* requirement of public service for continued state licensure."[51] In 1992, in a report co-sponsored by the Public Citizen Health Research Group and the National Alliance for the Mentally Ill, Torrey proposed that all mental health professionals be required, "as a condition of licensing, to do two hours of pro bono work a week at public mental health centers."[52] It is not clear how Torrey justifies making the licensure of mental health workers, but not that of other professionals, such as architects or allergists, contingent on rendering pro bono service to clients.

Finally, Torrey claimed: "They [deinstitutionalized patients] can live happily ever after in the community, but only when an aftercare and support system is provided."[53] The evidence points the other way. In a large project in California, researchers studied the posthospitalization life trajectories of some 400 former psychiatric inpatients living in sheltered care facilities and found that, after 10 years, fully 93 percent of them were still supported by Social Security payments. The investigators concluded that the psychiatrists' claims about the rehabilitation of deinstitutionalized mental patients are completely false:

> Many of these people do not possess the most common papers by which people identify themselves . . . . The most striking feature of this cohort is the stability of its disability . . . . The character and persistence of their mental disorder leads us to believe that prior to the era of deinstitutionalization they would have been the responsibility of state and county mental health departments.[54]

In short, deinstitutionalized mental patients are dependents who continue to require that others supply shelter and food for them. In one form or another, psychiatry continues to fulfill that need.

WHAT DOES THE DESTITUTE MENTAL PATIENT WANT?

Most people believe that psychotic persons have delusions and hallucinations, engage in senseless or unmotivated acts, and deny their illness. The truth is simpler and more painful. What psychotic persons do and say makes perfectly good sense, but is so disturbing that we prefer not to hear or understand it. Such refusal by a normal person to recognize the method in the mad Other's behavior may be an existentially reasonable option. But he who does not want to understand the Other has no right to say that what the Other does or says makes no sense. Revealingly, a journalist visiting Harvey, an ex-mental patient, in his subway station home, reports: "Every time I saw Harvey I offered to escort him to the hospital. He always refused . . . . He was obviously unable to understand my offers to help."[55] I think it was the other way around, the reporter being unable or unwilling to understand what Harvey wanted and why he wanted it. The proverb tells us that actions speak louder than words. Indeed, actions speak loudest when a person addresses an interlocutor who refuses to listen to him.[56]

Putting Ourselves in the Patient's Shoes

Psychiatrists study mental patients to diagnose their derangements, not to discover their desires. There are no Gallup polls to inform us whether deinstitutionalized mental patients prefer to live in mental hospitals or be relocated in an unfamiliar domicile chosen for them. However, a study by the National Institute of Mental Health revealed "that over one third of the discharged patients interviewed preferred hospital life to the alienation and loneliness they often found living on their own."[57] In another study, researchers at the Bronx State Hospital asked 220 patients how many of their fellow patients on their ward "would rather go on living here [in the hospital]." Seventeen percent replied "most"; 18 percent, "some"; 46 percent, a "few"; and 18 percent, "none." The researchers concluded that "many patients are loathe to be discharged from the hospital, while others return on many occasions."[58]

Actually, we do not need studies to recognize that some mental patients prefer to live outside mental hospitals and go to great lengths to stay out; that some prefer to live in mental hospitals and go to great lengths to get in and stay in; and that many others dislike both options. Comedienne Lily Tomlin's fictitious bag lady, Tess, articulates this ambivalence:

> I made these potholders when I was inside [the mental hospital] to keep from going bats. . . . I didn't like it there, but boy, I don't like it out here either. The reason I got in is somebody told 'em I think I'm God. They don't like anyone thinkin' they're God, 'cause they think they're God.[59]

The psychiatrists are not amused. They believe that seriously ill mental patients must be medicated and, if they refuse to take the drugs prescribed for them, must be involuntarily hospitalized and drugged against their will. Stephen Rachlin, deputy director of the Meyer-Manhattan Psychiatric Center, articulates this position forthrightly: "Liberty to be

psychotic is no freedom at all. . . . the right to treatment is more fundamental than that of unrestricted liberty. The paramount civil right of
the patient should be that of adequate treatment, provided in a suitable
environment."[60]

In my previous writings I have dealt at length with the situation of
persons who do not want to be in mental hospitals. Here, I want to offer
a few observations about the predicament of those who want to stay in
mental hospitals or want to be readmitted to them.

"Please Let Me Come Back!"

Many deinstitutionalized patients, especially if they have spent long
periods in mental hospitals, beseech psychiatrists to let them remain in
the hospital or readmit them. The following account is typical.*

Rodney Forster, a 64-year-old man diagnosed as schizophrenic, had
spent virtually all his adult life in a mental hospital in Wales. Involuntarily discharged, Forster embarked on long bus trips back to the hospital, where the "nursing staff bathed him and gave him boiled eggs."
Not allowed to stay overnight, Forster began sleeping on the hospital
grounds. The police were called to remove him. Finally, "he was found
shivering in the shelter of a wall and died six days later."[61] After his
death, nurses at the hospital described him as a "a likeable rogue who
had no chance of survival in the outside world."

So long as psychiatrists control the definition of what constitutes a
home for the mental patient, it is absurd to speak of psychiatric reforms. Consider the situation into which Forster was placed:

> One psychiatric nurse who had cared for him said last week: "For 30-odd
> years Rodney had been totally protected. He only had to get out of bed in the
> morning, eat three meals, and get back into bed again." . . . Forster had en-
> joyed his protected life there—with regular excursions to a betting shop and
> a summer holiday with fellow patients . . . and he was anxious not to lose
> contact with the friends he regarded as his family.

The forcible eviction of desocialized patients from mental hospitals is
a moral scandal on par with the forcible involuntary mental hospitalization of persons who are not desocialized. The responsibility for both
rests squarely on the shoulders of psychiatrists.

---

* Although my source for this vignette is the London *Sunday Times,* this tragedy could
just as well have happened in the United States.

"I Will Make You Take Me Back!"

How can a person evicted from a public mental hospital get readmitted? He cannot simply ask to be hospitalized. Ironically, that is the strategy most certain to fail.[62] On the other hand, the person who threatens to harm himself or others is virtually guaranteed admission. It should not surprise us, then, that many mental patients engage in precisely such behavior. Sometimes they declare that their motive is to be rehospitalized. Unwilling to admit that destructive or self-destructive behavior may be a rational and effective strategy, psychiatrists insist that the behavior is a symptom of the recurrence of the patient's mental illness, which justifies rehospitalizing him.

In his essay, "Arson: An Unforeseen Sequela of Deinstitutionalization," Jeffrey Geller describes several persons who deliberately set fires to prevent being discharged from the hospital or to secure readmission to it. He writes:

> A category of arson not described in earlier classification schemes has emerged: arson by consumers of public sector mental health services who want to communicate a wish and/or a need for a change in the location of these services. Fires may be set to return to a state hospital, to preclude placement from the hospital to a "less restrictive" setting, or to express dissatisfaction with one's current locus of services. [One of the patients stated that] she had set the fire to get into the hospital . . . . She had previously used fire setting to gain entry to the hospital.[63]

Another patient set fires repeatedly, the last time "after having been discharged to a community residence, [when] she set a fire to be reinstitutionalized." Nevertheless, Geller insists that these fires "are ascribable only to psychosis."[64] Although arson is one of the most dangerous crimes—Geller's fire-setters killed two people and injured several others—not a single one of the 13 arsonists whose cases he reports was convicted of a crime. Several were found not guilty by reason of insanity; others were declared incompetent to stand trial; in one case, the charges were dismissed.[65]

These stories exemplify one of the ways mental patients often succeed in turning the tables on psychiatrists. In the past, psychiatrists coerced individuals to be their involuntarily hospitalized patients. Today, mental patients coerce psychiatrists to be their involuntary doctors in hospitals to which the doctors do not want to admit them.[66] As usual, psychiatrists turn a blind eye to this spectacle as a power struggle for control, and define it instead as a medical struggle against mental disease.

Unfortunately, the professional mental patient has learned that the most effective method for gaining more than temporary housing in a mental hospital is by murdering someone:

> Daniel Thornton is a 34-year-old schizophrenic. . . . his case management broke down . . . [he] began to deteriorate. In desperation, his brother took him to San Francisco General Hospital, where he received more medication and was released. It didn't help. On December 1 [1985], Daniel stabbed a 75-year-old woman to death. He told police it was the only way he knew to get the psychiatric care he needed.[67]

Some would-be patients take a less violent and more direct route, holding up psychiatrists at gunpoint, demanding not money but mad-housing. In Miami, "A man with a shotgun took a doctor and two patients hostage in the psychiatric ward of a veteran's hospital." A medical center official promptly declared that there was "no motive for the incident." This claim was contradicted by a bystander, who told the press: "He [the gunman] said to the doctor: 'I'm going to get into the hospital, one way or another,' and the doctor says, 'You've got it.'"[68]

Journalists call such crimes "bizarre." Psychiatrists claim that defendants accused of such crimes are not responsible for their behavior, juries acquit them as not guilty by reason of insanity, and judges order them housed in psychiatric facilities. The public—secure in the knowledge that never before in history have mental patients received such enlightened and effective treatment—basks in the warm glow of rectitude that accompanies the conviction of doing good while being right.

11

THE FUTILITY OF PSYCHIATRIC REFORM

I wished to warn the people against the greatest of all evils—a blind and furious spirit of innovation, under the name of reform. . . . I hoped to see the surest of all reforms, perhaps the only sure reform— the ceasing to do ill.

—*Edmund Burke*[1]

Ever since individuals deemed to be insane were first incarcerated in madhouses, each new method of coercing them—from replacing chains with commitment laws, or exchanging camisoles for chemicals—has been romanticized as a reform and defined as a "patient liberation." Indeed, one of the most ironic features of psychiatric history is that the greatest oppressors of the mental patient—Philippe Pinel, Eugen Bleuler, Karl Menninger—are officially venerated as their most compassionate champions.[2] In their zeal to diagnose and doctor madness, psychiatrists have tried everything except eschewing coercion and treating the patient as a responsible person.

DEINSTITUTIONALIZATION: ITS MYTHIC HISTORY

Since the 1950s, hundreds of thousands of mental patients have been discharged from the hospitals that had been their homes. Many more, who formerly would have been committed, reside in institutions not formally designated as mental hospitals. The story of this transformation, called "deinstitutionalization," is already a part of the mythic social history of America, the truth about it recast as a crusade to liberate the mentally ill, much as the truth about the Civil War was recast as a crusade to liberate the slaves.

The Policy of Drugging and Deinstitutionalization

According to the psychiatrically correct version of the history of deinstitutionalization, as the decade of the 1950s drew to an end, psychiatrists realized that mental illness is like any other illness, that state hospitals are antitherapeutic institutions, and that the new antipsychotic drugs controlled the symptoms of serious mental illnesses. Accordingly, psychiatrists discharged large numbers of mental hospital patients from the asylums and discouraged the admission of new patients. As legend has it, mental patients were "freed from the confines of large state hospitals and released instead to small neighborhood programs."[3]

The falsification of the history of deinstitutionalization is thus embedded in the very language in which it is told. Psychiatrists did not "discharge" their patients. They evicted them from the only homes they had. I should add here that a person housed in a public mental hospital has, of course, no property rights to the dwelling in which he resides. I use the term *evict* because most chronic mental patients begin their psychiatric careers involuntarily, by being committed, and then often become voluntary squatters. We must keep in mind that after psychiatry passed through its brief, initial phase as the private trade in lunacy, it became a form of de facto poor relief disguised as the care and treatment of the mentally ill. Actually, the real function of the public insane asylum was to house and feed individuals unable or unwilling to support themselves. Unlike poor relief proper, which began as outdoor relief, "psychiatric poor relief" began as indoor relief, and for the better part of three hundred years continued to be limited to it. Since the 1960s, a huge new apparatus of psychiatric outdoor relief has supplemented a slightly reduced investment in the traditional indoor relief of mental patients.

The justifications for incarcerating and decarcerating mental patients are mirror images of one another. The rationale for institutionalization is that the patient is so seriously ill he requires hospital treatment; his objection to hospitalization proves how sick he is and justifies confining him against his will. The rationale for deinstitutionalization is that protracted residence in the state mental hospital is so deleterious to the patient's welfare he must be released to the community; his objection to being discharged proves how sick he is and justifies drugging him against his will outside the hospital.

It is not possible to understand the ugliness of the policy of drugging and deinstitutionalization unless we recognize that, once more in the history of psychiatry, it is something psychiatrists have done to involuntary mental patients. In the past, psychiatrists used their power to imprison individuals in mental hospitals for life. Now they use their power to drug patients for life.

HELPFUL DRUGS, HARMFUL CRITICS

In the spring of 1954 I was drafted into the Navy and assigned to the Bethesda Naval Medical Center. The move to Bethesda and my subsequent appointment in Syracuse afforded me a welcome opportunity to disengage myself from the Chicago Institute for Psychoanalysis and the full-time practice of psychoanalysis, and devote myself, at least part time, to undertaking a systematic critique of the principles and practices of psychiatry. By coincidence, I began to publish my critique of psychiatry at about the same time that American psychiatry embraced drugs and deinstitutionalization.

During the years immediately following the war, psychiatry was an odd couple, one partner warehousing impoverished nonproducers in snake pits, the other giving dynamic psychotherapy to successful producers in his private office. Drugs and deinstitutionalization rescued this absurd combination of somatic therapy in the hospital and psychotherapy in the office by transforming both into a homogenized biological-coercive psychiatry-plus-talk-therapy.[4] Although the old pillars of civil commitment and the insanity defense continued to support the new psychiatry as well, routine drug treatment in and out of the mental hospital together with outpatient commitment were added to shore up the weakening infrastructure.

The usual half-life of a psychiatric revolution is about one generation, the period required for the cures fueling false therapeutic claims to be unmasked as worthless or harmful. Insulin shock and lobotomy rose and fell in less time than that. As the 1980s drew to a close, disenchantment with deinstitutionalization (but not yet with antipsychotic drugs) set in, critics denouncing the dumping of the homeless mentally ill on the streets. Neuroleptic drugs and psychiatric enlightenment were credited for the alleged benefits of deinstitutionalization, while I and the antipsychiatry movement were blamed for its baneful consequences.

"The Man who Brought You Deinstitutionalization"

By disjoining the dubious benefits of new psychiatric treatments from the demonstrable harms they cause, psychiatrists have always managed to enjoy an astonishing lack of blame for their blunders. The reason for this is that psychiatry's most harmful practices have been the most helpful for the society it serves. Social critics have thus dealt gingerly with the disasters that were the predictable products of psychiatry's vaunted therapeutic triumphs, as if holding psychiatrists responsible for harming their involuntary patients would be tantamount to society holding itself responsible for injuring its most helpless members. The snake pits were blamed on public indifference and insufficient funding. Lobotomy was dismissed as a tragic but honest medical mistake. Deinstitutionalization is attributed to my malign influence.

The fact that I value responsibility and liberty more highly than mental health is proof enough of my guilt. In the words of Rael Jean Isaac and Virginia C. Armat, the authors of *Madness in the Streets*, "But for all his emphasis on the alleged brutality of psychiatry, it is Szasz's ideology that is truly inhumane."[5] Psychiatrists and the media succeeded in persuading many people that deinstitutionalization was my idea and that I had the influence to implement it. "If ever there was anyone who almost single-handedly was responsible for the current mess involving the homeless mentally ill," writes Mary D. Bublis, M.D., "Szasz—with his 'urgings' to 'empty the state hospitals' back in the 60's and 70's—could be that person."[6]

Although I am persona non grata in psychiatry, and although coercive psychiatric practices are now more popular than ever, Isaac and Armat lay the blame for deinstitutionalization squarely at my feet and call its cruel consequences "The Triumph of Thomas Szasz."[7] Their thesis is that, persuaded by *Law, Liberty, and Psychiatry*, "the mental health bar has substantially realized the vision of Thomas Szasz." As evidence, they point out that the law has made "dangerous acts the sine qua none for commitment."[8] This policy—which is contrary to my view that involuntary mental hospitalization ought to be abolished and that criminals ought to be punished by the criminal justice system—supports my contention that involuntary mental hospitalization is social control, not medical treatment. Milton Rosenbaum, formerly chairman of psychiatry at the Albert Einstein Medical Center in New York, agrees: "Prior to the Mental Health Act of 1963, critics of the system claimed its covert function was social control. Ironically, today's emphasis on dangerousness makes the criticism a reality."[9]

Perhaps Isaac and Armat misrepresent my views the better to buttress their enthusiasm for psychiatric coercions. "Our laws," Isaac complains, "make it impossible to treat the mentally ill against their will . . . in mental illness the diseased organ is the brain."[10] In neurological illness, such as epilepsy and Parkinsonism, the diseased organ is also the brain, but that does not justify treating patients suffering from these disease against their will.[11] Isaac and Armat conclude with this slander: "The counterculture denied the very existence of mental illness. . . . [as] formulated in the prolific writings of psychiatrist Thomas Szasz. . . . The anti-psychiatry movement that shut state hospitals created an inhumane world on the streets."[12] Bracketing me with the counterculture implies that I endorse licentious behavior. I advocate self-discipline, respect for others, and accepting responsibility for one's own behavior.[13]

In 1988, when *Contemporary Psychology* reviewed my book, *Insanity*, the review was titled: "From the Man Who Brought You Deinstitutionalization." The reviewer, John Monahan, a professor of law, wrote:

> The crux of Szasz's philosophic position is that psychiatric and psychological practice should be based not on what he derisively refers to as "coercive paternalism," but on the more lofty "principle of free contract." The problem he seems unable to recognize is that this ideological preference is fundamentally at odds with the social preferences that have shaped our public policy for the past 50 years. Freedom of contract has been in decline.[14]

It is easier to declare that freedom of contract has been in decline (which is true) than to show that the behaviors called "mental illnesses" are brain diseases or that individuals called "mental patients" are not moral agents (which are falsehoods). Moreover, although I carefully distinguish between voluntary and involuntary psychiatric interventions, Monahan disregards this fundamental distinction and dismisses my views with the conclusion: "'Szaszian' has become an adjective that connotes lack of subtlety in thought and an excess of polemics in argument."[15]

The success of the psychiatric loyalists' efforts to blame me for the deleterious consequences of deinstitutionalization is illustrated by the fact that even conservative writers—for example, Roger Scruton, Professor of Aesthetics at Birkbeck College in London and editor of the *Salisbury Review*—"credit" me for this policy. Scruton writes: "It is worth pointing out that the thinking represented by Szasz has been so successful that US law has been revised so as to forbid compulsory hospitalization of the insane. The chaotic and disturbing result of this change can be witnessed in every major American city."[16] Scruton's misconceptions also mirror the success of the carefully cultivated psychiatric canard that involuntary mental hospitalization has become so rare as to be irrelevant. Actually, more people are now committed to mental hospitals than ever before in

American history.[17] But the patients are allowed to stay in the hospital only for a short time, and are evicted as soon as they show any sign of adapting to their new environment. "I felt sick inside," a state hospital psychologist tells a reporter, "because I knew that as soon as he [the committed patient] demonstrated even the slightest sign of improvement, we'd be forced to send him back out to the street."[18] Then the cycle of hospitalization and discharge is repeated, over and over again, depriving the mental patient of a stable environment both within and without the insane asylum.

STILL, THE CURE IS COERCION*

While the media celebrates the discovery of the chemical causes and cures of mental illnesses, psychiatrists and their allies are preoccupied with the politics of housing the chronic mental patient. On the face of it, housing people does not seem to be a medical procedure. Nor would it be accepted as a treatment unless it were tacitly understood that, in a psychiatric context, housing means incarceration. An editorial in the *New York Times*, titled "How to house the mentally ill," explains:

> Across the nation, the mentally ill living on the streets number in the hundreds of thousands. Many of them fear the public shelters now available but are too dysfunctional to take advantage of new cheap housing on their own. Mental health workers know how to get them off the street. . . . New York City now operates an outreach program empowered to hospitalize the homeless mentally ill, *even against their will.*[19]

Disenchantment with deinstitutionalization has prompted psychiatrists to renew their attack on their old foe, freedom. After criticizing my views, Paul Applebaum, an authority on legal psychiatry, states: "That freedom *per se* will not cure mental illness is evident from the abject condition of so many of the deinstitutionalized."[20] Applebaum's assertion that freedom does not cure mental illness illustrates the cynicism with which he treats psychiatry's cardinal claim that mental illness is an illness. Freedom does not cure cancer or heart disease. Why, then, should we expect it to cure mental illness? Because if freedom does not cure

---

* Although there is no evidence that Galileo ever said *"E pur si muove"* ("Still, it moves"), the phrase has become famous as his alleged rejoinder to the Inquisition.

mental illness, then we can use that fact to justify coercive psychiatric drugging and deinstitutionalization. Declares Applebaum:

> [We need] greater authority for the state to detain and treat the severely mentally ill for their own benefit, even if they pose no immediate threat to their lives or those of others. . . . Our intervention, though depriving them of the right to autonomy in the short term, may enhance that quality in the long run. In such circumstances, benevolence and autonomy are no longer antagonistic principles.[21]

Richard Lamb, a prominent advocate for the coercive psychiatric treatment of the homeless, takes this argument a step further. He maintains that certain mental patients have a right to be deprived of their rights:

> Many homeless mentally ill persons will not accept services even with assertive outreach case management. . . . if homeless persons with major mental illnesses are incompetent to make decisions with regard to accepting treatment . . . then outreach teams including psychiatrists should bring all of these patients to hospitals, involuntarily if need be. . . . these persons have *a right to involuntary treatment.* . . . A very important right that I believe needs to be recognized.[22]

Rediscovering the Psychiatric Plantation

Along with psychiatrists, conservative and liberal social observers alike have also rediscovered the charms of the old psychiatric plantations. James Q. Wilson declares: "Take back the streets. Begin by reinstitutionalizing the mentally ill."[23] Charles Krauthammer agrees: "Getting the homeless mentally ill off the streets is an exercise in morality, not aesthetics. . . . Most of the homeless mentally ill . . . are grateful for a safe and warm hospital bed."[24] But if they are grateful, why do they have to be coerced? Remarking on the plight of the "solitary homeless persons who live on the streets," George Will opines: "Most are mentally ill." How does he know? He knows, because "many were in institutions."[25] Marvin Olasky, a professor of journalism, also recommends resurrecting the state hospital system. He writes:

> We need to move from sentimentality to clear thinking about the problem of the mentally ill . . . [who] are on the streets because of the astoundingly sentimental deinstitutionalization movement that swept through state mental hospitals during the mixed-up days of the 1960s, when some had faith that the insane were really sane and vice versa.[26]

Olasky's statement is plainly wrong. If the sane had been considered insane, then they would have been treated as such. So eager is Olasky to ignore the vexing problem of psychiatric coercion that he concludes:

> The solution to this problem [of the homeless mentally ill] only seems diffi-
> cult because of an [sic] pervasive unwillingness to categorize. But it is clear
> to anyone who walks the streets that the insane homeless who are unable to
> help themselves desperately need asylum, both in the current meaning of
> the word and in its original meaning of safety.[27]

Originally, the term *asylum* denoted a safe haven for individuals seek-ing protection from their adversaries. After the asylum became the in-sane asylum, it turned into an institution in which the inmates were incarcerated by their adversaries, in the name of helping them. The new meaning of the term is thus the exact opposite of the old meaning. It is simply impossible to combine or reconcile these two meanings of the word. Moreover, mental hospitals are notoriously unsafe places, for pa-tients and staff alike. Finally, Olasky's assertion that our problem re-garding the mentally ill is our "pervasive unwillingness to categorize" is nothing less than an Orwellian inversion of the language of psychiatry.

The views I have cited are supported by many of the foremost medical scientists in the United States. In *Late Night Thoughts on Listening to Mahler*, Lewis Thomas tells us that listening to Mahler late at night makes him think of the comforts of the state hospital—for the Other:

> But now it is becoming plain that life in the state hospitals, bad as it was, was
> better than life in the subways or in the doorways of downtown streets, late
> on cold nights with nothing in the shopping bag to keep body warm, and no
> protection at all against molestation by predators or the sudden urge to self-
> destruction. . . . We should restore the state hospital system, improve it,
> expand it if necessary, and spend enough money to ensure that the patients
> who must live in these institutions will be able to come in off the streets.[28]

Thomas is unwilling to see that the psychiatrists are themselves preda-tors. After all, it is they who coerce the patients.

PSYCHIATRY: WHEN CHANGE IS SYNONYMOUS WITH REFORM

In Shakespeare's world, there was no psychiatric coercion.[29] In ours, it is the preferred technique of social control. To understand how we got from there to here, let us take a glimpse at the history of psychiatry *as* the history of so-called reforms.

The Cyclical Character of Psychiatric Abuses and Reforms

The history of psychiatry, unlike the history of medicine, exhibits a distinctive pattern of cycles of patient abuse and institutional reform. Each cycle is characterized by the psychiatrist's staunch claim that he is a genuine medical healer, that his involuntary subjects are sick patients, that the buildings in which the subjects are imprisoned are hospitals, and that the inmates' detention and subjection constitute medical treatments.

The cycles begin with the confinement of the insane in private madhouses. Soon, their proprietors are accused of incarcerating sane persons. The abuse is attributed to the profit motive. The solution is the public madhouse system, managed by physicians on the public payroll, supervised by authorities accountable to the public.

Once established, the public mental hospital system turns out to be a method for warehousing society's undesirables. Its managers and staff are even more corrupt and sadistic than the keepers of private madhouses had been. The problem is attributed to insufficient funding and inadequate doctors. The solution is spending more money on psychiatry and more time on training psychiatrists.

Meanwhile, mental hospitals multiply and flourish. Psychiatrists claim therapeutic success for one new intervention after another. Mental patients are subjected to bleeding, cupping, tranquilizing chairs, ice-cold showers, threats of drowning, and other sadistic measures. After a few decades, the treatments are rejected as useless or harmful.[30]

Toward the end of the nineteenth century, genetic explanations of diseases become fashionable. Psychiatrists declare that earlier therapeutic enthusiasms were naive and misplaced. Insanity is an incurable, hereditary disease. Once a person is insane, he is destined to remain so for the rest of his life. The prominent psychiatrists of this era, exemplified by Emil Kraepelin, do not pretend to cure their patients. Instead, they model themselves after the pioneering pathologists who studied cadavers and classified diseases.* In short, the great state hospital psychiatrists were nosologists. They studied living corpses, called chronic mental patients, and classified their alleged diseases, creating mythological entities such as dementia praecox, manic-depressive illness, paranoia, and schizophrenia. Almost a century ago, psychiatry's most celebrated madman, Judge Paul Schreber, faulted his psychiatrist, the famous German psychiatrist Paul Flechsig, for focusing on diseases

---

* Adolf Meyer, the man who brought scientific psychiatry to the United States, was a Swiss pathologist.

rather than persons. In his *Memoirs,* Schreber wrote: "[Flechsig] *did not understand the living human being* and had no need to understand him, because . . . he dealt only with corpses."[31]

During the nineteenth century, society opened a second front in its war against mental illness. Psychiatrists and jurists joined forces and expanded the hitherto limited scope of civil commitment and the insanity defense. Coerced psychiatric examinations and psychological testing were introduced into every nook and cranny of the social fabric, from schools to divorce courts. The closer the alliance of psychiatry with the law and with education grew, the more indispensable coerced psychiatric interventions seemed to become.[32]

After World War I, medical scientists made rapid advances in controlling infectious and metabolic diseases, notably the contagious diseases of childhood and diabetes. Psychiatrists imitated these discoveries by introducing into the practice of psychiatry so-called somatic treatments, such as insulin coma, convulsions caused by metrazol and electricity, and lobotomy.

And so we arrive at the present scene, drugs and deinstitutionalization. Once again, politicians and psychiatrists clamor for mental health reforms. Now they claim that the patients are sicker than we thought they were; that mental illness makes them refuse to take the medications that make their maladies manageable; that the drugs previously hailed as having revolutionized the treatment of chronic mental illness are "ineffective or inadequate for as many as 60 to 80 percent of the patients";[33] that it was a mistake to give mental patients freedom, which they only abuse by not taking the drugs that keep them sane and law abiding. The reforms proposed are predictable: More money for mental health programs and for research on new psychiatric drugs; more legal and medical control of mental patients; more mental health education to teach the truth about mental illness.

Psychiatric Reform, Soviet Style

Fashionable rhetoric to the contrary notwithstanding, deinstitutionalization has nothing to do with drugs or civil rights. I have tried to show that just as ascribing mental illness and dangerousness to mental patients serves as a pretext for institutionalizing the patients, so attributing therapeutic efficacy to neuroleptic drugs and civil libertarian concerns to psychiatrists serves as a pretext for deinstitutionalizing them. The story of psychiatric reforms during the dissolution of the former Soviet Union further supports this interpretation.

In 1988, with the stroke of a pen, Soviet politicians removed "2 million people from the government's list of mental patients as part of the reforms intended to prevent psychiatric abuse of healthy people."[34] For a moment at least, Communist psychiatrists acknowledged what no capitalist psychiatrist would ever admit, namely, that they knowingly incarcerated sane people in insane asylums: "M. M. Kabanov, a Leningrad psychiatrist, acknowledged that in the past some doctors decided to send people to institutions, for instance for reading Bulgakov's works or for reading Pasternak's verses and poems. Such mistakes will not be repeated."[35] Unfortunately, what Kabanov calls "mistakes" were not mistakes at all. They were the results of Soviet psychiatrists' implementing formerly politically correct psychiatric policies, according to which that kind of deviant behavior could legitimately be diagnosed as a mental illness justifying commitment. Similarly, deinstitutionalization is neither a medical triumph nor a medical failure, but simply the result of American psychiatrists' implementing presently prevailing politically correct psychiatric policies, according to which chronic mental patients properly numbed with neuroleptic drugs can be legitimately discharged from mental hospitals.

Nomen Est Omen

The futility of psychiatric reforms is inherent in the key terms of the psychiatric vocabulary. The language of mental illness makes us search for the etiology of this putative disease, which we duly discover in some trendy cause, such as heredity, masturbation, the schizophrenogenic mother, child abuse, a metabolic or neurochemical defect—each seemingly true, only to prove false. This language also makes us search for the treatment of this dread disease, which we duly discover in some fashionable cure, such as sterilizing the eugenically unfit, antimasturbatory measures, psychoanalysis, chemical and electrical seizures, brain operations, family therapy, neuroleptic drugs—each seemingly effective, only to prove worthless or harmful. Finally, the language of mental illness makes us search for the proper place in which to store the mental patient, which we duly discover to be the private madhouse, the state mental hospital, the community mental health center, the general hospital, the halfway house—each hailed as the most humane and therapeutically effective setting for the purpose, only to be soon discredited as inappropriate and harmful.

Nevertheless, psychiatry and the media continue to bedazzle a public eager to believe in the impersonal nature and miraculous cures of mental illness. For more than two hundred years, the scenario conveying this theme has remained constant, with appropriate modernizations of the actors' lines. It is a story of the imprisoned patient's coerced validation of himself as a mentally ill patient, of those who imprison him as physicians, and of his prison as a hospital. In the past, the patient had to play his part by submitting to insulin shock, electroshock, and lobotomy. Today, he must play it by ingesting toxic chemicals called "antipsychotic drug treatment," participating in periodic meetings called "group therapy," or going through the hoops of some other performance scripted by the psychiatrists. The observer sees people called "patients" ingesting antipsychotic drugs and participating in group therapy, and is misled into believing that he is witnessing the cure of the sick. In fact, he is witnessing a medical-social ritual, the providers of homes for the homeless disguising the banality of their enterprise as proof of the powers of psychiatry.

CIVIL LAW AS AN INSTRUMENT OF IMPRISONMENT

Among the values that animated eighteenth- and nineteenth-century English society, the sanctity of contract ranked near the top. This contractarian-individualist ideal, whose origins reach back to the Magna Carta, protected the individual from being defrauded by his neighbor and being despoiled by his sovereign, and promoted the production of goods and services, generating domestic peace and material prosperity. The resulting polity guaranteed the security of private property and the safety of personal liberty. The practice of imprisoning defaulting debtors arose and flourished in this soil.[36]

Among the values that animate American society today, health, especially mental health, ranks near the top. Most people believe not only that mental health is a requisite for happiness, but that only the mentally healthy can properly engage in the pursuit of happiness. Prevented by illness, especially mental illness, from engaging in this hunt, the sick person must receive professional help before he can become a fit pursuer of happiness. This therapeutic faith—which is actually a scientistic reincarnation of faith in salvation through grace—protects the modern, secularized individual from the dangers he fears most, namely, disease and death. The overidealization of health encourages clinical interventions and generates medical and psychiatric treatments. Coercive psychiatric practices arose and flourished in this soil.

In short, similar social expectations and legal mechanisms supported the confinement of debtors in prisons, epileptics in colonies, and mental patients in hospitals. Despite the crucial role of civil law procedures in depriving each of these classes of persons of liberty, historians of economics and psychiatry have downplayed or even ignored this element. I submit they have done so because intuitively they have

realized that, in the Anglo-American political system, civil law sanctions constitute a fundamentally inappropriate and unjust mechanism
for depriving individuals of liberty. In his encyclopedic review of English law, O. R. McGregor noted that "the history of debt and debtors
hardly even features in social or legal monographs."[37] I have documented the expunging of the epileptic colony from the history of psychiatry earlier in this volume.[38] Moreover, no psychiatric historian has
even noted the moral-political dilemmas inherent in the *civil* character
of the civil commitment process. I submit that the similarities between
the fictions used to confine debtors and commit mental patients highlight the fact that while these measures are indispensable for supporting the dominant ethic of the society of which they are a part, they also
reveal their inescapable incompatibility with the fundamental moral
premises of Anglo-American law.

Reform versus Abolition

The so-called mentally ill homeless person illustrates the problem the
chronic mental patient poses in and to American society today. The issue
is epitomized by the case of the legendary New York City bag lady, Joyce
Brown, a.k.a. Billie Boggs, who had camped in front of an upper East Side
ice cream shop, urinated and defecated on the street, and thus injured
nearby business proprietors and passersby in their property rights. Commenting on the Brown case, Carl Horowitz, a scholar at the Heritage
Foundation, begins by writing eloquently about the need to restore respect for property rights in contemporary American society. Blind to psychiatry's hostility to those very rights, he thus actually seeks the better
protection of our besieged property rights through greater reliance on
the use of psychiatric sanctions. Horowitz emphasizes that Brown's behavior was deliberately disruptive, describes how the city's mental health
bureaucracy "removed her from the street and placed her into a hospital
for her own safety," castigates the New York Civil Liberties Union and the
judge who heard her protest against psychiatric imprisonment for freeing
her, and then concludes: "The legal system granted more rights to a
demented derelict than to property-holding entrepreneurs harmed by
her."[39] This is wrong and wrong-headed. Joyce Brown was not demented;
she knew what she was doing and, as a reward for her exploits, was in-
vited to lecture at Harvard Law School. Also, Horowitz knows, or ought
to know, that Brown was not committed "for her own safety," but for the
benefit of the community; and he is mistaken in stating that Brown was
"granted rights." Our legal system does not grant adults a right to liberty,
because they already possess that right; it only revokes the right to liberty

(for certain offenses) or restores it (if the deprivation did not conform to due process).

I cite the Brown case because it illustrates our collective enthusiasm for avoiding the use of the criminal justice system as a means of controlling a large class of lawbreakers, many of whom commit crimes against both property and persons. In view of this, it is especially ironic that Horowitz ends his comments on the Brown case with this reminder: "As Ludwig von Mises recognized, where civil behavior cannot be defined or enforced, liberty and property are easily destroyed."[40] Precisely. But protecting liberty and property from those who disrespect or destroy them ought to be the task of judges, juries, and prison guards, not psychiatrists, psychologists, and social workers. And the means of enforcing such protection should be the criminal justice system, not the mental health system.

As we saw, the debtor's prison could not be reformed. It could only be abolished. Similarly, coercive psychiatry cannot be reformed. Moreover, hardly anyone now wants to abolish it. People are so accustomed to subjecting others, and also themselves being subjected, to coercive psychiatric interventions that they cannot contemplate living without such meddling. Abandoning the illusory safety net of psychiatric sanctions would, indeed, require difficult personal and social readjustments.

The mental hospital system endures because it fulfills important personal and social needs. It segregates and supports adult dependents—who embarrass, burden, and disturb their families and the community. It incarcerates and incapacitates troublesome lawbreakers—who embarrass, burden, and disturb the judicial and penal systems. And, most importantly, it performs these functions by means of civil law sanctions—in a manner that pleases and pacifies the consciences of politicians, professionals, and the majority of the people. Hence, not only is there is no popular interest in abolishing involuntary psychiatric interventions, but, on the contrary, there is intense pressure—especially from the parents of mental patients, the judiciary, and the media—to reinforce the institution of psychiatry.

EPILOGUE

The dawning of all great truths on the consciousness of humanity has usually to pass—says Tolstoy—through three characteristic stages. The first is: "This is so foolish that it is not worth thinking about." "The second: "This is immoral and contrary to religion." The third: "Oh! This is so well known that it is not worth talking about."
                                                                    —*Michael Polanyi*[1]

Despite the mental health professional's passionate commitment to coercion, my critique of psychiatric power has apparently left a mark, at least on some psychiatrists of my generation.* In 1988, two years before his death, Karl Menninger—the psychiatrist who reigned supreme as the undisputed leader of his profession during the postwar years and whose views I systematically criticized in my writings—acknowledged that perhaps I was right, after all.[2] In a letter, Menninger wrote:

Dear Dr. Szasz:

I am holding your new book, *Insanity: The Idea and Its Consequences*, in my hands. I read parts of it yesterday and I have also read reviews of it. I think I know what it says but I did enjoy hearing it said again. I think I understand better what has disturbed you these years and, in fact, *it disturbs me, too, now*. We don't like the situation that prevails whereby a fellow human being

---
* Younger generations seem to have been spared the confrontation.

is put aside, outcast as it were, ignored, *labeled*, and said to be "sick in his mind.". . .[3]

In a language at once touching and melancholy, Menninger briefly reviewed the history of psychiatry, the tenor of his remarks illustrated by the following sentence: "Added to the beatings and chainings and baths and massages came treatments that were even more ferocious: gouging out parts of the brain, producing convulsions with electric shocks, starving, surgical removal of teeth, tonsils, uteri, etc."[4] Menninger graciously concluded:

Well, enough of those recollections of early days. You tried to get us to talk together and take another look at our material. I am sorry you and I have gotten *apparently* so far apart all these years. We might have enjoyed discussing our observations together. *You* tried; you wanted me to come there, I remember. I demurred. *Mea culpa.*[5]

From my reply, it is enough to cite here that I noted, also not without some sadness, that I long felt that our differences were irreconcilable:

because I realized that you wanted to hold on to the values of free will and responsibility and were struggling to reconcile them with psychiatry. For myself, I felt sure, long before I switched my residency from medicine to psychiatry, that this was impossible, that psychiatry was basically wrong. . . .[6]

Commenting on Menninger's letter, Ralph Slovenko, a professor of law and pupil of Menninger, writes:

For nearly thirty years psychiatrist Thomas Szasz has been the harshest critic of his own field. The publication of his book, *The Myth of Mental Illness,* in 1961, sparked debate over the nature of "mental illness." The impact of the book cannot be overstated. With it, the terms of our discussion about mental illness have been totally altered.[7]

My urgings that psychiatrists confront the legitimacy of their power have forced them to chew on a bone that got stuck in their throat. They can neither swallow it, that is, acknowledge that they are the only medical specialists whose practice rests on coercion; nor can they spit it out, that is, repudiate the use of psychiatric coercions. Fortunately, the force of my argument was not lost on nonpsychiatrists. "Whenever I tease psychiatrists about their . . . inability to answer charges that mental illness is a myth," writes John Harris, professor of philosophy at the

University of Manchester, "they always answer by showing me really distressed, unhappy people who need help which no other branch of medicine is offering. If this is a convincing answer, it is not so on the level of theory."[8]

RETHINKING THE JUSTIFICATION FOR DEPRIVING INDIVIDUALS OF LIBERTY

In the course of the nineteenth century, the English people realized that they could no longer postpone reconciling their political priorities with the practice of imprisoning delinquent debtors.* Their dilemma lay in the fact that some imprisoned debtors were paupers, whose creditors stood to gain nothing financially from their indefinite detention; while others were prosperous, owning assets that could have been used to satisfy the legitimate demands of the defrauded creditors. It was clear that justice could be better served than by indiscriminately depriving debtors of liberty while letting propertied debtors foil their creditors. The debtor, qua debtor, was restored to liberty, allowed to resume a productive existence, and enabled to repay some of his indebtedness. Some debtors continued to be punished, not by their creditors by means of civil law for insolvency, but by the state by means of the criminal law for fraud. The debtor's prison disappeared and was replaced by bankruptcy laws.

I believe we are on the threshold of a similar situation with respect to the incarceration of persons qua mental patients. Before long, we shall have to reconcile our political priorities with certain embarrassing facts about this practice. Our dilemma is that some mental patients are criminals, who should be punished for their offenses by the criminal law, instead of being civilly sentenced to involuntary treatment for nonexistent diseases.† Most mental patients are innocent of lawbreaking and hence entitled to protection from coercive psychiatric interference in their lives. Were the problem of involuntary mental hospitalization reframed in such terms, mental illness qua (mental) illness would no longer justify depriving a person of liberty in a mental hospital, just as in England after 1869 unsatisfied debt qua debt no longer justified loss of liberty in a debtor's prison. Instead of trying to reform debtor's

---

* I return here to a theme I discuss more fully in Chapter 2.
† The typical homeless mental patient, whose story makes the newspapers, deprives others of their rights, for example, by assault or interference with their businesses.

prisons, the English people reformed their attitudes toward those confined in them, treating the formerly imprisoned debtor as a person first, and as a delinquent debtor second. Similarly, instead of trying to reform commitment laws and mental hospitals, we ought to reform our attitudes toward individuals presently subjected to coercive psychiatric interventions, viewing the subject as a person first, and as a mental patient second.

To replace debtor's prisons with bankruptcy procedures, people had to accept that imprisoning the debtor is counterproductive, because it prevents him from working and thus repaying at least some of his debts; and they had to conclude that the relationship between unsatisfied creditor and insolvent debtor could be better regulated by means of bankruptcy procedures than by the use of debtor's prisons. Unfortunately, while the abolition of debtor's prisons eliminated the evils associated with depriving debtors of liberty by means of the civil law, declaring bankruptcy became the economic equivalent of a successful plea of temporary insanity. Both the debtor who defaults and the defendant who pleads insanity is—prima facie, de facto—guilty of injuring others. Hence, in my opinion, each ought to be accused of the particular offense he has committed and punished by means of criminal law sanctions—mildly or severely, depending on the circumstances.

Replacing the practice of committing persons as mental patients with the practice of treating them as responsible persons would require a similar metamorphosis of professional and popular opinion. People would have to accept that involuntary mental hospitalization is counterproductive, because it deprives the subject of dignity and liberty, excuses him from responsibility for his behavior, and prevents him from learning by suffering the consequences of his selfish or unwise actions; and they would have to conclude that the relationship between sane family members and their insane relatives—or between the state and certain rule violators—could be better regulated by means of regular criminal and civil law sanctions than by special mental health law procedures. Only then could the practice of involuntarily hospitalizing persons qua mental patients be abolished.

If civil commitment were abolished, mental hospitals as we know them would disappear. Regardless of their psychiatric diagnosis, persons who break the law would have to be accused of a crime, tried, and, if found guilty, punished in the criminal justice system; whereas persons innocent of crime would have to be left unmolested by the legal and psychiatric systems. Only then would mental illness be destigmatized and psychiatrists resemble regular physicians whose practice is limited to treating voluntary patients.

The Challenge: Care without Coercion

Whether we admit it or not, we have a choice between caring for others by coercing them and caring for them only with their consent. At the mo- ✘ ment, care without coercion—when the ostensible beneficiary's problem is defined as mental illness—is not an acceptable option in profession-ally correct deliberations on mental health policy. The conventional ex-planation for shutting out this option is that the mental patient suffers from a brain disease that annuls his capacity for rational cooperation. My explanation, which I tried to articulate and support in this volume, is that, because it makes us feel noble, we would rather pity the Other as a patient than respect him as a person. Our inability to place respect above compassion calls to mind Hayek's discerning warning about our fear of freedom: "Freedom granted only when it is known beforehand that its effects will be beneficial is not freedom . . . . Our faith in freedom does not rest on the foreseeable results in particular circumstances, but on the belief that it will, on balance, release more forces for the good than for the bad."[9]

It is dishonest to pretend that caring coercively for the mentally ill invariably helps him, and that abstaining from such coercion is tanta-mount to "withholding treatment" from him. Every social policy en-tails benefits as well as harms. Although our ideas about benefits and harms vary from time to time, all history teaches us to beware of bene-factors who deprive their beneficiaries of liberty. ✘

REFERENCES

Complete references for books are listed in the Bibliography.

EPIGRAPH

1. Shakespeare, W. *Hamlet,* Act 3, Scene 4, lines 179–180.

PREFACE

1. Burke, E. "Speech on conciliation with America" [1775], in Burke, E. *The Political Philosophy of Edmund Burke,* 114.
2. In this connection, see Becker, G. S. *A Treatise on the Family,* especially 8–9.
3. Augustine, St. "Letters XCIII, 5–10," in *The Political Writings of St. Augustine,* 193–194. In this connection, see also Smith, G. H., *Atheism, Ayn Rand, and Other Heresies.*
4. Ibid., 202–203.
5. For the failure of "economic compassion," see Lee, D. R. and R. B. McKenzie, *Failure and Progress.*
6. Stephen, Sir J. F. "Doing good" [1859], in *Liberty, Equality, Fraternity,* 302–303.
7. I touch on the problem of coercive paternalism outside the family throughout this book, especially in Chapters 4, 7, and 8.

INTRODUCTION

1. Orwell, G. *Down and Out in Paris and London,* 251–252.
2. For a compelling analysis of the political dimensions of this phenomenon, see Minogue, K. *The Liberal Mind* and *Alien Powers.*

3. Hale, Sir M. Quoted in Bartlett, J. *Familiar Quotations,* 1039.

4. Aristotle. *Nicomachean Ethics,* in *The Basic Works of Aristotle,* 957, 1109.

5. Arendt, H. "On humanity in dark times: Thoughts about Lessing" (1959), in Arendt, H. *Men in Dark Times,* 15.

6. Arendt, H. *On Revolution,* 80.

7. Ibid., 85.

8. Rousseau, J. J. Quoted in Arendt, H. *On Revolution,* 73.

9. See Szasz, T. S. "Mental illness and mental incompetence," in *A Lexicon of Lunacy,* 111–126.

10. Olivecrona, H. Quoted in Swazey, J. "Egas Moniz," in Gillespie, C. C., ed. *Dictionary of Scientific Biography,* Vol. 4, 286–287.

11. In this connection, see Ryn, C. G. *The New Jacobinism,* especially 94.

12. The only group of persons we acknowledge to be unwanted are unborn children or neonates. According to Dr. Jocelyn Elders, director of the Arkansas Department of Health and President Clinton's nominee for Surgeon General, "60 percent of American children are 'unplanned and unwanted.'" Quoted in Brown, F. J. "Life and death in Arkansas." *National Review* (April 26, 1993): 38–41, 40. See also Chapter 4.

13. Lewis, C. S. "The humanitarian theory of punishment" [1949], in Lewis, C. S. *God in the Dock,* 287–294; 292–293. See also Szasz, T. S. "Justice in the Therapeutic State" [1970], in *The Theology of Medicine,* 118–133.

14. Shakespeare, W. *Timon of Athens,* Act 1, Scene 1, line 108.

15. See Hoffer, P. C. and N. E. H. Hull. *Murdering Mothers.*

16. See Szasz, T. S. *The Manufacture of Madness;* and Bayer, R. *Homosexuality and American Psychiatry.*

CHAPTER 1: THE IDIGENT

1. Smith, A. *The Wealth of Nations,* 245.

2. Matthew 26:11.

3. Godfrey, W. H. *The English Almshouse,* 15.

4. Ibid., 16. My main focus in this chapter is the history of poor relief in England.

5. Salgado, G. *Cony-Catchers and Bawdy Baskets,* 9, 10. For a similarly nearly endless list of names for mental patients, see Szasz, T. S. *A Lexicon of Lunacy.*

6. Beier, A. L., *Masterless Men,* 9.

7. Little, D., *Religion, Order, and Law,* 212.

8. Coke, Sir E. Quoted in ibid., 210–211.

9. Little, D. Ibid., 211.

10. MacPherson, C. B. *The Political Theory of Possessive Individualism,* 286–287.

11. Bulwer, E. L. *England and the English,* 124. In this connection, see also Lightning, R. H. *Ealing and the Poor.*

12. Jones, K. *A History of the Mental Health Services,* 21.

13. Ibid., 26.

14. "Poor Law," *Encyclopaedia Britannica*, 14th ed., Vol. 18, 226–232, 229.

15. Himmelfarb, G. *The Idea of Poverty*, 76.

16. Toynbee, A. Quoted in ibid., 77.

17. Asked what accounts for the high incidence of mental illness in the United States, an Iranian physician ranked first "the concept of freedom." Hakimi, J. "A foreign psychiatrist looks at American psychopathology." *Resident and Staff Physician*, April 1970, 131–139, 131.

18. Franklin, B. Quoted in Himmelfarb, G. *The Idea of Poverty*, 5.

19. See Macfarlane, A. *The Origins of English Individualism*, 168; and Webber, C. and A. Wildavsky. *A History of Taxation and Expenditure in the Western World*, 234.

20. The phrase is Alfred Marshall's; see Marshall, A. Quoted in Himmelfarb, G. *The Idea of Poverty*, 77.

21. Foucault, M. *Madness and Civilization*, 49.

22. Himmelfarb, G. *Poverty and Compassion*, 134.

23. Himmelfarb, G. *The Idea of Poverty*, 183.

24. Ibid., 186.

25. See Chapter 11.

26. Bentham, J. Quoted in Himmelfarb, G. *The Idea of Poverty*, 79.

27. Crowther, M. A. *The Workhouse System, 1834–1929*, 18.

28. Ibid., 523.

29. Bentham, J. Quoted in Himmelfarb, G. *The Idea of Poverty*, 81.

30. Tocqueville, A. de. Quoted in ibid., 151.

31. Crabbe, G. Quoted in ibid., 187.

32. Nicholls, G. Quoted in ibid., 4.

33. Himmelfarb, G. *The Idea of Poverty*, 32.

34. Smith, A. Quoted in Hont, I. and M. Ignatieff. "Needs and justice in the *Wealth of Nations*: An introductory essay," in Hont, I. and M. Ignatieff, eds. *Wealth and Virtue*, 1–44, 1.

35. Tocqueville, A. de. Quoted in Himmelfarb, G. *The Idea of Poverty*, 147.

36. Naylor, S. W. "One in 10 Americans now use food stamps." *Syracuse Herald-American*, March 21, 1993, A-11.

37. Rector, R. "America's poverty myth." *The Wall Street Journal*, September 3, 1992.

38. Tobias, A. "Now, the good news about your money." *Parade*, April 4, 1993, 4–5, 5.

39. Orwell, G. *Down and Out in Paris and London*.

40. See American Psychiatric Association, *DSM-III-R*.

41. Disraeli, B. Quoted in Himmelfarb, G. *The Idea of Poverty*, 182.

42. Himmelfarb, G. *The Idea of Poverty*, 166.
43. "Social Welfare," *Encyclopaedia Britannica*, 14th ed., Vol. 20, 772–782, 779.
44. See Goffman, E. *Asylums*.
45. Himmelfarb, G. *The Idea of Poverty*, 188.
46. Ibid., 187.
47. See Szasz, T. S. *Insanity*, 275–369.
48. Quoted in ibid., 179.
49. Ibid., 530.

CHAPTER 2: THE DEBTOR

1. Pound, R. *An Introduction to the Philosophy of Law*, 163.
2. Rossiter, C. Introduction, in *The Federalist Papers*, xv.
3. Hamilton, A. "No. 7: Hamilton," in ibid., 65.
4. Madison, J. "No. 44: Madison," in ibid., 282.
5. Pound, R. *An Introduction to the Philosophy of Law*, 161.
6. Bentham, J. *Defense of Usury*, 102–103.
7. Holdsworth, Sir W. *A History of English Law*, Vol. VIII, 230.
8. Exodus 22:25–27, in *The Holy Bible*. Revised Standard Version. Subsequent Biblical quotations are from this source.
9. Leviticus 25:35–37.
10. Deuteronomy 15:1–3 and 23:19–20.
11. Psalms 37:26 and 112:5; Proverbs 19:17.
12. Luke 6:35.
13. See Gross, J. *Shylock*; and Simpson, L. "There, they could say, is the Jew." *New York Times Book Review*, April 4, 1993, 7, 9.
14. Nelson, B. *The Idea of Usury*, 32.
15. Ibid., 43.
16. Calvin, J. Quoted in Bouwsma, W. J. *John Calvin*, 196.
17. Ibid., 198.
18. Nelson, B. *The Idea of Usury*, 76.
19. Bouwsma, J. *John Calvin*, 197.
20. Ibid., 96.
21. Calvin, J. Quoted in Nelson, B. *The Idea of Usury*, 76.
22. Johnson, P. "Blessing capitalism." *Commentary*, May 1993, 33–36, 34.
23. Ibid.
24. Penn, W. Quoted in Friedman, J. "Locke as politician." *Critical Review* 2 (1988): 64–101, 70.
25. See Little, D. *Religion, Order, and Law*, especially Chapter 3.
26. For a detailed account of this complicated story, see Atiyah, P. S. *The Rise and Fall of Freedom of Contract*.

27. Bentham, J. *Defense of Usury*, 1–2; emphasis added.

28. Holdsworth, Sir W. *A History of English Law*, Vol. VIII, 231.

29. Atiyah, P. S. *The Rise and Fall of Freedom of Contract*, 190.

30. Walker, R. *Some Objections Humbly Offered to the Consideration of the Hon. House of Commons*, 2. See also Anonymous, *The Unreasonableness and Ill Consequence of Imprisoning the Body for Debt*.

31. Ogg, D. *England in the Reigns of James II and William III*, 20, 23.

32. Neild, J. *An Account of the Rise, Progress, and Present State of the Society for the Discharge and Relief of Persons Imprisoned for Small Debts throughout England and Wales*, 599.

33. Johnson, S. *The Idler*, 6 January 1759, No. 38, in Johnson, S. *The Idler and the Adventurer*, 119.

34. Quoted in Haagen, P. H. "Eighteenth-century English society and the debt law," in Cohen, S. and A. Scull, eds. *Social Control and the State*, 227.

35. Quoted in Ogg, D. *England in the Reign of James II and William III*, 11. For my similar suggestion regarding mental patients, see Szasz, T. S. "Whither psychiatry?" [1966], in Szasz, T. S. *Ideology and Insanity*, 218–245.

36. Johnson, S. *The Idler*, 16 September 1758, No. 22, in Johnson, S. *The Idler and the Adventurer*, 70.

37. Ibid., 71.

38. McGregor, O. R. *Social History and the Law Reform*, 35–36.

39. Holdsworth, Sir W. *A History of English Law*, Vol. XI, 524.

40. "Prison Discipline," in *Encyclopaedia Britannica*, 8th ed., Vol. 18, 574–575.

41. Labaton, S. "Bankruptcy is better in America." *New York Times*, January 23, 1990.

42. Hertell, T. *Remarks on the Law of Imprisonment for Debt*, 10.

43. Ibid., 14, 24.

44. Ibid., 33.

45. Greenhouse, S. "Warsaw's economic plan: Prosperity as goal, with freedom to fail." *New York Times*, December 31, 1989; see also Brenner, R. "Don't frighten the East Bloc bureaucrats." *The Wall Street Journal*, December 26, 1989.

46. Labaton, S. "Bankruptcy is better in America." *New York Times*, January 23, 1990.

47. Resnick, R. "The deadbeat state." *Forbes*, July 8, 1991, 62; and Rohter, L. "Rich debtors find shelter under a populist Florida law." *New York Times*, July 25, 1993, 1, 26.

48. Lux, H. "Today's fast track: Bankruptcy." *New York Times*, August 7, 1990.

49. Smokers with lung cancer suing tobacco manufacturers and gamblers who lose money suing casinos are other examples. See also Frum, D. "Find the deep pocket." *Forbes*, March 29, 1993, 44–45.

50. Friday, C. and L. Reibstein. "Taking the banker to court: Burned borrowers charge 'lender liability.'" *Newsweek*, May 8, 1989, 44.

51. Ibid.

52. See Haagen, P. H. "Eighteenth-century English society and the debt law," in Cohen, S. and A. Scull, eds. *Social Control and the State,* 222.

CHAPTER 3: THE EPILEPTIC

1. Galton, Sir F. Quoted in Chase, A. "Hitler did not distort any of Galton's eugenic concepts . . . " *Medical Tribune,* March 15, 1978, 22, emphasis added.

2. See for example, Adams, R. D. and M. Victor. *Principles of Neurology,* 233–254; Dichter, M. A. "The epilepsies and convulsive disorders," in Braunwald, E. et al., eds. *Harrison's Principles of Internal Medicine,* Vol. 2, 1921–1930; Goldenson, E. S. et al. "Epilepsy," in Rowland, L. P., ed. *Merritt's Textbook of Neurology,* 629–650; Walton, J. *Brain's Diseases of the Nervous System,* 609–630; and Kaplan, H. I., A. M. Freedman, and B. J. Sadock, eds. *Comprehensive Textbook of Psychiatry/III.*

3. 66 Stat. 182, 8 U.S.C., par. 118[a] (1952). Also excludable were "psychopaths," a category that included homosexuals. See Szasz, T. S. *The Manufacture of Madness,* 245–259.

4. Matthew 17:14–18.

5. Lennox, W. G. *Epilepsy and Related Disorders,* Vol. 1, 34.

6. Reynolds, J. R. *Epilepsy.* Quoted in Hunter, R. and I. Macalpine, eds. *Three Hundred Years of Psychiatry,* 1047.

7. Maudsley, H. Quoted in Hill, D. "Historical Review," in Reynolds, E. H. and M. R. Trimble, eds. *Epilepsy and Psychiatry,* 1–11, 4.

8. See Szasz, T. S. *Insanity,* 240–242.

9. Maudsley, H. *Responsibility in Mental Disease,* 41.

10. Ibid., 156, 165.

11. See Temkin, O. *The Falling Sickness,* 366–367.

12. See Goodman, L. and A. Gilman. *The Pharmacological Basis of Therapeutics,* 155.

13. Deutsch, A. *The Mentally Ill in America,* 383.

14. Shanahan, W. T. "History of the establishment and development of the Craig Colony for Epileptics located at Sonyea, N.Y." *Epilepsia,* 3 (1911): 153–161. The origin of the name *Sonyea* is shrouded in mystery. The village is in what used to be Seneca country, and some claim it is an Indian name. But David B. Schwartz states that the colony came first and the village later, and that Sonyea stands for State of New York Epileptic Asylum. See Schwartz, D. B. *Crossing the River,* 77.

15. Shanahan, W. T. "History of the development of special institutions for epileptics in the United States." *Psychiatric Quarterly* 2 (1928): 422–434, 423, emphasis added.

16. Ibid., emphasis added.

17. Grant, R. "Special Centres," in Reynolds, E. H. and M. R. Trimble, eds. *Epilepsy and Psychiatry*, 347–355, 350.

18. Letchworth, W. P. *Care and Treatment of Epileptics*, 71, emphasis added.

19. Ibid., 20–21.

20. Bramwell, E. "The sane epileptic and the colony system." *Scottish Medical and Surgical Journal* 18 (1906): 331–337, 331.

21. Barr, M. W. "President's annual address." *Journal of Psycho-Asthenics* 2 (September, 1987): 5–13, 1897, 13.

22. Sprattling, W. E. "An ideal colony for epileptics." *Proceedings of the National Conference of Charities & Correction*, Annual Meetings, 1903, 259–271.

23. Johnson, A. "The segregation of defectives: Report of Committee on Colonies for segregation of defectives." *Proceedings of the National Conference of Charities & Correction*, Annual Meetings, 1903, 245–253; 246.

24. Ibid., 251, 253.

25. Galton, Sir F. Quoted in Chase, A. "Hitler did not distort any of Galton's eugenic concepts . . . " *Medical Tribune*, March 15, 1978, 22, emphasis added.

26. Galton, F. Quoted in Forrest, D. W. *Francis Galton*, 136.

27. Galton, F. *Memories of My Life*, 323.

28. Southard, E. E. "The feeble-minded as subjects of research in efficiency." *Proceedings of the National Association of Charities & Correction*, Annual Meetings, 1915, 315, 319. In this connection, see also Smith, J. D. *Minds Made Feeble*.

29. Wagenen, B. van. "Surgical sterilization as a eugenic measure," *Journal of Psycho-Asthenics* 18 (June 1914): 185–196, 187.

30. Ibid., 194–195.

31. See Szasz, T. S. *Sex by Prescription*.

32. Arnold, G. B. "A brief review of the first thousand patients eugenically sterilized at the State Colony for Epileptics and Feebleminded," *Journal of Psycho-Asthenics* 43 (1938): 56–63, 57.

33. Ibid., 61.

34. Ibid., 62.

35. Alexander, F. G. and S. Selesnick. *The History of Psychiatry*, 281.

36. Bleuler, E. *Dementia Praecox, or the Group of Schizophrenias*, 175.

37. Bunker, H. A. "American psychiatric literature during the past one hundred years," in Hale, J. K., ed. *One Hundred Years of American Psychiatry*, 258–259.

38. For a discussion of the origin of electric shock treatment, see Szasz, T. S. "From the slaughterhouse to the madhouse." *Psychotherapy* 8 (Spring 1971): 64–67.

39. American Psychiatric Association. *DSM-III*.

40. *Physicians' Desk Reference*, 44th ed., 988–990.

41. McElroy, S. L. "Anticonvulsant treatment of psychiatric disorders updated." *Psychiatric Times* 7 (January 1990): 1, 35–37, 1.

42. Hill, D. "Historical review," in Reynolds, E. H. and M. R. Trimble, eds. *Epilepsy and Psychiatry*, 5.

43. Colaizzi, J. *Homicidal Insanity, 1800–1985*, 91.

44. Ibid.

45. Ibid.

46. Deutsch, A. *The Mentally Ill in America*, 383–384, emphasis added.

47. Zabriskie, E. G. "Epilepsy," in Cecil, R. L., ed. *A Textbook of Medicine*, 5th ed., 1626, 1631.

48. Adams, R. D. "Idiopathic epilepsy," in Wintrobe, M. M. et al., eds. *Harrison's Principles of Internal Medicine*, 7th ed., 1868.

49. Forster, F. M. and H. E. Booker. "The epilepsies and convulsive disorders," in Joynt, R. J., ed. *Clinical Neurology*, rev. ed., 58.

50. Epilepsy Foundation of America. "Protecting your legal rights," in Gumnit, R. J. *Living Well with Epilepsy*, 135–141, 135, 139.

51. Trimble, M. R. "Greater understanding perceived of link between epilepsy and psychiatry." *Psychiatric Times* 6 (February 1989): 16, 25, 16.

52. Lennox, W. G. *Epilepsy and Related Disorders*, Vol. 2, 1043, 1047.

53. Livingston, S. "Epilepsy and murder" (Editorial). *Journal of the American Medical Association* 188 (April 13, 1964): 164.

54. Heck, D. G. "The successful adult with epilepsy," in Gumnit, R. J. *Living Well with Epilepsy*, 94–104, 101.

55. Hamilton, S. W. "The history of American mental hospitals," in Hall, J. K., ed. *One Hundred Years of American Psychiatry, 1844–1944*, 123–124, emphasis added.

56. Ibid., 124.

CHAPTER 4: THE CHILD

1. Yeats, W. B. "The stolen child," in McDonagh, D. and L. Robinson, eds. *The Oxford Book of Irish Verse*, 130.

2. See generally, Boswell, J. *The Kindness of Strangers*. For child-rearing practices as forms of child abuse, see Miller, A. *For Your Own Good*. For a contemporary version of foster home placement as a form of child abandonment, see Chase, N. F. "Susanna: The myth of the 'saved' child." *On the Issues*, 16 (Fall 1990): 10–15, 41–43.

3. Boswell, J. *The Kindness of Strangers*, 27.

4. See Szasz, T. S. *Insanity*.

5. Leviticus 20:1–2; and 2 Kings 23:10.

6. See Szasz, T. S. *The Myth of Psychotherapy*, especially 129–131.

7. Boswell, J. *The Kindness of Strangers*, 77–79.

8. Ibid., 235.

9. Ibid., 241.

10. Ibid.

11. Ibid., 298.

12. Today, children are sometimes abused by a combination of religious and psychiatric bureaucracies. For example, see Farnsworth, C. H. "Orphans of the 1950's, telling of abuse, sue Quebec." *New York Times International,* May 21, 1993, A-3.

13. Boswell, J. *The Kindness of Strangers,* 9.

14. Ibid., 423.

15. Porter, B. "I met my daughter at the Wuhan foundling hospital." *New York Times Magazine,* April 11, 1993, 24 ff.

16. See Werry, J. S. "Child psychiatric disorders: Are they classifiable?" *British Journal of Psychiatry,* 161 (1992): 472–480, 478.

17. Associated Press. "5-year-old who drove car held in hospital." *Syracuse Herald American,* November 1, 1992, A-12.

18. Ibid.

19. Simmons, J. E. *Psychiatric Examination of Children,* 21.

20. Markowitz, J. "The nature of the child's initial resistances to psychotherapy," in Haworth, M., ed. *Child Psychotherapy,* 190.

21. Pearson, G. H. J. *A Handbook of Child Psychoanalysis,* 71.

22. Ibid., 73.

23. See Szasz, T. S. *Schizophrenia,* especially Chapter 1.

24. American Psychiatric Association. *DSM-III,* 63–64.

25. Ibid., 49.

26. Freud, S. "On psychotherapy" [1905], SE, Vol. 7, 263–264, 293.

27. Freud, S. "Recommendations to physicians practicing psycho-analysis" [1912], SE, Vol. 12, 120.

28. See Szasz, T. S. *The Ethics of Psychoanalysis,* and "The man behind the couch," *The Wall Street Journal,* April 21, 1988.

29. Freud, A. *Normality and Pathology in Childhood,* 34.

30. Ibid., 35.

31. Ibid., 120–121, 122.

32. Heller, P. *A Child Analysis with Anna Freud,* xxv, xxiv, xxvii. See also Heller, P. *Anna Freud's Letters to Eva Rosenfeld,* and Burlingham, J. H. *The Last Tiffany.*

33. Appel, R. "Review" of Graf-Nold, A. *Der Fall Hermine Hug-Hellmuth: Eine Geschichte der frühen Kinderpsychoanalyse* (München: Verlag Internationale Psychoanalyse, 1988), *Frankfurter Algemeine Zeitung,* January 4, 1989; the translation is mine. For a somewhat similar current example, see McCabe, M. "Palo Alto doctor sees daughter behind death plot: He says she suffers delusions of sex abuse and has threatened to kill both parents." *San Francisco Chronicle,* November 26, 1992, A-26.

34. MacLean, G. and U. Rappen. *Hermine Hug-Hellmuth*. MacLean dismisses Hug-Hellmuth's use of the base rhetoric of psychoanalysis in the service of demeaning her nephew, asserting, "This [the analysis] is a false rumor at best." See MacLean, G. "The role of Hermine Hug-Hellmuth: An exchange." *Academy Forum* (The American Academy of Psychoanalysis) 36 (Winter, 1992): 8–9, 8.

35. Longmate, N. *The Workhouse*, 166.

36. Richardson, T. T. *The Century of the Child*, 11.

37. English, P. C. "Pediatrics and the unwanted child in history: Foundling homes, disease, and the origins of foster care in New York City, 1860 to 1920." *Pediatrics* 73 (May 1984): 699–711, 701, 707.

38. Rothman, D. J. *The Discovery of the Asylum*, 209.

39. 69 Stat. 381 (July 28, 1955), 381.

40. Bauder, D. "Report rips care for disturbed kids." *Syracuse Herald-Journal*, March 15, 1993, B-3.

41. Ibid.

42. Gardner, G. E. "History of Child Psychiatry," in Freedman, A. M., H. I. Kaplan, and B. J. Sadock, eds. *Comprehensive Textbook of Psychiatry—II*, 2nd ed., Vol. 2, 2032–2036, 2032.

43. Kennedy, F. "The problem of social control of the congenital defective: Education, sterilization, euthanasia." *American Journal of Psychiatry* 99 (July 1942): 13–16, 14, 16.

44. Ibid., 2034.

45. Fr·ud, A. *Psychoanalysis for Teachers and Parents*, 95–96.

46. Ro-s, V. Quoted in Heller, P. *Anna Freud's Letters to Eva Rosenfeld*, 22, emphasis added.

47. Between 1989 and 1992, the cost of treating child psychiatric patients in Arizona rose by more than 400 per cent. See Young, A. "Child mental-health costs soar." *Arizona Republic*, March 18, 1993, B-1, B-3.

48. Morrison, P. Quoted in Gibbs, N. "How America has run out of time." *Time*, April 24, 1989, 58–67, 61.

49. See for example, Chilnick, L. "27 percent of private mental hospital patients are teenagers." *Medical Tribune*, October 1, 1980, 3.

50. "Increase seen in youth psychiatric hospitalization." *American Medical News*, September 11, 1987, 44.

51. Ibid.

52. Kovar, L. C. *Wasted Lives*, 206.

53. Schiffman, J. R. "Children's wards: Teen-agers end up in psychiatric hospitals in alarming numbers." *The Wall Street Journal*, February 3, 1989.

54. Ibid.

55. Darnton, N. "Committed youth: Why are so many teens being locked up in private mental hospitals?" *Newsweek*, July 31, 1989, 66–72.

56. Johnson, J. "Mental disorders measured in young: Study says 12% of the people under 18 are impaired." *New York Times,* June 8, 1989.

57. Freudenheim, M. "Business and health: Mental health costs soaring." *New York Times,* October 7, 1986.

58. "Insane demand." *Research Weekly,* Prudential Bache Securities, July 27, 1987, 1.

59. Hospital plans to wean teens from Satanism." *Arkansas Democrat,* September 7, 1989.

60. Ibid.

61. Irwin, M. "Literature Review," in Schulman, J. L. and M. Irwin, eds. *Psychiatric Hospitalization of Children,* 36–37.

62. See Szasz, T. S. "The Ethics of Suicide" [1971], in *The Theology of Medicine,* 68–85, and "The case against suicide prevention," *American Psychologist* 41 (July 1986): 806–812.

63. Donaldson, J. Y. and J. A. Davis. "Evaluating the suicidal adolescent," in McIntire, M. S. and C. R. Angle, eds. *Suicide Attempts in Children and Youth,* 35.

64. Ibid., 37.

65. Sometimes the entire issue of a psychiatric journal is devoted to adolescent suicide. See, for example, Spurlock, J., guest editor. "Adolescent psychiatry." *Psychiatric Annals* 20 (March 1990).

66. McIntire, M. S. "The epidemiology and taxonomy of suicide," in McIntire, M. S. and C. R. Angle, eds. *Suicide Attempts in Children and Youth,* 123.

67. Pfeffer, C. R. "Clinical assessment of suicidal behavior in children," in Sudak, H. S., A. B. Ford, and N. B. Rushforth, eds. *Suicide in the Young,* 175, 179.

68. Kenney, E. M. and K. J. Krajewski. "Hospital treatment of the adolescent suicidal patient," in McIntire, M. S. and C. R. Angle, eds. *Suicide Attempts in Children and Youth,* 71.

69. Sudak, H. S., A. B. Ford, and N. B. Rushforth, "Therapies and intervention: A review," in Sudak, H. S., et al., eds. *Suicide in the Young,* 417–426, 417.

70. Ibid.

71. Ibid.

72. Ibid., 417–418.

73. Ibid., 424.

74. Kenney, and Krajewski, op. cit., 71.

75. See Szasz, T. S. *Psychiatric Justice.*

76. *In re Gault,* 387 U.S. 1, 1967.

77. Ibid., 49–50. In this connection, see also my discussion of the use of civil law sanctions in Chapter 2 and the Epilogue.

78. Ibid., 61.

79. See Miller, J. "Number of youths hospitalized for psychiatric care on the rise." *Psychiatric Times* 6 (July 1989): 33–34.

80. Ibid. See also Weithorn, L. A. "Mental hospitalization of troublesome youth: An analysis of skyrocketing admission rates." *Stanford Law Review* 40 (February 1988): 788–826.

81. McFadden, R. D. "Boy, 14, is put in psychiatric ward after report of AIDS exposure." *New York Times,* June 12, 1987.

82. A good case could be made for most schools, especially contemporary American public schools, disserving children. But that is another subject. See, for example, Brimelow, P. and L. Spencer. "The National Extortion Association?" *Forbes,* June 7, 1993.

83. Pekow, C. "The other Dr. Bettelheim: The revered psychologist had a dark, violent side." *Washington Post,* August 26, 1990.

84. 'Beno Brutalheim'? A revered child psychologist comes under attack for abusive methods." *Time,* September 10, 1990, 59; see also Bernstein, R. "Accusations of abuse haunt the legacy of Dr. Bruno Bettelheim." *New York Times,* November 4, 1990, and Mesic, P. "The abuses of enchantment." *Chicago,* August 1991, 82–103.

CHAPTER 5: THE HOMELESS

1. Morrow, L. "The bright cave under the hat." *Time,* December 24, 1990, 78.

2. Morris, C. *The Discovery of the Individual, 1050–1200,* 2.

3. Quoted in Morson, G. S. "Coping with utopia," *American Scholar* (Winter 1992): 132–138; 132.

4. Lukacs, J. "The bourgeois interior," *American Scholar* 39 (Autumn 1970): 619–639, 619.

5. Rybczynski, W. *Home,* 25.

6. Richardson, L. "Chronicle." *New York Times,* January 2, 1992, A-22.

7. Dowd, M. "A shy, sensitive guy trying to get by in lib city." *New York Times,* March 24, 1993, C-1, C-10.

8. Mencken, H. L. *The Impossible H. L. Mencken,* 126–127.

9. Hesse, H. *Reflections,* 166.

10. See, for example, Dugger, C. W. "Judge orders homeless man hospitalized: His aggressive behavior cited in commitment." *New York Times,* December 23, 1992, B-1, B-2.

11. Macfarlane, A. *The Origins of English Individualism,* 15.

12. Steiner, G. "Afterword," in Mann, T. *The Confessions of Felix Krull,* 321–331; 322.

13. "Making More Homeless" (Editorial). *The Wall Street Journal,* January 24, 1992. In this connection, see Hazlitt, H. "Why some are poorer." *Econ Update,* 6: 1, 9–11 (September 1991), and O'Rourke, J. *Parliament of Whores,* 123–141.

14. See Brown, P. L. "The architecture of those called homeless." *New York Times,* March 28, 1993, 1, 32.

15. Birman, I. Quoted in Lubin, P. "How to dismantle Communism." *National Review* (December 8, 1989): 29–33, 29–30.

16. Melcher, M. "What rough beast slouches toward Moscow?" *Strategy Weekly* (Prudential-Bache), December 6, 1989, 25–29, 28.

17. See Chapters 6 and 8.

18. In this connection, see especially Orwell, G. *Down and Out in Paris and London.* This deeply moving book illustrates the incredible parochialism of the current American view linking homelessness to mental illness.

19. Carroll, G. "Growing old behind bars: Some cellblocks are more nursing home than jail." *Newsweek,* November 29, 1989, 70.

20. Hazlett, T. "Rent controls and the housing crisis," in Johnson, M. B., ed. *Resolving the Housing Crisis,* 278.

21. Hayek, F. A. *The Constitution of Liberty*, 343.

22. Pilon, R. "Property rights and a free society," in Johnson, M. B., ed. *Resolving the Housing Crisis,* 369.

23. See generally, Lee, D. R. "Government policy and the distortions in family housing," in Peden, J. R. and F. R. Glahe, eds. *The American Family and the State.*

24. "Making more homeless" (Editorial). *The Wall Street Journal,* January 24, 1992.

25. Between 1983 and 1993, New York City spent more than $3.5 billion on sheltering the homeless, the annual cost of the operation rising from less than $60 million to more than $500 million. See Dugger, C. W. "Setbacks and surprises temper a mayor's hopes to house all." *New York Times,* July 5, 1993, 1, 24.

26. Brokaw, T. Quoted in "Most alarming statistic." *Time,* October 17, 1988, 22.

27. Whittemore, H. "We can't pay the rent." *Parade,* January 10, 1988, 4–6; and "The numbers racket: How polls and statistics lie." *U.S. News & World Report,* July 11, l988, 44–47; 46.

28. Mathews, J. "Rethinking homeless myths." *Newsweek,* April 6, 1992, 29.

29. Cohen, N. L. Quoted in "Homeless mentally ill: Distinct psychiatric subgroup." *Clinical Psychiatry News* 16 (January 1988):20.

30. Moran, M. "Treating patients on their turf." *Psychiatric News* 24 (January 5, 1990): 14, emphasis added.

31. Ibid.

32. Ibid.

33. Kolata, G. "Twins of the street: Homelessness and addiction." *New York Times,* May 22, 1989.

34. Kolata, G. "Drug addicts among the homeless: Case studies of some 'lost dreams.'" *New York Times,* May 30, 1989. Ibid.

35. Lewin, T. "Nation's homeless veterans battle a new foe: Defeatism." *New York Times,* December 31, 1987.

36. French, H. W. "Medicaid rules revised against hospital fraud." *New York Times,* October 29, 1989.

37. Ibid.

38. Hilfiker, D. "Are we comfortable with the homeless?" *Journal of the American Medical Association* 262 (September 8, 1989): 1375–1376, 1375. In this connection, see also, for example, Perrone, J. "AMA guidelines help doctors treat family violence cases." *American Medical News,* February 3, 1992, 2.

39. Hilfiker, op. cit., emphasis added.

40. Erlandson, G. "Homelessness: Vatican—adequate shelter is a 'universal right.'" *The Catholic Sun,* February 17–23, 1988, 8.

41. Ibid.

42. Szasz, T. S. *Schizophrenia,* 141–184.

43. "MHLP granted $2 million." *Psychiatric News* 22 (December 18, 1987): 7.

44. Mechanic, D. and L. H. Aiken. "Improving the care of patients with chronic mental illness." *New England Journal of Medicine* 317 (December 24, 1987): 1634–1638, 1637; see also Mechanic, D. "Foreword," in Hudson, C. G. and A. J. Cox, eds. *Dimensions of State Mental Health Policy,* ix-xi.

45. Dugger, C. W. "New York report finds drug abuse rife in shelters." *New York Times,* February 16, 1992.

46. Gelberg, L., et al. "Mental health, alcohol and drug use, and criminal history among homeless adults." *American Journal of Psychiatry* 145 (February 1988): 191–196, 191.

47. Navarro, M. "Sensibility of New York becomes offended as a nuisance becomes common." *New York Times,* November 25, 1989, 1, 26, 26.

48. Ritter, B. *Covenant House,* 8. For a more detailed account of Father Ritter's exploits, see Szasz, T. S. *Our Right to Drugs,* 86–87.

49. Quoted in Moehringer, J. R. "Unit seizures in drug raids imperil many." *New York Times,* January 7, 1989.

50. Ibid.

51. Cited in Crane, E. "President's message: Are America's liberties evaporating?" *Cato Policy Report* 11 (November/December, 1989): 2.

52. See Szasz, T. S. *Our Right to Drugs,* 22–25.

CHAPTER 6: THE ORIGIN OF PSYCHIATRY

1. Chekhov, A. "Ward No. 6," in *Seven Short Stories by Chekhov,* 130.

2. See generally, Parry-Jones, W. Ll. *The Trade in Lunacy.*

3. Tennessee Williams, who never forgave himself for failing to prevent his sister's lobotomy, wrote: "Confinement [in a mental hospital] has always been the greatest dread of my life." Williams, T. *Memoirs,* 294.

4. See Macalpine, I. and R. Hunter. *George III and the Mad Business;* and Szasz, T. S. *Law, Liberty, and Psychiatry.*

5. I take up this subject again in Chapters 7 and 8.

6. The members of ex-mental patient movements systematically reject the patient role. One typical manifesto proclaims: "'Mental health' system survivors are people who are neither 'crazy' nor 'mentally ill' nor genetically

distinguishable from anyone else. We are now, and always have been, fully human. . . . We call ourselves survivors. . . ." "What's Wrong with the 'Mental Health System'," A Draft Policy Prepared for the Re-evaluation Counseling Communities (Seattle, WA: Rational Island Publishers, 1991): 8–9. Mimeographed.

7. Neugebauer, R. "Diagnosis, guardianship, and residential care of the mentally ill in medieval and early modern England." *American Journal of Psychiatry* 146 (December, 1989): 1580–1584 , 1580.

8. Ibid., 1582.

9. See Chapter 7; and Szasz, T. S. *Insanity.*

10. See Orrell, M., B. Sahakian, and K. Bergmann."Self-neglect and frontal lobe dysfunction." *British Journal of Psychiatry* 155 (January, 1989): 101–105; and Vostanis, and C. Dean. "Self-neglect in adult life." *British Journal of Psychiatry* 161 (August, 1992): 265–267.

11. For a critical analysis of the similarities and differences between infants and the insane, see Chapter 7.

12. Foucault, M. *Madness and Civilization.*

13. Porter, R. *Mind-Forg'd Manacles*, 8, 9, emphasis added.

14. In this connection, see especially, St. Augustine. *The Political Writings of St. Augustine*, 197–217; see also Szasz, T. S. *The Manufacture of Madness* and *Insanity*, 294–304.

15. See generally, Parry-Jones, W. Ll. *The Trade in Lunacy.*

16. Ibid., 241.

17. Ibid.

18. Porter, R. *Mind-Forg'd Manacles*, 88.

19. Quoted in ibid.

20. See Chapters 9 and 10.

21. Hunter, R. and I. Macalpine. *Three Hundred Years*, 196.

22. Cheyne, G. *The English Malady.*

23. Ibid., 1.

24. Ibid., 111.

25. Ibid., 261–262.

26. Defoe, D. *Augusta Triumphans* (1728), in Hunter, R. and I. Macalpine. *Three Hundred Years*, 266–267.

27. In this connection, the story of late nineteenth-century critiques of German psychiatry is instructive. See Lothane, Z. *In Defense of Schreber*, 260–316.

28. Chekhov, A. "Ward No. 6" [1892], in *Seven Short Stories by Chekhov*; quoted from abridged version, reprinted in Szasz, T.S., ed. *The Age of Madness*, 124–126.

29. See Szasz, T. S. *A Lexicon of Lunacy*, Chapter 1.

30. Bucknill, J. C. *The Psychology of Shakespeare*, in Hunter, R. and I. Macalpine. *Three Hundred Years of Psychiatry*, 1064–1068.

31. Ibid., 1065.

32. Ibid.

33. Shakespeare, W. *Macbeth*, Act 5, Scene 3, lines 36–39.

34. Ibid., lines 36–44.

35. Ibid., lines 45–46.

36. Shakespeare, W. *Hamlet*, Act 3, Scene 1, lines 47–49.

37. Ibid., lines 49–54.

38. Shakespeare, W. *Othello*, Act 1, Scene 3, lines 323–331.

39. DePorte, M. *Nightmares and Hobbyhorses*, 56.

40. Swift, J. *A Tale of a Tub* [1704], in Ross, A. and D. Woolley, eds. *Jonathan Swift*, 62–164, 147–148, emphasis in the original.

41. Hobbes, T. *Leviathan*, 62.

42. Swift, J. *A Tale of a Tub*, in Ross and Woolley, op. cit., 141.

43. Ehrenpreis, I. *Swift*, Vol. 3, 580.

44. O'Donoghue, E. G. *The Story of Bethlehem Hospital*, 249; and Probyn, C. T. *Jonathan Swift*, 57.

45. O'Donoghue, op. cit., 250.

46. Swift, J. "Verses on the Death of Dr. Swift," in Ross and Woolley, op. cit., 530.

47. Mossner, E. C. "Swift, Jonathan (1667–1745)," in *The Encyclopedia of Philosophy*, Vol. 8, 52.

48. Swift, J. "Verses on the Death of Dr. Swift," in Ross and Woolley, op. cit., 516.

CHAPTER 7: ECONOMICS AND PSYCHIATRY

1. Smith, A. *The Wealth of Nations*, 119, emphasis added.

2. See Lachman, L. M. "The significance of the Austrian school of economics in the history of ideas," in Ebeling, R. M., ed. *Austrian Economics*, 17–39.

3. Wieser, F. von. *Social Economics*, 3; for a comprehensive review, see Ebeling, R. M., ed. *Austrian Economics*.

4. Mises, L. von. *Human Action*, 3, 11, 13.

5. See Szasz, T. S. *The Myth of Mental Illness, Ideology and Insanity*, and *Insanity*.

6. Becker, G. S. and K. M. Murphy. "A theory of rational addiction," *Journal of Political Economy*, 96 (August 1988): 675–700; and Becker, G. S. *Human Capital, The Economic Approach to Human Behavior*, and *A Treatise on the Family*.

7. Becker, G. S. *A Treatise on the Family*, ix-x, emphasis in the original.

8. Becker, G. S. *The Economic Approach to Human Behavior*, 145.

9. Ibid., 154. See also Becker, G. S. "The Economic Way of Looking at Life." *Law and Economics Working Paper No. 12* (2d Series), January 1993 (Chicago: The University of Chicago), 5–6.

10. See Szasz, T. S. *Insanity.*

11. Strauss, L. and J. Cropsey, eds. "Adam Smith, 1723–1790," in *History of Political Philosophy,* 607–630.

12. Smith, A. *Lectures on Justice, Police, Revenue, and Arms* (1763/1896). Quoted in West, E. G. *Adam Smith,* 87.

13. Smith, A. *The Theory of Moral Sentiments.* Quoted in ibid., 78.

14. Smith, A. *Lectures.* Quoted in ibid., 79.

15. See Boaz, D. and E. H. Crane, eds. *Market Liberalism.*

16. See Chapter 6.

17. Murray Rothbard is an exception. See Rothbard, M. *For a New Liberty,* 90–93. Today, many libertarians also reject psychiatric coercions and excuses.

18. Friedman, M. "Using the market for social development," *The Cato Journal* 8 (Winter 1989): 567–579, 568–569.

19. Eisenberg, L., "For-profit psychiatric hospitals." *American Journal of Psychiatry* 144 (March 1987): 396. For similar views, see, for example, Gralnick, A. "Psychiatric care in Cuba." *Psychiatric Times,* March 1988, 36; Waitzkin, H. "A Marxist analysis of the health care systems of advanced capitalist countries," in Eisenberg, L. and A. Kleinman, eds. *The Relevance of Social Science for Medicine,* 333–369, 349–350; and Callahan, D. Quoted in Friedrich, O. "Does helping really help?" *Time,* December 21, 1987, 45.

20. Mises, L. von. *Human Action,* 729.

21. Smith, A. Quoted in West, op. cit., 16.

22. Madison, J. "Property," in *The Writings of James Madison,* Vol. 6, 103; for a more sustained analysis of this theme, see Szasz, S. M. "Resurfacing the road to serfdom." *Freeman* 41 (February 1991): 46–49.

23. Garrett, G., "The people's pottage," excerpted from *The People's Pottage* (Caldwell, ID: Caxton Printers, 1953), in *Freedom Daily* 4 (July 1933): 29–32, 32.

24. See Szasz, T. S. *Ceremonial Chemistry* and *Our Right to Drugs.*

25. See Chapter 2.

26. Hobbes, T. *Leviathan,* 127.

27. Ibid., 202.

28. Locke, J. *The Second Treatise of Government,* in Locke, J. *Two Treatises of Government,* 350.

29. Mill, J. S. *On Liberty,* 14.

30. Ibid., 18.

31. Ibid., 99–100.

32. Ibid., 100, emphasis added.

33. Stephen, J. F. *Liberty, Equality, Fraternity,* 68–69.

34. Friedman, M. *Capitalism and Freedom,* 33.

35. See generally, Szasz, T. S. *Law, Liberty, and Psychiatry, Psychiatric Justice,* and *Insanity.*

36. C. S. Lewis never tired of emphasizing this distinction. See especially, *The Abolition of Man* and *The Screwtape Letters and Screwtape Proposes a Toast.*

37. The classic paper on the subject is Rosenhan, D. L. "On being sane in insane places," *Science* 179 (1973): 250–258. See also Mann, T. *Felix Krull*; Feynman, R. P. "Uncle Sam Doesn't Need *You!*" in *"Surely You're Joking, Mr. Feynman!"* 156–163; and Szasz, T. S. "Psychiatric classification as a strategy of personal constraint" [1966], in *Ideology and Insanity*, 190–217.

38. Mises, L. von. *Human Action*, 95.

39. Ibid., 148–149, emphasis added.

40. Ibid., 185.

41. Ibid., emphasis added.

42. Ibid., 316.

43. See Szasz, T. S. *Our Right to Drugs.* Happily, there are some diehard holdouts. See, for example, King, F. "New Age hypochondria." *National Review,* March 29, 1993, 80.

44. See also Chapter 2.

45. Minogue, K. "Pisher's progress." *National Review,* December 31, 1989, 38–39, 38.

46. Ibid., 39.

47. Shakespeare, W. *Julius Caesar,* Act 2, Scene 1, line 18.

48. See, for example, Lane, H. *The Mask of Benevolence*; Konner, M. "Misreading the signs." *New York Times Book Review,* August 2, 1992, 11; and Shapiro, J. P. "Disabling 'Jerry's Kids.'" *U.S. News & World Report,* September 14, 1992, 39–40.

CHAPTER 8: ADULT DEPENDENCY: IDLENESS AS ILLNESS

1. Calvin, J. Quoted in Little, D. *Religion, Order, and Law,* 59, emphasis in the original.

2. See, for example, Goleman, D. "More than 1 in 4 U.S. adults suffers a mental disorder each year." *New York Times,* March 17, 1993, C-13.

3. See, for example, Sigerist, H. E. *Medicine and Health in the Soviet Union,* 96.

4. Churchill, W. Quoted in King, F. "New Age hypochondria." *National Review,* March 29, 1993, 80.

5. Davidson, J. D. and W. Rees-Mogg. *The Great Reckoning,* 81.

6. In this connection, see Raico, R. "Liberalism, Marxism, and the state." *The Cato Journal* 11 (Winter 1992): 390–404.

7. Ibid., 103.

8. Calvin, J. Quoted in Little, D. *Religion, Order, and Law,* 60, 64, emphasis in the original.

9. Ibid., 59. See the epigraph at the head of this chapter.

10. Veblen, T. "The instinct of workmanship," in Lerner, M., ed. *The Portable Veblen,* 306–323, 313. This reference to Veblen should not be misconstrued as an endorsement of his views on economics. In this connection, see

Mencken, H. L. "Professor Veblen" [1919], in Mencken, H. L. *A Mencken Chrestomathy*, 265–275.

11. Chekhov, A. P. "Letter to Alexey S. Suvorin," December 9, 1890, in A. Yarmolinsky, ed. *The Portable Chekhov*, 622.

12. See Modrow, J. *How to Become a Schizophrenic*.

13. Barham, P. *Schizophrenia and Human Values*, 194.

14. Ibid., 190.

15. Kantor, A. "The 100 faces of John: Syracusan fights to find himself among dozens of personalities buried within his tormented psyche." *Syracuse Herald-Journal*, June 3, 1992, C1 & C3.

16. "NAMI members on employment," *NAMI Advocate* 13 (July-August 1992): 3. Twenty-two percent of the relatives remained unaccounted for in the survey.

17. Rosenfeld, J. E., A. Glassberg, and M. Sherrid. "Administration of ECT 4 years after aortic aneurysm dissection." *American Journal of Psychiatry* 145 (January 1988): 128–129.

18. Quoted in Seldes, G. *The Great Quotations*, 354.

19. Bauer, P. T. *Reality and Rhetoric*, 158; and Schoeck, H. *Envy*.

20. Carlson, A. "What has government done to our families?" *Essays in Political Economy* (The Ludwig von Mises Institute) 13 (November 1991): 1–12, 2.

21. Quoted in ibid., 7. See also Carlson, A. "The economics of children," *The Free Market* 10 (April 1992): 1, 7.

22. Szasz, T. S. *Law, Liberty, and Psychiatry*, 212–222; and generally, *The Therapeutic State*.

23. See Chapter 1.

24. Ortega y Gasset, J. *Man and Crisis*, 13.

CHAPTER 9: THE NEW PSYCHIATRIC DEAL

1. Shaw, G. B. Preface, in *Saint Joan*, 39–40.

2. Szasz, T. S. *Insanity*.

3. Blain, D. Quoted in Johnson, A. B., *Out of Bedlam*, 30, emphasis added.

4. For an excellent exposé of the new "homes" for the mentally ill, see "The care takers." *Detroit News*, May 2, 1993, 1-A, 10-A–13-A.

5. Cited in Visotsky, H. M. "The great American roundup," *New England Journal of Medicine* 317 (December 24, 1987): 1662–1663, 1963.

6. White, W. A. Quoted in Zwerling, I. "The mental hospital as a basis for community psychiatry," in Arieti, S., ed. *American Handbook of Psychiatry*, Vol. 2, 686–696, 686.

7. Solomon, H. C. Quoted in ibid.

8. For an in–depth discussion of this subject, see Szasz, T. S. *The Myth of Psychotherapy*, especially 101–157; and Yerushalmi, Y. H., *Freud's Moses*.

9. See Szasz, T. S. *The Ethics of Psychoanalysis* and *Anti-Freud*.

10. Freud, S. In *The Complete Letters of Sigmund Freud to Wilhelm Fliess,* 398.

11. Ibid., 461.

12. Freud, S. Quoted in Clark, R. W. *Freud,* 339. In this connection, see generally, Roazen, P., *Freud and His Followers.*

13. Freud, S. *An Autobiographical Study,* in SE, Vol. XX, 52, emphasis added.

14. See Szasz, T. S. *The Myth of Psychotherapy* and *Anti-Freud.* For a characteristically psychiatric misinterpretation of the influence of psychoanalysis on American psychiatry, see Torrey, E. F. *Freudian Fraud.*

15. See generally, Szasz, T. S. *Anti-Freud;* for a specific example, see "'As a will turns': A real-world soap." *Chicago Tribune,* September 6, 1988, C-3.

16. Freud, S. Quoted in Lieberman, E. J. *Acts of Will,* 228.

17. In this connection, see Murray, C. *Losing Ground;* and Szasz, T. S. *Ceremonial Chemistry* and *Our Right to Drugs.*

18. "1993 Appropriations for National Institutes of Health." *Chronicle of Higher Education,* October 14, 1992, A-27. See also Johnson, A. B. *Out of Bedlam,* 28.

19. Kennedy, J. F. Quoted in Torrey, E. F. *Nowhere To Go,* 108.

20. Ibid.

21. 69 Stat. 381 (July 28, 1955), in *U.S. Statutes at Large, 1955,* 381–383; cited in Joint Commission on Mental Illness and Health (JCMIH), *Action for Mental Health,* v.

22. Ibid., 382.

23. Ibid. Hereafter also cited as the *Report.*

24. Ibid., 277.

25. In this connection, see Hayek, F. A. *The Counter-Revolution of Science.*

26. JCMIH, *Action for Mental Health,* 39, emphasis added.

27. Ibid., 53–54.

28. Szasz, T. S. *The Myth of Mental Illness.*

29. Flynn, L. "The brain is back in the body," *NAMI Advocate* 13 (July/August 1992): 16.

30. Herrick, K. W. "Social Security," in *Encyclopedia Americana,* Vol. 25, 132–137; and Bernstein, M. C. and J. B. Bernstein. *Social Security,* especially Chapter 11.

31. Dickey, B. and M. D. Cohen. "Financing state mental health programs: Issues and options," in Hudson, C. G. and A. J. Cox, eds. *Dimensions of State Mental Health Policy,* 211–229; 212.

32. "Taking a scalpel to medicine." *Newsweek,* June 24, 1985, 56–58, 57.

33. Sharfstein, S. S. "Privatization: Economic opportunity and public health" (Editorial). *American Journal of Psychiatry* 145 (May 1988): 611–612, 611.

34. U.S. Department of Health and Human Services. *Social Security Bulletin,* Annual Statistical Supplement, 1991, 68.

35. See Szasz, T. S. *Insanity.*

36. Anderson, J. R. "Social Security and SSI benefits for the mentally disabled." *Hospital and Community Psychiatry* 33 (April 1982): 295–298, 295.

37. Ibid., 296.

38. U.S. Department of Health and Human Services, *Social Security Bulletin, Annual Statistical Supplement,* 1991, 300. See also Weaver, C. L. "Disability insurance's crippling costs." *The Wall Street Journal,* July 23, 1992.

39. Johnson, A. B. *Out of Bedlam,* 98.

40. Szasz, T. S. "Some observations on the use of tranquilizing agents," *A.M.A. Archives of Neurology and Psychiatry* 77 (January 1957): 86–92, 91.

41. Scull, A. T. *Decarceration,* 80.

42. Laborit, H. Quoted in Johnson, A. B. *Out of Bedlam,* 40.

43. Kline, N. Quoted in Brody, J. "A simple salt promises relief of mania." *New York Times,* April 2, 1970.

CHAPTER 10: RE-STORING THE MENTAL PATIENT

1. Nash, O. Quoted in Burkett, D. "Are our commonest diseases preventable?" *Pharos* 54 (Winter 1991): 19–21, 21. I have been unable to locate the source of this quotation or otherwise verify it. It may be spurious.

2. Singer, H. D. "The organization of a state hospital," *Mental Hygiene* 2 (July 1918): 426–431, 426.

3. Bockoven, J. S. *Moral Treatment in Community Mental Health,* 198–199.

4. Miller, S. O. "Historical perspectives on state mental health policy," in Hudson, C. G. and A. J. Cox, eds. *Dimensions of State Mental Health Policy,* 19–39; 22.

5. Schinnar, A. P., A. B. Rothbard, R. Kanter, and Y. S. Jung. "An empirical literature review of definitions of severe and persistent mental illness." *American Journal of Psychiatry* 147 (December 1990): 1602–1608, 1602, 1603.

6. Goldman, H. H., A. A. Gattozzi, and C. A. Taube. "Defining and counting the chronically mentally ill." *Hospital & Community Psychiatry* 32 (January 1981): 21–27, 22. See also Goldman, H. H., N. H. Adams, and C. A. Taube. "Deinstitutionalization: The data demythologized." *Hospital and Community Psychiatry* 34 (February): 129–134.

7. Yager, T., ed. *The Future of Psychiatry as a Medical Specialty,* 2, 82–83.

8. See Dear, M. J. and J. R. Wolch. *Landscapes of Despair,* especially 66.

9. 69 Stat. 381 (July 28, 1955), 381.

10. Moss, F. E. and V. J. Halamandaris. *Too Old, Too Sick, Too Bad,* xiv.

11. Ibid., 104.

12. Tarini, P. "Elderly's unmet need: Geriatric psychiatry." *American Medical News,* March 2, 1990, 11, 13.

13. Ibid., 13.

14. Bishop, K. "Studies find drugs still overused to control nursing home elderly." *New York Times,* March 13, 1989; "Free nursing home patients"

(Editorial). *New York Times*, March 7, 1992; and "Heavy psychotropic drug use found in rest homes." *Clinical Psychiatry News* 17 (May 1989): 7.

15. McCarthy, M. J. "Grim prospect: Older people will do anything to avoid life in nursing home." *The Wall Street Journal*, December 3, 1992, A-1, A-4.

16. Goldsmith, M. F."From mental hospitals to jails: The pendulum swings." *Journal of the American Medical Association* 250 (December 9, 1983): 3017–3018, 3017.

17. Torrey, E. F., et al. *Criminalizing the Seriously Mentally Ill*, iv; Hilts, P. J. "Mentally ill jailed on no charges, survey says." *New York Times*, September 10, 1992; "Many seriously mentally ill confined in jails, not getting help." *Psychiatric News* 27 (October 2, 1992): 11, 23, 11. See also Buie, J. "NAMI deplores abuse of jails as hospitals: For 30,000 people, 'treatment' equals jail." *NAMI Advocate* 13 (October 1992): 1, 12.

18. Grinfeld, M. J. "Task force to report on jailed mentally ill." *Psychiatric Times* 9 (November 1992): 1, 28–30, 28.

19. Ibid.

20. Creno, C. "Mentally ill seek jail time to get care." *Arizona Republic*, August 13, 1992, A-1.

21. Creno, C. "Help for some, 'the Hole' for others." *Arizona Republic*, August 14, 1992, A-1.

22. "Population ups and downs." *Correction* 17 (April 1952): 15; "Population ups and downs." *Correction* 25 (July-August 1960): 32; Bureau of Justice Statistics, "Prisoners 1982 in State and Federal Institutions on December 31, National Prisoner Statistics Bulletin, 1984; Raab, S. "Jails to grow by 1,000 beds in New York." *New York Times*, May 13, 1991.

23. LaFraniere, S. "Influx of inmates floods California, other states." *Washington Post*, April 27, 1991.

24. Butterfield, F. "U.S. expands its lead in the rate of imprsonment." *New York Times*, February 11, 1992, A-16; Banks, R. "One man in 25." *New York Times Book Review*, August 20, 1992, 5.

25. Malcolm, A. H. "More cells for more prisoners, but to what end?" *New York Times*, January 18, 1991; Butterfield, F. "Are American jails becoming shelters from the storm?" *New York Times*, July 19, 1992, E-4; and Banks, R. "One man in 25." *New York Times Book Review*, August 30, 1992, 5.

26. "U.S. leads world in imprisonment." *New York Times*, January 7, 1991; and see Szasz, T. S. *Our Right to Drugs*, 116–120.

27. "U.S. leads world in imprisonment." *New York Times*, January 7, 1991.

28. Cazentre, D. and C. Miller. "Hutchings patient kills woman because she'd rather be in jail." *Syracuse Herald-Journal*, November 18, 1992, A-1, A-9; and Cazentre, D. "State agencies investigate Hutchings slaying." *Syracuse Herald-Journal*, November 19, 1992, E-1.

29. See Menninger, K. *The Crime of Punishment*.

30. See Thornburn, K. M. "The corrections department: The forgotten branch of the mental health system." *Hawaii Medical Journal* 48 (March 1989): 91–92, 92. See also Halpern, A. "Misuse of post-acquittal hospitalization for punitive purposes," 1992. Mimeographed, courtesy of the author.

31. In this connection, see also Chapter 5.

32. Craig, T. J. "Economics and inpatient care." *Psychiatric Annals* 18 (February 1988): 75–78, 75; see also Beigel, A. and S. S. Sharfstein. "Mental health care providers: Not the only cause or only cure for rising costs." *American Journal of Psychiatry* 141 (May 1984): 668–672, 668.

33. Johnson, A. B. *Out of Bedlam*, 103.

34. Schoenholtz, J. C. "Public hospitals can't handle the mentally ill" (Letter). *New York Times*, January 19, 1991; and "The white elephants of mental health" (Editorial). *New York Times*, October 10, 1992, 20.

35. Quoted from *U.S. News & World Report*, February 8, 1993, and *Charlotte (NC) Observer*, November 2, 1992, cited in *PsychoHeresy Awareness Letter* 1 (March-April 1993): 3.

36. Johnson, A. B. *Out of Bedlam*, 103–104.

37. Dorwart, R. A. and M. Schlesinger. "Privatization of psychiatric services." *American Journal of Psychiatry* 145 (May 1988): 543–553, 545–546.

38. See for example, King, T. R. "National Medical will restructure a troubled unit." *The Wall Street Journal*, April 24, 1994, A-6. In March 1993, the Texas Senate passed a bill mandating "New criminal penalties for hospitals, companies, or individuals that offer bounties for patient referrals." Stutz, T. "Senate OKs 8 bills on mental hospitals." *Dallas Morning News*, March 25, 1993.

39. Taylor, J. H. "Tranquilizers, anyone?" *Forbes*, December 10, 1990, 214–216, 214.

40. Ibid. See also Cowley, G., et al. "Money madness: Are private psychiatric hospitals resorting to kidnapping in their quest for paying patients?" *Newsweek*, November 4, 1991, 50–52.

41. Ibid., 216.

42. Freiman, M. P. and L. I. Sederer. "Transfer of hospitalized psychiatric patients under Medicare's prospective payment system." *American Journal of Psychiatry* 147 (January 1990): 100–105, 100–101, 104.

43. Dorwart, R. A. and M. Schlesinger. "Privatization of psychiatric services." *American Journal of Psychiatry* 145 (May 1988): 543–553, 543–544, emphasis added.

44. Sharfstein, S. S. "Privatization: Economic opportunity and public health" (Editorial). *American Journal of Psychiatry* 145 (May 1988): 611–612, 611.

45. See Krucoff, C. "Psychiatrist of the streets: E. Fuller Torrey, treating Washington's homeless." *Washington Post*, May 24, 1984, D-1, D-15.

46. Torrey, E. F. "Homelessness and mental illness." *USA Today* (Magazine), March 1988, 26–27.

47. Torrey, E. F. *Nowhere To Go*, 15; subsequent excerpts are from the same source.

48. Torrey, E. F., et al. "Washington's grate society: Schizophrenics in the shelters and on the street." *Public Citizen* (Washington, DC: Health Research Group, April 23, 1985), 9–10.

49. Ibid., 4.

50. Ibid., 19.

51. Torrey, E. F. "Thirty years of shame: The scandalous neglect of the mentally ill homeless." *Policy Review*, Spring 1989, 10–15, 14. It never occurs to Torrey that pro bono work may not help its impoverished beneficiaries. See Macey, J. R. "Not all pro bono work helps the poor." *The Wall Street Journal*, December 30, 1992, 30.

52. Torrey, E. F. Quoted in Hilts, J. "Mentally ill jailed on no charges, survey shows." *New York Times*, September 10, 1992.

53. Ibid., 11, emphasis added.

54. Segal, S. and P. L. Kotler. "Sheltered-care residents ten years later: I. Extent of disability." Mental Health and Social Welfare Research Group, University of California, Berkeley, CA 94720. Unpublished manuscript, August, 1989; cited by permission.

55. Landau, E. *The Homeless*, 54.

56. See Szasz, T. S. "Crazy talk: Thought disorder or psychiatric arrogance?" *British Journal of Medical Psychology* 66 (1993): 61–67; and generally, Szasz, T. S. *Insanity*.

57. Cited in Landau, E. *The Homeless*, 56–57.

58. Mayer, J. E. and A. Rosenblatt. "Clash in perspectives between mental patients and staff." *American Journal of Orthopsychiatry* 44 (April 1974): 432–441, 437–438; see also Rosenblatt, A. "Providing custodial care for mental patients: An affirmative view." *Psychiatric Quarterly* 48 (1974): 14–25.

59. Allen, S. *Funny People*, 272–273.

60. Rachlin, S. "With liberty and psychosis for all." *Psychiatric Quarterly* 48 (1974): 1–11.

61. Caseby, R. and M. Durham. "The lonely man killed by a taste of freedom." *Sunday Times* (London), November 5, 1989, A-7; subsequent quotes are from this source.

62. For an ironic twist on this dilemma, see Barbanel, J. "System to treat mental patients is overburdened." *New York Times*, February 22, 1988.

63. Geller, J. "Arson: An unforeseen sequela of deinstitutionalization." *American Journal of Psychiatry* 141 (April 1984): 504–508, 507, 505.

64. Ibid.

65. Ibid.

66. See for example, Braginsky, B. M., M. Grosse, and K. Ring. "Controlling outcomes through impression-management: An experimental study of the manipulative tactics of mental patients." *Journal of Consulting Psychology* 30

(1966): 295–300; Braginsky, B. M., D. D. Braginsky, and K. Ring. *Methods of Madness*; Ludwig, A. M. and F. Farrelly. "The weapons of insanity." *American Journal of Psychotherapy* 21 (1967): 737–749, and Snyder, C. R., R. L. Higgins, and R. J. Stucky. *Excuses*, especially, 221–240.

67. Morgenthau, T., et al. "Abandoned." *Newsweek*, January 6, 1986, 14– 19, 17.

68. "Man takes hostages to get into hospital." *Syracuse Herald-Journal*, December 27, 1983, A-4.

CHAPTER 11: THE FUTILITY OF PSYCHIATRIC REFORM

1. Burke, E. "Letter to William Elliott" [1795], in Burke, E. *The Philosophy of Edmund Burke*, 166.

2. See for example, Weiner, D. B. "Philippe Pinel's 'Memoir on Madness' of December 11, 1794: A fundamental text of modern psychiatry." *American Journal of Psychiatry* 149 (June 1992): 725–732; for my critique, see Szasz, T. S. *The Manufacture of Madness*.

3. Lewin, T. "The seriously ill and the 'worried well'." *New York Times Book Review*, December 18, 1988, 14.

4. See for example, Levy, S. T. and C. B. Nemeroff. "From psychoanalysis to neurobiology." *National Forum* 73 (Winter 1993): 18–21.

5. Isaac, R. J. and V. C. Armat. *Madness in the Streets*, 37. For a critique of this book, see Farber, S. *Madness, Heresy, and the Rumor of Angels*, 247–249. For a more sympathetic interpretation of my views, see Vice, J. *From Patients to Persons*.

6. Bublis, M. D., "Szasz award" (Letters). *Psychiatric News*, May 15, 1992, 16.

7. Isaac, R. J. and V. C. Armat. *Madness in the Streets*, 155. Apparently, Isaac sees no inconsistency between her support of coercive psychiatry and her opposition to coercive utopians. See Isaac, R. J. and E. Isaac. *Coercive Utopians*.

8. Ibid.

9. Rosenbaum, M. "Violence in psychiatric wards." *General Hospital Psychiatry* 13 (1991): 115–121, 119.

10. Isaac, R. J. "The mentally ill don't know they're sick." *New York Times*, March 2, 1991.

11. See Chapter 3.

12. Isaac, R. J. "'Right' to madness: A cruel hoax." *Los Angeles Times*, December 15, 1990; and Isaac, R. J. and V. C. Armat. *Madness in the Streets*, 14–15. However, see Dear, M. J. and J. R. Wolch. *Landscapes of Despair*, who, in a book-length study of deinstitutionalization, do not even mention the antipsychiatry movement.

13. See for example, Szasz, T. S. *Insanity* and *The Untamed Tongue*. For a refutation of the misinterpretation of my psychiatric critique, exemplified by Isaac and Armat's book, see Grenander, M. E. "The sleep of reason." *American Scholar*, Winter 1992, 156.

14. Monahan, J. "From the man who brought you deinstitutionalization." *Contemporary Psychology* 33 (June 1988): 492.

15. Ibid.

16. Scruton, R. "Editorial Note," in Legutko, R. "Do liberals love liberty?" *Salisbury Review,* September 1988, 30.

17. Roth, L. H. "Four studies of mental health commitments." *American Journal of Psychiatry* 146 (February 1989): 135–137.

18. Landau, E. *The Homeless,* 62.

19. "How to house the mentally ill" (Editorial). *New York Times,* October 26, 1989, emphasis added.

20. Applebaum, P. "Crazy in the streets." *Commentary,* May 1987, 34–39, 38.

21. Ibid., 39.

22. Lamb, R. "Will we save the homeless mentally ill?" *American Journal of Psychiatry* 147 (May 1990): 649–651, 650; quoted in Isaac, R. J. and V. C. Armat. *Madness in the Streets,* 160, emphasis added.

23. Wilson, J. Q. Quoted approvingly in Will, G. F. "Nature and the male sex." *Newsweek,* June 17, 1991, 70.

24. Krauthammer, C. "Brown v. Board of Re-education: How to save the homeless mentally ill." *New Republic,* February 8, 1988, 22–25.

25. Will, G. "Community has right to remove homeless." *Post-Standard* (Syracuse), November 19, 1987.

26. Olasky, M. *The Tragedy of American Compassion,* 211.

27. Ibid., 211.

28. Thomas, L. *Late Night Thoughts on Listening to Mahler's Ninth Symphony,* 99–100.

29. See Chapter 6.

30. See Szasz, T. S. *The Myth of Psychotherapy.*

31. Schreber, D. P. *Memoirs of My Nervous Illness,* 55, emphasis in the original; cited in, and in this connection see further, Lothane, Z. *In Defense of Schreber,* 467 ff.

32. See for example, "Arrest,"in *Encyclopaedia Britannica,* 14th ed., Vol. 2, 473–474.

33. According to Alan Breier, research psychiatrist at the National Institute of Mental Health; quoted in Acker, C. "New drugs quiet world for those with schizophrenia." *Detroit Free Press,* June 29, 1993.

34. "Soviets to trim list of 'mental patients': End of abuses would mean reclassifying 2 million people." *Arizona Republic,* February 12, 1988.

35. Ibid.

36. See Chapter 2.

37. McGregor, O. R. *Social History and Law Reform,* 49.

38. See Chapter 3.

39. Horowitz, C. F. "The 'homeless' vs. property." *The Free Market* 10 (September 1992): 1, 6, 8, 8.

40. Ibid.

EPILOGUE

1. Polanyi, M. *Full Employment and Free Trade,* v.
2. In this connection, it is worth noting that in his 1992 Nobel Lecture in Economic Science, Gary Becker singled out Karl Menninger's views on crime as mental illness for criticism. See Becker, G. "The Economic Way of Looking at Life." *Law and Economics Working Paper No. 12* (2d Series), January 1993 (Chicago: The University of Chicago), 5–6.
3. Menninger, K. "Reading notes." *Bulletin of the Menninger Clinic* 53 (July 1989): 350–351, 350.
4. Ibid., 351.
5. Ibid.
6. Szasz, T. S. "Letter to Karl Menninger," October 12, 1988, ibid., 352.
7. Slovenko, R. "Dr. Karl Menninger and Dr. Thomas Szasz: Were they apart on 'mental illness'?" *AAPL [American Academy of Law and Psychiatry] Newsletter* 16 (April 1991): 21–22, 21. In this connection, see generally, Robitscher, J., *The Powers of Psychiatry.*
8. Harris, J., J. L. T. Birley, and K. W. M. Fulford. "The proposal to classify happiness as a psychiatric disorder." *British Journal of Psychiatry* 162 (1993): 539–542, 540.
9. Hayek, F. von. *The Constitution of Liberty,* 31. Almost a century earlier, Lord Acton declared: "Liberty is not a means to a higher political end. It is itself the highest political end." Quoted in *Bartlett's Familiar Quotations,* 16th ed., 52.

BIBLIOGRAPHY

Adams, R. D. and M. Victor, *Principles of Neurology*, 3rd ed. (New York: Mc-Graw Hill, 1985).

Ahmed, P. I. and S. C. Plog, eds., *State Mental Hospitals: What Happens When They Close?* (New York: Plenum, 1976).

Alexander, F. G. and S. T. Selesnick, *The History of Psychiatry: An Evaluation of Psychiatric Thought and Practice from Prehistoric Times to the Present* (New York: Harper & Row, 1966).

Allen, S., *Funny People* (New York: Stein and Day, 1981).

American Psychiatric Association, *Diagnostic and Statistical Manual of Mental Disorders*, 3rd ed. (Washington, DC: American Psychiatric Association, 1980). Hereafter cited as *DSM-III*.

Anonymous, *Account of the Rise and Progress of the Asylum, Proposed to Be Established, near Philadelphia, for the Relief of Persons Deprived of the Use of Their Reason* (Philadelphia: Kimber and Conrad, 1814).

Anonymous, *The Unreasonableness and Ill Consequence of Imprisoning the Body for Debt. Prov'd from the Laws of God and Nature, Human Policy and Interest* (London: T. Read and J. Purser, 1729).

Archer, T., *The Pauper, the Thief, and the Convict: Sketches of Some of Their Homes, Haunts, and Habits* [1865], facsimile reprint (New York: Garland Publishing, 1985).

Arendt, H., *The Burden of Our Time* (London: Secker & Warburg, 1951).

Arendt, H., *On Revolution* (New York: Viking, 1965).

Arendt, H., *Men in Dark Times* (New York: Harcourt, Brace & World, 1968).

Arieti, S., ed., *American Handbook of Psychiatry,* 2nd ed. (New York: Basic Books, 1974).

Aristotle, *The Basic Works of Aristotle,* ed. by R. McKeon (New York: Random House, 1941).

Arney, W. R. and B. J. Bergen, *Medicine and the Management of Living: Taming the Last Great Beast* (Chicago: University of Chicago Press, 1984).

Artaud, A., *Antonin Artaud: Selected Writings,* ed. with an Introduction by S. Sontag, trans. by H. Weaver (New York: Farrar, Straus and Giroux, 1976).

Atiyah, P. S., *The Rise and Fall of Freedom of Contract* (New York: Clarendon Press, 1979).

Auchincloss, L., *The Vanderbilt Era: Profiles of a Gilded Age* (New York: Scribner's, 1989).

Augustine, St., *The Political Writings of St. Augustine,* ed. by H. Paolucci (Chicago: Gateway/Regnery, 1962).

Barham, P., *Schizophrenia and Human Value: Chronic Schizophrenia, Science, and Society* (Oxford: Blackwell, 1984).

Barrow, R. L. and H. D. Fabing, *Epilepsy and the Law,* 2nd ed. (New York: Harper & Row, 1966).

Bartlett, J., *Familiar Quotations,* 12th ed., ed. by C. Morely (Boston: Little, Brown, 1951).

Bartlett, J., *Familiar Quotations,* 16th ed., ed. by J. Kaplan (Boston: Little, Brown, 1992).

Barzun, J., *Science: The Glorious Entertainment* (New York: Harper & Row, 1964).

Bastiat, F., *Economic Sophisms* [1845/1851], trans. by A. Goddard (Princeton, NJ: D. Van Nostrand, 1964).

Bauer, P. T., *Dissent on Development: Studies and Debates in Development* (London: Weidenfeld and Nicolson, 1971).

Bauer, P. T., *Equality, the Third World, and Economic Delusion* (London: Weidenfeld and Nicolson, 1981).

Bauer, P. T., *Reality and Rhetoric: Studies in Economic Development* (London: Weidenfeld and Nicolson, 1984).

Bayer, R., *Homosexuality and American Psychiatry: The Politics of Diagnosis* (New York: Basic Books, 1981).

Becker, C. L., *The Heavenly City of the Eighteenth-Century Philosophers* [1932] (New Haven: Yale University Press, 1971).

Becker, G. S., *Human Capital: A Theoretical and Empirical Analysis, with Special Reference to Education* [1964], 2nd ed. (Chicago: University of Chicago Press, 1975).

Becker, G. S., *The Economic Approach to Human Behavior* (Chicago: University of Chicago Press, 1976).

Becker, G. S., *A Treatise on the Family* [1981], enlarged ed. (Cambridge, MA: Harvard University Press, 1991).

Beier, A. L., *Masterless Men: The Vagrancy Problem in England, 1560–1640* (London: Methuen, 1985).

Bentall, R. P., ed., *Reconstructing Schizophrenia* (London: Routledge, 1990).

Bentham, J., *Defence of Usury; Shewing the Impolicy of the Present Legal Restraints on the Terms of Bargains* (London: Payne and Foss, 1818).

Bentham, J., *The Works of Jeremy Bentham*, ed. by J. Bowring (Edinburgh: William Tait, 1843).

Berlin, I., *Four Essays on Liberty* (London: Oxford University Press, 1969).

Berlin, I., *Concepts and Categories: Philosophical Essays*, ed. by H. Hardy (New York: Viking, 1979).

Bernstein, M. C. and J. B. Bernstein, *Social Security: The System That Works* (New York: Basic Books, 1988).

Black, H. C., *Black's Law Dictionary*, rev. 4th ed. (St. Paul: West, 1968).

Bleuler, E., *Dementia Praecox, or the Group of Schizophrenias* [1911], trans. by J. Zinkin (New York: International Universities Press, 1950).

Boaz, D. and E. H. Crane, eds., *Market Liberalism: A Paradigm for the 21st Century* (Washington, DC: Cato Institute, 1993).

Bockoven, J. S., *Moral Treatment in the Community* (New York: Springer, 1972).

Boswell, J., *The Kindness of Strangers: The Abandonment of Children in Western Europe from Late Antiquity to the Renaissance* (New York: Pantheon, 1988).

Bouwsma, W. J., *John Calvin: A Sixteenth Century Portrait* (New York: Oxford University Press, 1988).

Braginsky, B. M., D. D. Braginsky, and K. Ring, *Methods of Madness: The Mental Hospital as a Last Resort* (New York: Holt, Rinehart & Winston, 1969).

Braunwald, E., et al., eds., *Harrison's Principles of Internal Medicine*, 11th ed. (New York: Mc-Graw Hill, 1987).

Brydall, J., *Non Compos Mentis: Or, the Law Relating to Natural Fools, Mad-Folks, and Lunatick Persons, Inquisited, and Explained, for Common Benefit* (London: I. Cleave, 1700), Facsimile reprint (New York: Garland, 1979).

Buchanan, J. M., *The Limits of Liberty: Between Anarchy and Leviathan* (Chicago: University of Chicago Press, 1975).

Buchanan, J., R. Tollison, and G. Tullock, eds., *Towards a Theory of the Rent-Seeking Society* (College Station, TX: Texas A&M University Press, 1980).

Bucknill, J. C., *The Psychology of Shakespeare* (London: Longman, 1859), quoted in Hunter, R. and I. Macalpine, *Three Hundred Years of Psychiatry*, 1064–1068.

Bulwer, E. L., *England and the English* [1833], ed. by S. Meacham (Chicago: University of Chicago Press, 1970).

Burdett, H. C., *Hospitals and Asylums of the World: Their Origin, History, Construction, Administration, Management, and Legislation* (4 vols.; London: J. & A. Churchill, 1891–1893).

Burke, E., *Further Reflections on the Revolution in France* [1789–1796], ed. by D. E. Ritchie (Indianapolis: Liberty Fund, 1992).

Burke, E., *The Philosophy of Edmund Burke, A Selection from His Speeches and Writings,* ed. by L. I. Bredvold and R. G. Ross (Ann Arbor, MI: University of Michigan Press, 1960).

Burke, E., *The Political Philosophy of Edmund Burke,* ed. by I. Hampsher-Monk (London: Longman, 1987).

Burke, E., *Reflections on the Revolution in France* [1790], ed. by C. C. O'Brien (Baltimore: Penguin, 1969).

Burlingham, M. J., *The Last Tiffany: A Biography of Dorothy Tiffany Burlingham* (New York: Atheneum, 1989).

Bury, J. B., *The Idea of Progress: An Inquiry into Its Growth and Origin* [1932] (New York: Dover, 1955).

Busfield, J., *Managing Madness: Changing Ideas and Practice* (London: Hutchinson, 1986).

Butterfield, H., *The Whig Interpretation of History* [1931] (New York: Norton, 1965).

Bynum, W. F., R. Porter, and M. Shepherd, eds., *The Anatomy of Madness: Essays in the History of Psychiatry* (3 vols.; London: Tavistock, 1985–1988).

Cecil, R. L., ed., *A Textbook of Medicine,* 5th ed., rev. (Philadelphia: Saunders, 1942).

Celine, L. F., *The Life and Work of Semmelweis* [1924], in Celine, L. F., *Mea Culpa and The Life and Work of Semmelweis,* trans. by R. A. Parker (New York: Howard Fertig, 1979).

Chadwick, O., *The Secularization of the European Mind in the Nineteenth Century* (New York: Cambridge University Press, 1975).

Chekhov, A. P., *Seven Short Stories by Chekhov,* trans. by B. Makanowitzky (New York: Bantam Books, 1963).

Chekhov, A. P., *The Portable Chekhov,* ed. by A. Yarmolinsky (New York: Viking, 1965).

Cheyne, G., *The English Malady: Or, A Treatise of Nervous Diseases of All Kinds, as Spleen, Vapours, Lowness of Spirits, Hypochondriacal, and Hysterical Distempers, etc.* (London: Strahan & Leake, 1733).

Clark, R. W., *Freud: The Man and the Cause* (London: Jonathan Cape and Weidenfeld & Nicolson, 1980).

Cohen, N. L., ed., *Psychiatry Takes to the Streets: Outreach and Crisis Intervention for the Mentally Ill* (New York: Guilford Press, 1990).

Cohen, S. and A. Scull, eds., *Social Control and the State* (New York: St. Martin's Press, 1983).

Colaizzi, J., *Homicidal Insanity, 1800–1985* (Tuscaloosa: University of Alabama Press, 1989).

Collier, P. and D. Horowitz, *The Kennedys: An American Drama* (New York: Summit, 1984).

Collinson, G. D., *A Treatise on the Law Concerning Idiots, Lunatics, and Other Persons Non Compotes Mentis* (London: W. Reed, 1812).

Coles, G., *The Learning Mystique: A Critical Look at Learning Disabilities* (New York: Ballantine Books, 1987).

Coulter, J., *Approaches to Insanity: A Philosophical and Sociological Study* (New York: Wiley, 1973).

Crowther, M. A., *The Workhouse System, 1834-1929: The History of an English Social Institution* (Athens, GA: University of Georgia Press, 1982).

Davidson, J. D. and W. Rees-Mogg, *The Great Reckoning* (New York: Summit Books, 1991).

Dear, M. J. and J. R. Wolch, *Landscapes of Despair: From Deinstitutionalization to Homelessness* (Princeton: Princeton University Press, 1987).

DePorte, M., *Nightmares and Hobbyhorses: Swift, Sterne, and Augustan Ideas of Madness* (San Marino, CA: Huntington Library, 1974).

Deutsch, A., *The Mentally Ill in America: A History of Their Care and Treatment from Colonial Times*, 2nd ed. (New York: Columbia University Press, 1952).

Dickens, C., *The Portable Dickens*, ed. by A. Wilson (New York: Penguin, 1983).

Dicey, A. V., *Lectures on the Relation between Law and Public Opinion in England* [1905, 1914], 2nd ed. (London: Macmillan, 1963).

Digby, A., *Pauper Palaces* (London: Routledge & Kegan Paul, 1978).

Edwards, P., ed., *The Encyclopedia of Philosophy* (8 vols.; New York: Macmillan/ Collier, 1967).

Ehrenpreis, I., *Swift: The Man, His Works, and the Age* (3 vols.; Cambridge: Harvard University Press, 1983).

Eisenberg, L. and A. Kleinman, eds., *The Relevance of Social Science for Medicine* (Boston: Reidel, 1981).

Encyclopedia Americana, International Edition (Danbury, CT: Grolier, 1990).

Encyclopedia of Philosophy, The, ed. by P. Edwards (8 vols.; New York: Macmillan and Free Press, 1967).

Farber, S., *Madness, Heresy, and the Rumor of Angels: The Revolt against the Mental Health System* (Chicago: Open Court, 1993).

The Federalist Papers: Hamilton, Madison, Jay [1788], Introduction by C. Rossiter (New York: Mentor, 1961).

Feynman, R. P., *"Surely You're Joking, Mr. Feynman!": Adventures of a Curious Character*, ed. by E. Hutchings (New York: Norton, 1985).

Formaini, R., *The Myth of Scientific Public Policy* (New Brunswick, NJ: Transaction Publishers, 1990).

Forrest, D. W., *Francis Galton: The Life and Work of a Victorian Genius* (New York: Taplinger, 1974).

Foucault, M., *Madness and Civilization: A History of Insanity in the Age of Reason* [1961], trans. by R. Howard (New York: Pantheon, 1965).

Foucault, M., *Foucault Live (Interviews, 1966–1984)*, ed. by Sylvere Lotringer, trans. by J. Johnson (New York: Semiotext[e], 1989).

Freedman, A. M., H. I. Kaplan, and B. J. Sadock, eds., *Comprehensive Textbook of Psychiatry–II*, 2nd ed. (Baltimore: Williams & Wilkins, 1975).

Freud, A., *Psychoanalysis for Teachers and Parents: Introductory Lectures* [1935], trans. by B. Low (New York: Norton, 1979).

Freud, A., *Normality and Pathology in Childhood: Assessments of Development* (New York: International Universities Press, 1965).

Freud, S., *The Standard Edition of the Complete Psychological Works of Sigmund Freud* (24 vols.; London: Hogarth Press, 1953–1974). Cited as SE.

Freud, S., *The Complete Letters of Sigmund Freud to Wilhelm Fliess, 1887–1904*, trans. and ed. by J. M. Masson (Cambridge, MA: Harvard University Press, 1985).

Friedman, M., *Capitalism and Freedom* (Chicago: University of Chicago Press, 1962).

Fromm, E., *Escape from Freedom* (New York: Rinehart, 1941).

Frost, R., The Death of a Hired Man [1914], in *The Oxford Book of American Verse*, ed. by F. O. Matthiessen (New York: Oxford University Press, 1950).

Galton, F. *Memories of My Life* (New York: Dutton, 1909).

Gillespie, C. C., ed., *Dictionary of Scientific Biography* (New York: Scribner's, 1971).

Gilmore, G., *The Death of Contract* (Columbus: Ohio State University Press, 1974).

Girard, R., *A Theater of Envy: William Shakespeare* (New York: Oxford University Press, 1991).

Glass, J. M., *Delusion: Internal Dimensions of Political Life* (Chicago: University of Chicago Press, 1985).

Godfrey, W. H., *The English Almshouse, With Some Account of Its Predecessor, the Medieval Hospital* (London: Faber and Faber, 1955).

Goffman, E., *Asylums: Essays on the Social Situation of Mental Patients and Other Inmates* (Garden City, NY: Doubleday Anchor, 1961).

Goffman, E., *Stigma: Notes on the Management of Spoiled Identity* (Englewood Cliffs, NJ: Prentice-Hall, 1963).

Goldstein, J., *Console and Classify: The French Psychiatric Profession in the Nineteenth Century* (New York: Cambridge University Press, 1987).

Goodman, L. and A. Gilman, *The Pharmacological Basis of Therapeutics: A Textbook of Pharmacology, Toxicology, and Therapeutics for Physicians and Medical Students* (New York: Macmillan, 1941).

Goodwin, D. K., *The Fitzgeralds and the Kennedys* (New York: Simon and Schuster, 1987).

Grob, G., *The Inner World of American Psychiatry, 1890–1940: Selected Correspondence* (New Brunswick, NJ: Rutgers University Press, 1985).

Gross, J., *Shylock: A Legend and Its Legacy* (New York: Simon & Schuster, 1993).

Gumnit, R. J., ed., *Living Well with Epilepsy* (New York: Demos Publications, 1990).

Hall, J. K., et al., eds., *One Hundred Years of American Psychiatry* (For the American Psychiatric Association; New York: Columbia University Press, 1944).

Hampsher-Monk, I., *The Political Philosophy of Edmund Burke* (London: Longman, 1987).

Hampson, N., *The Enlightenment* [1968] (New York: Penguin, 1984).

Hancock, G., *Lords of Poverty: The Power, Prestige, and Corruption of the International Aid Business* (New York: Atlantic Monthly Press, 1989).

Harrington, J., *The Political Works of James Harrington,* ed. with an Introduction by J. G. A. Pocok (New York: Cambridge University Press, 1977).

Haworth, M., ed., *Child Psychotherapy: Practice and Theory* (New York: Basic Books, 1964).

Hayek, F. A., *The Constitution of Liberty* (Chicago: University of Chicago Press, 1960).

Hayek, F. A., *The Counter-Revolution of Science: Studies in the Abuse of Reason* [1955] (New York: Free Press, 1964).

Heinroth, J. C., *Textbook of Disturbances of Mental Life, or Disturbances of the Soul and Their Treatment* [1818], trans. by J. Schmorak (2 vols.; Johns Hopkins University Press, 1975).

Heller, P., *A Child Analysis with Anna Freud* (Madison, CT: International Universities Press, 1989).

Heller, P., with Contributions by G. Bittner and V. Ross, *Anna Freud's Letters to Eva Rosenfeld,* trans. by M. Weigand (Madison, CT: International Universities Press, 1992).

Hertell, T., *Remarks on the Law of Imprisonment for Debt: Showing Its Unconstitutionality, and Its Demoralizing Influence on the Community* (New York: Gould & Banks, 1823).

Hesse, H., *Reflections,* selected from his books and letters by V. Michels, trans. by R. Manheim (New York: Farrar, Straus and Giroux, 1974).

Heymann, C. D., *A Woman Named Jackie* (New York: Lyle Stuart, 1989).

Highmore, A., *A Treatise on the Law of Idiocy and Lunacy* (London: J. Butterworth, 1807).

Himmelfarb, G., *The Idea of Poverty: England in the Early Industrial Age* (New York: Random House, 1983).

Himmelfarb, G., *Poverty and Compassion: The Moral Imagination of the Late Victorians* (New York: Knopf, 1991).

Hobbes, T., *Leviathan* [1651], ed. by M. Oakeshott, (New York: Macmillan/Collier, 1962).

Hoffer, P. C. and N. E. H. Hull, *Murdering Mothers: Infanticide in New England, 1558–1803* (New York: New York University Press, 1984).

Holdsworth, W., *A History of English Law*, ed. in part by A. L. Goodhart, and H. G. Hanbury, General Index by J. Burke, (17 vols.; London: Methuen, 1925–1972).

Holy Bible, The Revised Standard Version (New York: Meridian, 1964).

Hont, I. and M., Ignatieff, eds., *Wealth and Virtue: The Shaping of Political Economy in the Sottish Enlightenment* (Cambridge: Cambridge University Press, 1983).

Huber, P. W., *Liability: The Legal Revolution and Its Consequences* (New York: Basic Books, 1988).

Hudson, C. G. and A. J. Cox, eds., *Dimensions of State Mental Health Policy* (New York: Praeger, 1990).

Hunter, R. and I. Macalpine, eds., *Three Hundred Years of Psychiatry, 1535-1860: A History Presented in Selected English Texts* (London: Oxford University Press, 1963).

Isaac, R. J. and V. C. Armat, *Madness in the Streets: How Psychiatry and the Law Abandoned the Mentally Ill* (New York: Free Press, 1990).

Isaac, R. J. and E. Isaac, *The Coercive Utopians: Social Deception by America's Power Players* (Chicago: Regnery, 1983).

Jahoda, M., *Current Concepts of Positive Mental Health* (New York: Basic Books, 1958).

Johnson, A. B., *Out of Bedlam: The Truth About Deinstitutionalization* (New York: Basic Books, 1990).

Johnson, M. B., ed., *Resolving the Housing Crisis: Government Policy, Decontrol, and the Public Interest* (San Francisco: Pacific Institute, 1982).

Johnson, S., *The Idler and the Adventurer*, ed. by W. J. Bate, J. M. Bullitt, and L. F. Powell (New Haven: Yale University Press, 1963).

Joint Commission on Mental Illness and Health, *Action for Mental Health: Final Report of the Joint Commission on Mental Illness and Health, 1961* (New York: Basic Books, 1961).

Jones, K., *Mental Health and Social Policy, 1845–1959* (London: Routledge & Kegan Paul, 1960).

Jones, K., *A History of the Mental Health Services* (London: Routledge & Kegan Paul, 1972).

Jones, N., *God and the Moneylenders: Usury and Law in Early Modern England* (Oxford: Basil Blackwell, 1989).

Joynt, R. J., ed., *Clinical Neurology*, rev. ed. (Philadelphia: Lippincott, 1988).

Kaplan, H. I., A. M. Freedman, and B. J. Sadock, eds., *Comprehensive Textbook of Psychiatry/III*, 3rd ed. (3 vols.; Baltimore: Williams and Wilkins, 1980).

Kenny, A., *Will, Freedom, and Power* (New York: Barnes & Noble, 1976).

Kovar, L. C., *Wasted Lives: A Study of Children in Mental Hospitals and Their Families* (New York: Gardner Press, 1979).

Kraepelin, E., *Lectures on Clinical Psychiatry* (A Facsimile of the 1904 Edition), trans. by T. Johnstone (New York: Hafner, 1968).

Kramnick, I., *The Rage of Edmund Burke: Portrait of an Ambivalent Conservative* (New York: Basic Books, 1977).

Lamb, H. R., ed., *The Homeless Mentally Ill: A Task Force Report of the American Psychiatric Association* (Washington, DC: American Psychiatric Association, 1984).

Lamb, H. R., L. L. Bachrach, and F. I. Kass, eds., *Treating the Homeless Mentally Ill: A Report of the Task Force on the Homeless Mentally Ill* (Washington, DC: American Psychiatric Association, 1992).

Landau, E., *The Homeless* (New York: Julian Messner, 1987).

Lane, H., *The Mask of Benevolence: Disabling the Deaf Community* (New York: Knopf, 1992).

Latham, C. and J. Sakol, *The Kennedy Encyclopedia: An A-to-Z Illustrated Guide to America's Royal Family* (New York: New American Library, 1989).

Lee, D. R. and R. B. McKenzie, *Failure and Progress: The Bright Side of the Dismal Science* (Washington, DC: Cato Institute, 1933).

Lemert, E., *Human Deviance, Social Problems, and Social Control* (Englewood Cliffs, NJ: Prentice-Hall, 1967).

Lennox, W. G., *Epilepsy and Related Disorders* (2 vols.; Boston: Little, Brown, 1960).

Leonard, E. M., *The Early History of English Poor Relief* (Cambridge: Cambridge University Press, 1900).

Lerner, R. and M. Mahdi, eds., *Medieval Political Philosophy: A Sourcebook* (Ithaca, NY: Cornell University Press, 1972).

Letchworth, W. P., *Care and Treatment of Epileptics* (New York: G. P. Putnam's, 1900).

Lewis, C. S., *The Abolition of Man* (New York: Macmillan, 1947).

Lewis, C. S., *The Screwtape Letters and Screwtape Proposes a Toast* (New York: Macmillan, 1961).

Lewis, C. S., *God in the Dock: Essays on Theology and Ethics*, ed. by W. Hooper (Grand Rapids, MI: Eerdmans, 1970).

Lieberman, E. J., *Acts of Will: The Life and Work of Otto Rank* (New York: Free Press, 1985).

Lightning, R. H., *Ealing and the Poor: The Poor Law, the Workhouses, and Poor Relief in the Parish of St. Mary Ealing, from 1722 to 1800* (Ealing: Ealing Local Historical Society, Members Paper No. 7, 1966).

Lion, J. and W. H. Reid, *Assaults within Psychiatric Facilities* (New York: Grune & Stratton, 1983).

Little, D., *Religion, Order, and Law: A Study in Pre-Revolutionary England* (New York: Harper & Row, 1969).

Locke, J., *Two Treatises on Government* [1690], ed. by P. Laslett (New York: New American Library, 1965).

Longmate, N., *The Workhouse* (New York: St. Martin's Press, 1974).

Lothane, Z., *In Defense of Schreber: Soul Murder and Psychiatry* (Hillsdale, NJ: Analytic Press, 1992).

Love, E. G., *Subways Are for Sleeping* (New York: Harcourt, Brace, 1957).

Lukes, S., *Essays in Social Theory* (New York: Columbia University Press, 1977).

Macalpine, I. and R. Hunter, *George III and the Mad-Business* (New York: Pantheon, 1969).

Macfarlane, A., *The Origins of English Individualism: The Family, Prosperity, and Social Transition* (Oxford: Blackwell, 1978).

Mackay, C., *Extraordinary Popular Delusions and the Madness of Crowds* [1841, 1852] (New York: Noonday Press, 1962).

MacPherson, C. B., *The Political Theory of Possessive Individualism: Hobbes to Locke* [1962] (Oxford: Oxford University Press, 1962).

Madison, J., *The Writings of James Madison*, ed. by G. Hunt (9 vols.; New York: Putnam's 1900–1910).

Manderscheid, R. W. and S. A., Barrett, eds., *Mental Health, United States, 1987* (Rockville, MD: U.S. Department of Health and Human Services, n.d.).

Manderscheid, R. W. and M. A. Sonnenschein, eds., *Mental Health, United States, 1990* (Rockville, MD: U.S. Department of Health and Human Services, n.d.).

Mann, T., *Confessions of Felix Krull, Confidence Man* [1954], trans. by D. Lindley (New York: Signet/New American Library, 1957).

Mark, R. and P. D. Scott, *The Disease of Crime: Punishment or Treatment* (Edwin Stevens Lectures for the Laity (London: William Clowes & Sons, 1972).

Marrus, M. R., *The Unwanted: European Refugees in the Twentieth Century* (New York: Oxford University Press, 1985).

Maudsley, H., *Responsibility in Mental Disease*, 4th ed. (London: Kegan Paul, Trench, 1885).

McDonald, F., *Novus Ordo Seclorum: The Intellectual Origins of the Constitution* (Lawrence, KS: University Press of Kansas, 1985).

McDonagh, D. and L. Robinson, eds., *The Oxford Book of Irish Verse: XVIIth Century–XXth Century* (Oxford: Clarendon Press, 1958).

McGovern, C. M., *Masters of Madness: Social Origins of the American Psychiatric Profession* (Hanover, NH: University of Vermont Press and University Press of New England, 1985).

McGregor, O. R., *Social History and Law Reform* (London: Stevens & Sons, 1981).

McIntire, M. S. and C. R. Angle, eds., *Suicide Attempts in Children and Youth* (Hagerstown: Harper & Row, 1980).

Mead, G. H., *Mind, Self & Society: From the Standpoint of a Social Behaviorist* (Chicago: University of Chicago Press, 1934).

Mencken, H. L., *A Mencken Chrestomathy* (New York: Knopf, 1967).

Mencken, H. L., *The Impossible H. L. Mencken*, ed. by M. E. Rodgers (New York: Doubleday, 1992).

Menninger, K., *The Vital Balance: The Life Process in Mental Health and Illness* (New York: Viking, 1963).

Menninger, K., *The Crime of Punishment* (New York: Viking, 1968).

Mill, J. S., *On Liberty* [1859] (Chicago: Regnery, 1955).

Miller, A., *For Your Own Good: Hidden Cruelty in Child-Rearing and the Roots of Violence*, trans. by H. and H. Hannum (New York: Farrar, Straus and Giroux, 1983).

Miller, R. D., *Involuntary Civil Commitment of the Mentally Ill in the Post-Reform Era* (Springfield, IL.: Charles C. Thomas, 1987).

Minogue, K., *The Liberal Mind* (London: Methuen, 1963).

Minogue, K., *Alien Powers: The Pure Theory of Ideology* (New York: St. Martin's Press, 1985).

Mises, L. von, *Human Action: A Treatise on Economics* (New Haven: Yale University Press, 1949).

Modrow, J., *How to Become a Schizophrenic: The Case against Biological Psychiatry* (Everett, WA: Apollyon Press, 1992).

Montesquieu, B., de (Charles Secondat), *The Spirit of the Laws* [1748] (New York: Hafner, 1949).

Moore, F. E. and V. J. Halamandaris, *Too Old, Too Sick, Too Bad: Nursing Homes in America* (Germantown, MD: Aspen Systems, 1977).

Moore, R. I., *The Formation of a Persecuting Society: Power and Deviance in Western Europe, 950–1250* (Oxford: Basil Blackwell, 1987).

Morgan, R. E., *Disabling America: The "Rights Industry" in Our Time* (New York: Basic Books, 1984).

Morris, C., *The Discovery of the Individual, 1050–1200* (New York: Harper & Row, 1972).

Munthe, A., *The Story of San Michele* [1929] (New York: Dutton, 1957).

Murray, C., *Losing Ground: American Social Policy, 1950–1980* (New York: Basic Books, 1984).

Neild, J., *An Account of the Rise, Progress, and Present State of the Society for the Discharge and Relief of Persons Imprisoned for Small Debts throughout England and Wales* (London: John Nichols and Son, 1808).

Nelson, B., *The Idea of Usury: From Tribal Brotherhood to Universal Otherhood*, 2nd ed. (Chicago: University of Chicago Press, 1969).

O'Donoghue, E. G., *The Story of Bethlehem Hospital, From Its Foundation in 1247* (New York: Dutton, 1915).

Ogg, D., *England in the Reigns of James II and William III* (London: Oxford University Press, 1969).

Olasky, M., *The Tragedy of American Compassion* (Chicago: Regnery, 1992).

Oldys, W., ed., *The Harleian Miscellany: A Collection of Scarce, Curious, and Entertaining Pamphlets and Tracts*, some additional notes by T. Park (4 vols.; London: White and Co., 1809).

Ormiston, G. L. and R. Sassower, eds., *Prescriptions: The Dissemination of Medical Authority* (Westport, CT: Greenwood Press, 1990).

O'Rourke, P. J., *Parliament of Whores: A Lone Humorist Attempts to Explain the Entire U.S. Government* (New York: Atlantic Monthly Press, 1991).

Orszagh, L., *A Concise Hungarian-English Dictionary*, 8th ed., (Budapest: Akadémia Kiadó, 1979).

Ortega y Gasset, J., *The Revolt of the Masses* [1930], (New York: Norton, 1957).

Ortega y Gasset, J., *Man and Crisis*, trans. by M. Adams (New York: Norton, 1962).

Ortega y Gasset, J., *Concord and Liberty* [1941], trans. by H. Weyl (New York: Norton, 1963).

Ortega y Gasset, J., *Man and People* [1957], trans. by W. R. Trask (New York: Norton, 1963).

Orwell, G., *Down and Out in Paris and London* (New York: Harper & Brothers, 1933).

Orwell, G., *The Orwell Reader* (New York: Harcourt Brace, 1956).

The Oxford English Dictionary, 2nd ed., ed. by J. A. Simpson, and E. S. C. Weiner, (20 vols.; Oxford: Clarendon Press, 1989).

Palgrave. The New Palgrave: A Dictionary of Economics, ed. by J. Eatwell, M. Milgate, and P. Newman, (4 vols.; London: Macmillan, 1987).

Pangle, T. L., *Montesquieu's Philosophy of Liberalism: A Commentary on "The Spirit of the Laws"* (Chicago: University of Chicago Press, 1973).

Pangle, T. L., *The Spirit of Modern Republicanism: The Moral Vision of the American Founders and the Philosophy of John Locke* (Chicago: University of Chicago Press, 1988).

Parkman, G., *Proposal for Establishing a Retreat for the Insane, To Be Constructed by George Parkman, M.D.* (Boston: John Eliot, 1814).

Parry-Jones, W. Ll., *The Trade in Lunacy: A Study of Private Madhouses in England in the Eighteenth and Nineteenth Centuries* (London: Routledge & Kegan Paul, 1976).

Pearson, G. H. J., ed., *A Handbook of Child Psychoanalysis* (New York: Basic Books, 1968).

Peden, J. R. and F. R. Glahe, eds., *The American Family and the State* (San Francisco: Pacific Institute, 1986).

Peterson, D., ed., *A Mad People's History of Madness* (Pittsburgh: University of Pittsburgh Press, 1982).

Phelps, E. S., ed., *Altruism, Morality, and Economic Theory* (New York: Russell Sage Foundation, 1975).

Piven, F. F. and R. A. Cloward, *Regulating the Poor: The Functions of Public Welfare* (New York: Pantheon, 1971).

Podach, E. F., *The Madness of Nietzsche* [1930], trans. by F. A. Voigt (London: Putnam, 1931).

Polanyi, M., *Full Employment and Free Trade* (Cambridge: Cambridge University Press, 1948).

Porter, R., *Mind-Forg'd Manacles: A History of Madness from the Restoration to the Regency* (London: Athlone Press, 1987).

Porter, R., *A Social History of Madness: The World through the Eyes of the Insane* (New York: Weidenfeld & Nicolson, 1987).

Postman, N., *Crazy Talk, Stupid Talk: How We Defeat Ourselves by the Way We Talk—And What We Can Do About It* (New York: Delta, 1976).

Pound, R., *An Introduction to the Philosophy of Law* [1992] (New Haven: Yale University Press, 1954).

Poynter, J. R., *Society and Pauperism: English Ideas on Poor Relief, 1795–1834* (London: Routledge & Kegan Paul, 1969).

Probyn, C. T., *Jonathan Swift: The Contemporary Background* (New York: Barnes & Noble, 1979).

Reynolds, E. H. and M. R. Trimble, eds., *Epilepsy and Psychiatry* (London: Churchill Livingstone, 1981).

Reynolds, J. R., *Epilepsy: Its Symptoms, Treatment, and Relation to Other Chronic Convulsive Diseases* (London: Churchill, 1861).

Richardson, T. T., *The Century of the Child: The Mental Hygiene Movement and Social Policy in the United States and Canada* (Albany: State University of New York Press, 1989).

Rilke, R. M., *The Notebooks of Malte Laurids Brigge* [1910], trans. by Stephen Mitchell (New York: Vintage, 1985).

Roazen, P., *Freud and His Followers* (New York: Knopf, 1975).

Robinson, J. F., et al., eds., *Psychiatric Inpatient Treatment of Children* (Washington, DC: American Psychiatric Association, 1957).

Robitscher, J., *The Powers of Psychiatry* (Boston: Houghton Mifflin, 1980).

Rogers, W., *A Will Rogers Treasury: Reflections and Observations*, ed. by B. B. Sterling and F. N. Sterling (New York: Bonanza Books, 1982).

Ross, A. and D. Woolley, eds., *Jonathan Swift* (New York: Oxford University Press, 1984).

Rothbard, M. N., *For a New Liberty: The Libertarian Manifesto*, rev. ed. (New York: Collier, 1978).

Rothbard, M. N., *Individualism and the Philosophy of the Social Sciences*, Cato Paper No. 4 (San Francisco: Cato Institute, 1979).

Rothman, D. J., *The Discovery of the Asylum: Social Order and Disorder in the New Republic* (Boston: Little, Brown, 1971).

Rowland, L. P., ed., *Merritt's Textbook of Neurology*, 7th ed. (Philadelphia: Lea & Febiger, 1984).

Rousseau, J. J., *The Social Contract* [1762], in *The Social Contract and Discourses*, trans. by C. D. H. Cole (New York: Dutton, 1950).

Rybczynski, W., *Home: A Short History of an Idea* (New York: Viking, 1986).

Ryn, C. G., *The New Jacobinism: Can Democracy Survive?* (Washington, DC: National Humanities Institute, 1991).

Salgado, G., *Cony-Catchers and Bawdy Baskets: An Anthology of Elizabethan Low Life* (Harmondsworth: Penguin, 1972).

Salinger, J. D., *The Catcher in the Rye* [1945] (New York: Signet, 1951).

Schelling, T. C., *Choice and Consequence* (Cambridge: Harvard University Press, 1984).

Schneider, H. W., ed., *Adam Smith's Moral and Political Philosophy* (New York: Harper Torchbooks, 1970).

Schochet, G. J., *Patriarchalism in Political Thought: The Authoritarian Family and Political Speculation and Attitudes Especially in Seventeenth Century England* (New York: Basic Books, 1975).

Schoeck, H., *Envy: A Theory of Social Behaviour [1966]*, trans. by Michael Glenny and Betty Ross (New York: Harcourt, Brace & World, 1969).

Schreber, D. P., *Memoirs of My Nervous Illness* [1903], trans. and ed. by I. Macalpine, and R. A. Hunter, (London: Dawson, 1955).

Schulman, J. L. and M. Irwin, eds., *Psychiatric Hospitalization of Children* (Springfield, IL: Charles C. Thomas, 1972).

Schwartz, D. B., *Crossing the River: Creating a Conceptual Revolution in Community and Disability* (Cambridge, MA: Brookline Books, 1992).

Scull, A., *Decarceration: Community Treatment of the Deviant, a Radical View* [1977] (New Brunswick, NJ: Rutgers University Press, 1984).

Scull, A., *Social Order/Mental Disorder: Anglo-American Psychiatry in Historical Perspective* (Berkeley: University of California Press, 1989).

Segal, S. P. and U. Aviram, *The Mentally Ill in Community-Based Sheltered Care: A Study of Community Care and Social Integration* (New York: Wiley, 1978).

Seldes, G., ed., *The Great Quotations* (New York: Lyle Stuart, 1960).

Shand, A. H., *Free Market Morality: The Political Economy of the Austrian School* (New York: Routledge, 1990).

Shaw, G. B., *Saint Joan* [1924], ed. by S. Weintraub (Indianapolis: Bobbs-Merrill, 1971).

Sheaffer, R., *Resentment against Achievement: Understanding the Assault upon Ability* (Buffalo: Prometheus Books, 1988).

Sigerist, H. E., *Medicine and Health in the Soviet Union* (New York: Citadel Press, 1947).

Simmons, J. E., *Psychiatric Examination of Children*, 2nd ed. (Philadelphia: Lea & Febiger, 1974).

Simpson, J. B., ed., *Contemporary Quotations* (New York: T. Crowell, 1964).

Smith, A., *The Theory of Moral Sentiments* [1749], (Indianapolis: Liberty Classics, 1976).

Smith, A., *An Inquiry into the Nature and Causes of the Wealth of Nations* [1776], ed. by B. Mazlish (Indianapolis: Bobbs-Merrill, 1961).

Smith, A., *The Wealth of Nations, Books I–III* [1776], Introduction by A. Skinner (London: Penguin, 1987). Unless otherwise indicated, all page references are to this edition.

Smith, A., *The Wisdom of Adam Smith*, ed. by B. A. Rogge (Indianapolis: Liberty Press, 1976).

Smith, G. H., *Atheism, Ayn Rand, and Other Heresies* (Buffalo, NY: Prometheus Books, 1991).

Smith, J. D., *Minds Made Feeble: The Myth and Legacy of the Kallikaks* (Rockville, MD: Aspen Systems, 1985).

Snyder, C. R., R. L. Higgins, and R. J. Stucky, *Excuses: Masquerades in Search of Grace* (New York: Wiley, 1983).

Stangerup, H., *The Man Who Wanted to Be Guilty* [1982], trans. by D. Gress-Wright (London: Marion Boyars, 1991).

Stanlis, P. J., *Edmund Burke and the Natural Law* (Ann Arbor, MI: University of Michigan Press, 1965).

Stephen, J. F., *Essays, by a Barrister* (London: Smith, Elder, 1863).

Stephen, J. F., *Liberty, Equality, Fraternity [1874], and Three Brief Essays*, Foreword by R. A. Posner (Chicago: University of Chicago Press, 1991).

Stevenson, B., *The Macmillan Book of Proverbs, Maxims, and Famous Phrases* (New York: Macmillan, 1948).

Stone, I., ed., *Dear Theo: The Autobiography of Vincent Van Gogh* (New York: Signet, 1937).

Strauss, L. and J. Cropsey, eds., *History of Political Philosophy*, 2nd ed. (Chicago: Rand McNally, 1963).

Sudak, H. S., A. B. Ford, and N. B. Rushforth, eds., *Suicide in the Young* (Boston: John Wright-PSG, 1984).

Swift, J., *Jonathan Swift*, ed. by A. Ross, and D. Woolley, (Oxford: Oxford University Press, 1984).

Szasz, T. S., *The Myth of Mental Illness: Foundations of a Theory of Personal Conduct* [1961], rev. ed. (New York: Harper & Row, 1974).

Szasz, T. S., *Law, Liberty, and Psychiatry* [1963], with a new Preface (Syracuse: Syracuse University Press, 1989).

Szasz, T. S., *Psychiatric Justice* [1965], with a new Preface (Syracuse: Syracuse University Press, 1988).

Szasz, T. S., *The Ethics of Psychoanalysis: The Theory and Method of Autonomous Psychotherapy* [1965], with a new Preface (Syracuse: Syracuse University Press, 1988).

Szasz, T. S., *Ideology and Insanity: Essays on the Psychiatric Dehumanization of Man* (Garden City, NY: Doubleday Anchor, 1970).

Szasz, T. S., *The Manufacture of Madness: A Comparative Study of the Inquisition and the Mental Health Movement* (New York: Harper & Row, 1970).

Szasz, T. S., ed., *The Age of Madness: A History of Involuntary Mental Hospitalization Presented in Selected Texts* (Garden City, NY: Doubleday Anchor, 1973).

Szasz, T. S., *Ceremonial Chemistry: The Ritual Persecution of Drugs, Addicts, and Pushers* [1976], with a new Preface (Holmes Beach, FL: Learning Publications, 1985).

Szasz, T. S., *Schizophrenia: The Sacred Symbol of Psychiatry* [1976], with a new Preface (Syracuse: Syracuse University Press, 1988).

Szasz, T. S., *Psychiatric Slavery: When Confinement and Coercion Masquerade as Cure* (New York: Free Press, 1977).

Szasz, T .S., *The Theology of Medicine: The Political-Philosophical Foundations of Medical Ethics* [1977], with a new Preface (Syracuse: Syracuse University Press, 1988).

Szasz, T. S., *The Myth of Psychotherapy: Mental Healing as Religion, Rhetoric, and Repression* [1978], with a new Preface (Syracuse: Syracuse University Press, 1988).

Szasz, T. S., *Sex by Prescription* [1980], with a new Preface (Syracuse: Syracuse University Press, 1990).

Szasz, T. S., *The Therapeutic State: Psychiatry in the Mirror of Current Events* (Buffalo: Prometheus Books, 1984).

Szasz, T. S., *Insanity: The Idea and Its Consequences* (New York: Wiley, 1987).

Szasz, T. S., *The Untamed Tongue: A Dissenting Dictionary* (Lasalle, IL: Open Court, 1990).

Szasz, T. S., *Our Right to Drugs: The Case for a Free Market* (New York: Praeger, 1992).

Szasz, T. S., *A Lexicon of Lunacy: Metaphoric Malady, Moral Responsibility, and Psychiatry* (New Brunswick, NJ: Transaction Publishers, 1993).

Takaki, R., *Strangers from a Different Shore: A History of Asian Americans* (Boston: Little, Brown, 1989).

Tarsis, V., *Ward 7: An Autobiographical Novel,* trans. by K. Brown (London and Glasgow: Collins & Harvill, 1965).

Tawney, R. H., *Religion and the Rise of Capitalism: A Historical Study* [1922] (Gloucester, MA: Peter Smith, 1962).

Temkin, O., *The Falling Sickness: A History of Epilepsy from the Greeks to the Beginnings of Modern Neurology,* 2nd ed. (Baltimore: Johns Hopkins Press, 1971).

Thomas, L., *Late Night Thoughts on Listening to Mahler's Ninth Symphony* (New York: Viking, 1983).

Tocqueville, A. de, *Democracy in America* [1835–1840], The Henry Reeve text (2 vols.; New York: Vintage, 1945).

Tocqueville, A. de, *The Old Regime and the French Revolution* [1856], trans. by S. Gilbert (Garden City, NY: Doubleday Anchor, 1955).

Tollison, R. D. and R. E. Wagner, *Smoking and the State: Social Cost, Rent Seeking, and Public Policy* (Lexington, MA: Lexington Books, 1988).

Torrey, E. F., *Nowhere to Go: The Tragic Odyssey of the Homeless Mentally Ill* (New York: Harper & Row, 1988).

Torrey, E. F., *Freudian Fraud: The Malignant Effect of Freud's Theory on American Thought and Culture* (New York: HarperCollins, 1992).

Torrey, E. F., et al., *Criminalizing the Seriously Mentally Ill: The Abuse of Jails as Mental Hospitals* (Washington, DC: National Alliance for the Mentally Ill and Public Citizen's Health Research Group, 1992).

Trattner, W. E., *From Poor Law to Welfare State: A History of Social Welfare in America*, 3rd ed. (New York: Free Press, 1984).

Tuveson, E. L., *Redeemer Nation: The Idea of America's Millennial Role* (Chicago: University of Chicago Press, 1968).

Ullman, W., *The Medieval Idea of Law: As Represented by Lucas De Penna* (London: Methuen, 1946).

United States Statutes at Large, 1955, Vol. 69 (Washington, DC: United States Government Printing Office, 1955).

Van Gogh, V., *Dear Theo: The Autobiography of Vincent Van Gogh*, ed. by I. Stone (New York: Signet/New American Library, 1937).

Veblen, T., *The Theory of the Leisure Class: An Economic Study of Institutions* [1899] (New York: Mentor, 1953).

Veblen, T., *The Portable Veblen*, ed. by M. Lerner (New York: Viking, 1958).

Vice, J., *From Patients to Persons: The Psychiatric Critiques of Thomas Szasz, Peter Sedgwick, and R. D. Laing* (New York: Peter Lang, 1993).

Walker, R., *Some Objections Humbly Offered to the Consideration of the Hon. House of Commons, Relating to the Present Intended Relief of Prisoners* (London: E. Nutt, 1729).

Wall, C. E., ed., *A Matter of Fact: Statements Containing Statistics on Current Social, Economic, and Political Issues* (Ann Arbor, MI: Pierian Press, 1991).

Walton, J., *Brain's Diseases of the Nervous System*, 9th ed. (London: Oxford University Press, 1985).

Wear, A., ed., *Medicine in Society: Historical Essays* (Cambridge: Cambridge University Press, 1992).

Weaver, R., *Ideas Have Consequences* (Chicago: Phoenix Books, 1962).

Webber, C. and Wildavsky, A., *A History of Taxation and Expenditure in the Western World* (New York: Simon and Schuster, 1986).

West, E. G., *Adam Smith: The Man and His Works* (Indianapolis: Liberty Press, 1976).

White, R. W., Jr., *Rude Awakenings: What the Homeless Crisis Tells Us* (San Francisco: ICS Press, 1992).

Wieser, F. von, *Natural Value* [1888], trans. by Christian A. Malloch (New York: Kelley & Millman, 1956).

Wieser, F. von, *Social Economics* [1914], trans. by A. Ford Hinrichs (New York: Greenberg, 1927).

Williams, T., *Memoirs* [1975] (New York: Bantam, 1976).

Wintrobe, M. M. et al., eds., *Harrison's Principles of Internal Medicine,* 7th ed. (New York: McGraw-Hill, 1974).

Yager, J. ed., *The Future of Psychiatry as a Medical Specialty* (Washington, DC: American Psychiatric Association, 1989).

Yerushalmi, Y. H., *Freud's Moses: Judaism Terminable and Interminable* (New Haven: Yale University Press, 1991).

Young, R., *Personal Autonomy: Beyond Positive and Negative Liberty* (London: Croom Helm, 1986).

NAME INDEX

SUBJECT INDEX